OPEN DIALOGUE FOR PSYCHOSIS

This highly readable book provides a comprehensive examination of the use of Open Dialogue as a treatment for psychosis. It presents the basic principles and practice of Open Dialogue, explains the training needed to practice and explores how it is being developed internationally.

Open Dialogue for Psychosis includes first-hand accounts of the process by people receiving services due to having psychotic experiences, their family members and professionals who work with them. It explains how aspects of Open Dialogue have been introduced in services around the world, its overlap with and differentiation from other psychological approaches and its potential integration with biological and pharmacological considerations. The book concludes with a substantive section on the research available and its limitations.

Open Dialogue for Psychosis will be a key text for clinicians and administrators interested in this unique approach, particularly those who recognise that services need to change for the better and are seeking guidance on how this can be achieved. It will also be suitable for people who have experienced psychosis and members of their families and networks.

Nick Putman is a psychotherapist and practitioner, supervisor and trainer in Open Dialogue. He is the founder of Open Dialogue UK.

Brian Martindale is a psychiatrist and psychoanalyst based in the UK. He is past Chair of the International Society for Psychological and Social Approaches to Psychosis (ISPS) and co-founder of the European Federation of Psychoanalytic Psychotherapy (EFPP).

THE INTERNATIONAL SOCIETY FOR PSYCHOLOGICAL AND SOCIAL APPROACHES TO PSYCHOSIS BOOK SERIES

Series editors: Anna Lavis and Andrew Shepherd

Stretching back more than 50 years, the International Society for Psychological and Social Approaches to Psychosis (ISPS) has members in more than twenty countries. Central to its ethos is that the perspectives of individuals with lived experience of psychosis and their families and friends are key to forging more inclusive understandings of, and therapeutic approaches to, psychosis.

Over its history ISPS has pioneered a growing global recognition of the emotional, socio-cultural, environmental, and structural contexts that underpin the development of psychosis. It has recognised this as an embodied psycho-social experience that must be understood in relation to a person's life history and circumstances. Evidencing a need for interventions in which talking and listening are key ingredients, this understanding has distinct therapeutic possibilities. To this end, ISPS embraces a wide spectrum of approaches from psychodynamic, systemic, cognitive, and arts therapies, to need-adapted and dialogical approaches, family and group therapies and residential therapeutic communities.

A further ambition of ISPS is to draw together diverse viewpoints on psychosis, fostering discussion and debate across the biomedical and social sciences, as well as humanities. This goal underpins international and national conferences, and the journal Psychosis, as well as being key to this book series.

The ISPS book series seeks to capture cutting edge developments in scholarship into psychosis, providing a forum in which authors with diverse lived and professional experiences can share their work. It showcases a variety of empirical focuses and differing experiential and disciplinary perspectives. The books combine intellectual rigour with accessibility for readers across the ISPS community. We aim for the series to be a resource for mental health professionals, academics, policy makers, and for people whose interest in psychosis stems from personal or family experience.

To support its aim of advancing scholarship in an inclusive and interdisciplinary way, the series benefits from the advice of an editorial board:

For more information about ISPS, email isps@isps.org or visit our website, www.isps.org.

For more information about the journal *Psychosis* visit www.isps.org/index.php/publications/journal

OPEN DIALOGUE FOR PSYCHOSIS

Organising Mental Health Services to Prioritise
Dialogue, Relationship and Meaning

Edited by
Nick Putman and Brian Martindale

Routledge
Taylor & Francis Group

LONDON AND NEW YORK

First published 2022
by Routledge
2 Park Square, Milton Park, Abingdon, Oxon OX14 4RN

and by Routledge
605 Third Avenue, New York, NY 10158

Routledge is an imprint of the Taylor & Francis Group, an informa business

British Library Cataloguing-in-Publication Data
A catalogue record for this book is available from the British Library

Library of Congress Cataloging-in-Publication Data
Names: Putman, Nick, editor. | Martindale, Brian, editor.
Title: Open dialogue for psychosis: organising mental health
services to prioritise dialogue, relationship and meaning / edited by
Nick Putman & Brian Martindale. Description: First edition. |
Milton Park, Abingdon, Oxon; New York, NY: Routledge, 2021. |
Series: The international society for psychological and social
approaches to psychosis book series |
Includes bibliographical references and index.
Identifiers: LCCN 2020056625 (print) | LCCN 2020056626 (ebook) |
ISBN 9780815392323 (paperback) | ISBN 9780815392316 (hardback) |
ISBN 9781351199599 (ebook)
Subjects: LCSH: Psychoses. | Mental health services.
Classification: LCC RC512.O64 2021 (print) |
LCC RC512 (ebook) | DDC 362.2/6–dc23
LC record available at https://lccn.loc.gov/2020056625
LC ebook record available at https://lccn.loc.gov/2020056626

ISBN: 978-0-815-39231-6 (hbk)
ISBN: 978-0-815-39232-3 (pbk)
ISBN: 978-1-351-19959-9 (ebk)

Typeset in Times New Roman
by Newgen Publishing UK

THIS BOOK IS DEDICATED TO BIRGITTA
ALAKARE, MARKKU SUTELA AND KAUKO
HAARAKANGAS.

THE REVERBERATIONS OF THEIR
COMPASSION AND WISDOM CAN BE FELT
THROUGHOUT THIS BOOK.

CONTENTS

CONTENTS

CONTENTS

CONTENTS

CONTRIBUTORS

Editors/authors

Brian Martindale, Newcastle-upon-Tyne, UK. Psychiatrist and psychoanalyst. Past chair of ISPS (International Society for Psychological and Social Approaches to Psychosis) and founding editor of the ISPS book series. He co-founded the European Federation of Psychoanalytic Psychotherapy (EFPP) and has represented the Western European Zone to the World Psychiatric Association. He has considerable clinical experience in early intervention in psychosis and has published and lectured widely.

Nick Putman, London, UK. Founder, Open Dialogue UK (www. opendialogueapproach.co.uk). Psychotherapist and Open Dialogue practitioner, supervisor and trainer. Since leaving his career as a psychologist in the NHS, Nick has trained as a psychotherapist at the Philadelphia Association (PA) in London, living and working in therapeutic communities run by the PA and Arbours during his training. He now works in private practice and, due to a desire to see changes in the approach taken in public mental health services, established Open Dialogue UK in 2013 in order to develop trainings for staff working in such services, as well as services for families/networks.

Authors

Volkmar Aderhold, Hamburg, Germany. Physician of psychiatry, psychotherapy and psychotherapeutic medicine (now retired). Guest professor at the University Charité in Berlin. Developer of in-house Open Dialogue training programme for multi-professional teams, often including experts by experience. Has published widely on various subjects including the risks of using antipsychotics.

Jorma Ahonen, Helsinki, Finland. Trainer and supervisor in family therapy, organisational consultant at Dialogic Partner Co. Trainer in long-term international programmes of family therapy and Open Dialogue.

Birgitta Alakare, Tornio, Finland. Chief psychiatrist at Western Lapland Health Care District until 2014 (now retired). Family therapist and family therapy/Open Dialogue trainer.

Zelda Alpern, Burlington, VT, USA. Social worker/collaborative network approach coordinator at Counseling Service of Addison County in Vermont. Has been a hearer of voices and other sounds. Currently delighting in her child who is not yet three and already has many stories to tell and songs to sing.

Edward Altwies, New York, USA. Psychologist in private practice. Was a team leader and trainer on the Parachute NYC project, as well as a supervisor and practitioner on the Brooklyn Early Psychosis team. Trained Open Dialogue practitioner.

Darren Baker, PhD, London, UK. Principal clinical psychologist working in the NHS. Qualified trainer and practitioner in Open Dialogue.

Helene Brändli, Winterthur, Switzerland. Peer support worker in psychiatric practice. Has undertaken EX-IN (Experienced Involvement) training and Open Dialogue training and is now a trainer on EX-IN trainings. In her work she has focused on recovery and a reduction of violence and coercion in mental health services.

Frank Burbach, PhD, Somerset, UK. Clinical psychologist and head of outcomes, innovation and research at Healios. Currently developing family-oriented internet psychological therapies. For the previous 30 years has developed integrated family intervention services and family-inclusive mental health services in the NHS in Somerset, UK.

Simona Calzavara, London, UK. Social worker in an Early Intervention in Psychosis team. Previously specialised in substance misuse and work with older people and their carers.

Ana María Corredor, London, UK. Trainer at Recovery College, South West London and St George's Mental Health NHS Trust. Trained as psychologist (Colombia), dance movement therapist, and systemic practitioner (UK). Currently undertaking the Open Dialogue UK three-year training. Committed to dialogical applications beyond traditional Open Dialogue settings.

Lauren Cubellis, PhD, Berlin, Germany. Psychological anthropologist. Postdoctoral researcher in the Anthropology of Environment/Human Relations Laboratory, Humboldt University. Max Kade Postdoctoral Fellow, Berlin Program for Advanced German and European Studies at Free University, Berlin. Main research focus is on alternative treatment models for psychosis.

Mario Eugster, London, UK. Principal music therapist in the NHS. Manages arts therapists in acute and community services. Works with individuals, families and groups. Special interest in psychosis. Trainer and lead with the International Centre for Arts Psychotherapies.

Thomas Floeth, PhD (Sociology), Berlin, Germany. Chief Executive Officer of Pinel Netzwerk NGO, which offers developing nationwide community interventions for psychiatric crisis and offers training in Open Dialogue. Member of Board of Directors of Umbrella Association for Community Psychiatry (Dachverband Gemeindepsychiatrie).

Claudio Fuenzalida, PhD student (Clinical Linguistics), Elche, Spain. Psychologist and coordinator at Adolescent Unit in the Center of Interfamily Therapy. Currently promoting European programmes for interfamily and dialogical practices.

Laura Galbusera, Berlin, Germany. Clinical psychologist. Doctoral degree in psychiatry from the University of Heidelberg. Currently a researcher in Open Dialogue, psychotherapy for psychosis, and peer support at Brandenburg Medical School.

Anna Gastaldi, Savona, Italy. Peer support worker and Open Dialogue practitioner. Member of association 'Noi per Voi' Carcare. Completed one-year training in Open Dialogue in Turin.

Christopher Gordon, Boston, USA. Associate professor of psychiatry at Harvard Medical School. Psychiatrist, Massachusetts General Hospital, Boston. Chief Medical Officer, Emeritus, Advocates Inc, Framingham, MA. Clinical associate professor of psychiatry, University of Massachusetts Medical School. Private practice.

Niklas Granö, PhD, Helsinki, Finland. Chief psychologist at Helsinki University Hospital, Department of Adolescent Psychiatry.

Nils Greve, Cologne, Germany. Psychiatrist and psychologist. Chairman of Dachverband Gemeindepsychiatrie (German umbrella organisation of regional mental health centres). Leader of a multi-centre randomised controlled trial Open Dialogue research project. Trainer in systemic therapy. Past CEO of Solingen mental health centre.

Alan Hendry, Brighton, UK. Trainer, coach in mental health voluntary sector. Trainer of peer mentors. Personal experience of psychosis.

Katrin Herder, Solingen, Germany. Nurse, family therapist and trainer at Familientherapeutische Arbeitsgemeinschaft Marburg. Undertakes counselling for people with mental health problems and their families in the community, and crisis work.

Annie Hodgkins, Taunton, UK. Nurse at Somerset NHS Foundation Trust. Team manager for Somerset Team for Early Psychosis.

Petra Hohn, Stockholm, Sweden. Network therapist at Psykiatri Södra Stockholm. Head of two outpatient centres. Teaches dialogical practices at Stockholm University. Developer of trainings on dialogical approaches and family/network perspectives across Europe. Involved with the Parachute Project in Sweden during the nineties and more recently Parachute Project NYC.

Mark Hopfenbeck, Gjøvik, Norway. Assistant professor at Norwegian University of Science and Technology (NTNU). Social anthropologist specialising in health and social policy. For 15 years has been teaching postgraduate programmes focusing on Open Dialogue. Currently co-investigator on the ODDESSI trial and member of the Advisory Board for the HOPEnDialogue project.

Yasmin Ishaq, Kent, UK. Social worker/psychotherapist at Kent and Medway NHS and Social Care Partnership Trust. Service lead for the Kent Open Dialogue service. Trainer in dialogic practice for families. Has worked in the public sector in health and social care for 30 years.

Val Jackson, Wakefield, UK. Systemic psychotherapist. Trainer and supervisor on the Peer Supported Open Dialogue, Social Network and Relationship Skills course. Conducted a small trial in Open Dialogue in the Leeds Early Intervention in Psychosis Service in 2013.

Ritva Jacobsen, Greater Oslo, Norway. Nurse. Degree in clinical health care. Project manager at the division of mental health, Akershus University Hospital. Open Dialogue practitioner, training to be a trainer. Open Dialogue researcher.

Pia Birgitte Jessen, Stokmarknes, Norway. Family and network therapist at GOD DIALOG clinic. Worked with Open Dialogue since the beginning of 1990, implementing it in psychiatric health services until 2017. Has since started a clinic based on Open Dialogue.

Bengt Karlsson, Drammen, Norway. Family therapist, professor of mental health and leader of Center of Mental Health and Substance Abuse. Teaches, researches and publishes about Open Dialogue approaches in different Norwegian contexts.

Miriam Kyselo, Berlin, Germany. Professor of philosophy. Doctoral degree in cognitive science from the University of Osnabrück. Research on self, embodiment and enactive cognition at Technische Universität (TU) Berlin.

Mett Marri Lægsgaard, PhD, Aarhus, Denmark. Psychologist. Chief consultant and project manager with DEFACTUM, a centre that aims for quality improvement in social work through innovation, development and evaluation. Counsellor for leaders and social workers researching their own practice.

Kirsty Lee, Kent, UK. Writer/ecologist. Board member of the Open Dialogue Champions network aiming to raise awareness of Open Dialogue. Sits on the ODDESSI trial Lived Experience Advisory Panel. Interested in how we can connect with the natural world in ways that can improve mental and physical wellbeing.

Anja Lehmann, PhD (Psychology), Berlin, Germany. Behavioural therapist and supervisor at St Hedwig Hospital, Charité University Medicine Berlin. Involved in Open Dialogue and other approaches in various clinical settings since 2005. Trainer in Open Dialogue.

Marcello Macario, Savona, Italy. Psychiatrist and head of Community Mental Health Centre of Carcare (local health authority of Savona). Chair, Italian Hearing Voices Network. Trained in Open Dialogue (three-year training in London).

Rolf Michels, Itzehoe, Germany. Psychiatrist, Psychotherapist at Zentrum für Psychosoziale Medizin. Psychiatrist and psychotherapist in charge of a hospital-based service for clients with psychotic disorders. Came into contact with Open Dialogue 10 years ago and completed the international trainers' training in Helsinki in 2018.

Brenda Miele Soares, Massachusetts, USA. Social worker and Vice-President of Behavioral Health Services at Advocates Inc, Framingham, MA. Certified Open Dialogue practitioner. Award for Excellence in Program Leadership from the Massachusetts' Association for Behavioral Healthcare. Oversees a large number of services.

Amy Morgan, Massachusetts, USA. Licensed independent social worker. Certified Open Dialogue practitioner. Leader in developing community mental health services. Senior trainer at national and international level for those with lived experience to become trainers themselves.

Leslie Nelson, Vermont, USA. Trainer, consultant and supervisor at the Howard Centre in Vermont.

Mary Olson, PhD. Killingworth, CT, USA. Founder/director of the Institute for Dialogic Practice. Clinical professor, Yale School of Medicine; Fulbright Scholar. International lecturer and author of numerous chapters and articles. Elected to the American Academy of Family Therapists. Maintains a private practice in Connecticut.

James Osborne, Kent, UK. Consultant psychologist at Kent and Medway Partnership Trust. Lead of psychological practice across secondary care and specialist personality disorder services and Clinical Lead for Open Dialogue in Kent. A career in family approaches led to Open Dialogue.

Luigi Roberto Pezzano, Catania, Italy. Psychologist and family therapist at Mental Health Department of Catania. Board member of Italian Hearing Voices Network. Trained in Open Dialogue (one-year training).

Raffaella Pocobello, PhD (Clinical Psychology), Rome, Italy. Researcher at the Institute of Cognitive Science and Technology of the Italian National Research Council. Principal investigator of the HOPEnDialogue international study. Trainee in Open Dialogue in the UK.

Russell Razzaque, London, UK. Consultant psychiatrist and Director of Research at North East London NHS Foundation Trust (NELFT). Community consultant in a Peer-supported Open Dialogue team in Havering. Coordinates and teaches on NHS Open Dialogue training delivered by NELFT. Co-applicant and primary investigator in the National Institute for Health Research (NIHR) funded UK ODDESSI trial.

Mike Roth, London, UK. Long-time student of dialogical approaches. Currently on the three-year Open Dialogue training programme in London. Locum specialty doctor (psychiatry) at Medacs Healthcare.

Olga Runciman, Copenhagen, Denmark. Psychologist and owner at Psycovery. com. Offers help and support to those suffering from psychosis. An Open Dialogue family therapist with lived experience. Active in the hearing voices movement and a consultant for the World Health Organization and United Nations on human rights in psychiatry.

Reiulf Ø. Ruud, Stokmarknes, Norway. Psychiatrist, family and network therapist at GOD DIALOG clinic. Worked with Open Dialogue since the beginning of 1990, implementing it in psychiatric health services until 2017. Has since started a clinic based on Open Dialogue.

Werner Schütze, Hamburg, Germany. Child and youth psychiatrist. Former head of a psychiatric department where Open Dialogue was implemented. International trainer and supervisor in Open Dialogue.

Jaakko Seikkula, PhD, Helsinki, Finland. Professor in psychotherapy at University of Jyväskylä until 2018 (now retired). Clinical psychologist at Keropudas hospital in Tornio between 1981 and 1998. Main research interest has been in developing dialogical clinical practice for severe crises. In this he has sought to combine naturalistic research with the daily clinical practice and training of Open Dialogue.

Javier Sempere, Elche, Spain. Psychiatrist and medical director at Center of Interfamily Therapy. Specialist in family therapy, group therapy and multifamily therapy. Has published research into interfamily therapy.

Alexander Smith, Vermont, USA. Programme director for a rural community mental health programme in Vermont which he has worked with for the past 30 years. In recent years has helped support implementation of Open Dialogue-informed practices.

Jorunn Sørgård, Greater Oslo, Norway. Nurse. Degree in clinical health care. Project manager, department of specialised psychiatry, Akershus University Hospital. Trained Open Dialogue practitioner. Published research on Open Dialogue in Norwegian and English.

Sandra Steingard, Vermont, USA. Psychiatrist and Chief Medical Officer at the Howard Centre, Vermont. Clinical Associate Professor of Psychiatry at the Larner College of Medicine, University of Vermont. Trained in Open Dialogue at Institute for Dialogue Practice. Editor of *Critical Psychiatry: Controversies and Clinical Implications*, Springer, 2019.

Maria Sundvall, Stockholm, Sweden. Psychiatrist at Transcultural centre, Stockholm County Council. Former member of Södertälje first episode psychosis team.

Sully Swearingen, Salt Lake City, USA. Studying geology at Westminster College. Hobbies include snowboarding, skating and playing guitar. When he is not outside, you may find him reading a book by Edward Abbey or in a record store searching for new music.

Giuseppe Tibaldi, Modena, Italy. Psychiatrist at Mental Health Department Modena. Manager of a network of community mental health services. Psychotherapist. Researcher – board member of the Italian Society of Epidemiological Psychiatry. Trainer in Open Dialogue.

Iseult Twamley, West Cork, Ireland. Clinical psychologist. Clinical lead for Open Dialogue implementation in West Cork. Open Dialogue trainer and supervisor in Ireland and internationally. Lecturer and co-leader of Open Dialogue research at University College, Cork. From family and personal experience, passionate about collaborative and co-productive practices in mental health practice.

Veronica, PhD, Italy. Science teacher at public secondary school. Expert by experience.

Sebastian von Peter, Berlin, Germany. (Critical) psychiatrist. Professor at Brandenburg Medical School. Senior psychiatrist in a home treatment team, integrating Open Dialogue elements into daily practice. Leader of research team, using participatory approaches in the evaluation of mental health services and alternatives.

Margit Wallsten, Stockholm, Sweden. Psychologist and psychotherapist. Former member of Södertälje first episode psychosis team.

FOREWORD

Mental health has now finally emerged as a global priority and at last is recognised as being as important as physical health. However, there are serious questions and debates around the optimum mental health policies and approaches in which to invest and, at the same time, to not invest in. The publication of this book *Open Dialogue for Psychosis* is very timely, as the approach described can substantially and meaningfully contribute to those debates at a global level.

The history of mental healthcare and psychiatry has been quite dramatic over the last 150 years, with its pendulum-like shifts from theories and practices that could be caricatured as espousing a 'brainless mind' to the opposite: those espousing a 'mindless brain'. For example, over recent decades the biomedical model has been dominant, succeeding the previous dominance of psychoanalysis. However, there is ever increasing research evidence pointing to the limited effectiveness and possible harm of mainstream mental healthcare based on a biomedical approach to individual mental health disorders that often ignores and undermines broader societal issues and human rights concerns.

The bold promise was that the systematic application of the biomedical paradigm would lead to resolution of individual problems, improvements in quality of life, and an end to stigma and the discrimination of persons with mental health issues; but the evidence is increasingly thin for these claims. Hence there is a contemporary need to rethink many 'conventional wisdoms'.

One of the most worrying messages, documented by research and by testimonies of thousands of users and ex-users of mental health services, is the recognition that heavy reliance on a biomedical paradigm may actually reinforce vicious cycles of stigma, discrimination, social exclusion and coercion. Psychiatry, in contrast to other fields of medicine, has refused to accept the principle of informed consent as the basis of protection of the human rights of service users. The legal framework and practice of psychiatry continues to use and overuse 'exceptions' where it is quite easy to override the human rights of individuals, and to apply non-consensual measures.

Arguments of 'dangerousness' or 'medical necessity' are commonly used and coercion is widespread in all regions of the world, thereby toxifying relations between providers and users and adversely affecting the reputation and image of psychiatry. People who hear voices or who have any other signs of what is qualified as psychosis particularly and disproportionately suffer from discrimination, institutionalisation, coercion and overmedicalisation. Their human rights are often violated in the name of medicine and psychiatry.

Around the world innovative approaches need to be developed and mainstreamed that can overcome reliance on the legacy of coercion and disempowerment of those who use services. A human rights based approach is needed at the centre of mental health policies and services, free of coercion and the excessive use of the biomedical model.

Open Dialogue is one of the leading and most promising ways of providing such an approach and this book, with its many contributions conveying experiences of it from many regions, convincingly presents a way of organising mental health services for persons experiencing the most serious mental health issues, with minimal necessity for coercion.

This book provides a comprehensive description of all the principles of Open Dialogue and how these are put into practice, together with evidence of its benefits, and will provide a very important contribution to the necessary global discourse I have mentioned. It brings hope that there is a way out from the impasse of the current 'status quo'.

Open Dialogue is a good illustration of the synergy of two important principles used simultaneously. Firstly, services are structurally organised such that people in crisis receive support and care immediately. Secondly, this support and care is provided in a respectful and dignified way, with minimal need for non-consensual measures. The book demonstrates Open Dialogue's application through a variety of accounts and reflections from various regions and countries, and explores possibilities for combining Open Dialogue with other methods, including the neurobiological model.

Open Dialogue, as any other approach, is not a panacea, and there will always be a need for a broad variety of interventions to meet the differing needs of people with mental health issues and to overcome the crisis that mental health is currently facing globally. However, in the search for practices that are in line with modern human rights based approaches, Open Dialogue offers an avenue that is very inspiring and hopeful, and I can therefore strongly recommend this book to all those interested in thinking seriously about modernising the broad field of mental healthcare, including providers, users, family members and administrators.

Dainius Pūras
Professor, Clinic of Psychiatry, Vilnius University, Lithuania
Former (2014–2020) UN Special Rapporteur on the
right to physical and mental health

PROLOGUE

Nick Putman
(UK)

Given the rapid growth of interest in the Open Dialogue (OD) approach in recent years, there is clearly a need for a book that not only describes what the OD approach is, but also collates how it is being developed internationally. Several reasons for the growing interest in the approach can be identified. First and foremost, more and more people are becoming familiar with the approach and its evidence base, as this has been detailed in various journals and books since the 1990s. The research from Western Lapland clearly shows that a system of public mental health care, organised flexibly in order to ensure a rapid response in a time of need/crisis, with an emphasis on relationships, dialogue and meaning, can produce far better outcomes for people having psychotic experiences than we are used to seeing in conventional mental health services in regions such as Europe, North America and Australasia. Details of the research carried out to date, which now includes a 19-year follow-up of participants from earlier studies, can be found in Section 6. Clearly there is a need for further research of sufficient quality to address the question of the replicability of the approach in different settings, and details of new research projects that have this aim in mind can also be found in Section 6.

To understand the scale of the interest that is developing, though, I think we need to look beyond the Western Lapland evidence base, to the current service provision for people having psychotic experiences in the majority of psychiatric services in the regions mentioned above. The biomedical model has come to dominate service provision, especially for people having psychotic experiences, such that in many countries, including the UK, they are unlikely to be offered psychotherapeutic or family support (e.g. Haddock et al., 2014). In this model, psychotic experiences have largely been reduced to a theory of biochemical imbalance, for which there is scant aetiological evidence (see Read and Dillon, 2013, for a discussion of different models of psychosis/madness). For most of those diagnosed with psychosis or schizophrenia, treatment consists almost entirely of neuroleptic medication in the short term, and for many the long term too, with all of the concomitant problems of so-called 'side effects', which are prominent in the experience of most who take these medications, leading many to discontinue treatment (Lieberman et al., 2005). The United Nations has recently made a substantive critique of current mental health service provision:

> There is now unequivocal evidence of the failures of a system that relies too heavily on the biomedical model of mental health services, including the front-line and excessive use of psychotropic medicines, and yet these models persist.
>
> (United Nations, 2017)

Those of us who have adopted an essentially psychotherapeutic approach to working with individuals and families affected by psychotic experiences have commonly found a strong connection between a person's psychotic experiences and events that have taken place in their life, with trauma being a strong feature of their histories (Read et al., 2005; Varese et al., 2012). We therefore need no encouragement to adopt an approach such as OD, which offers a frame within which to make sense of psychotic experiences and life events that are related to these experiences.

What distinguishes OD in Western Lapland from other psychosocial approaches to people having psychotic experiences is that, in addition to being a therapeutic approach, it is also a way of organising a public mental health service. This was the greatest factor in my decision to travel to Lapland to study the approach in the first instance, and in my subsequent desire to develop training programmes for people working in public mental health services. For whilst I could see the value of developing my psychotherapy practice for people having psychotic experiences, I could also see the limitations of this approach, which include limited financial means and a reluctance (or inability) on the part of some people having such experiences to engage in psychotherapy. OD (as developed in Western Lapland), a publicly funded mental health service which employs a variety of means to engage flexibly with social networks affected by psychotic experiences, seemed to address many of the issues I was seeing/experiencing in my practice, and was therefore a natural place to put my attention and energy.

Given that this book is part of the ISPS series, the emphasis is placed on people having psychotic experiences (although some may prefer alternative words to describe their experiences and this is respected in the OD approach, where we aim to follow the language of family/network members). However, it is important to remember that, even though the research from Western Lapland has focused on people having psychotic experiences, the OD approach is actually used with all individuals/families experiencing a mental health crisis in Western Lapland, regardless of diagnosis. At the same time, we can ask ourselves whether there is something about the OD approach that is particularly well suited to people having psychotic experiences.

Having now been involved in the development of OD for the past eight years, in the UK and elsewhere, I can say something about the conversations that I've had with many mental health professionals from a variety of backgrounds, services and countries, who have come to seminars, conferences, training programmes and other events related to the approach. A dominant theme in such conversations has been how disaffected many professionals feel with the current state of service provision. Many find themselves having to adhere to a service model that does not correspond with their values, and that does not seem to them to be in the best interests of those with whom they work. When it comes to people having psychotic experiences, they often speak of excessive use of medications and a lack of psychotherapeutic/family work, as well as extensive bureaucracy and heavy workloads which affect their capacity to *be with* the people they work with. Many find themselves working in ways which differ significantly from the ways in which they imagined they would be working when they embarked on their career, or perhaps the way they used to be able to practise earlier in their careers, and see in OD an approach that is closer to their values and to what they think will be of most benefit. Some of these concerns have also been raised by service users and family members (at Open Dialogue UK events and elsewhere), and there is thus a significant, and I would suggest growing, body of people who want to see changes to mental health services.

Clearly, we still have a long way to go, in this struggle to 'humanise' our mental health services, as some have put it – but the contributions to this book highlight the fact that, within the OD field (not to mention other approaches), there have already been very many significant developments along these lines, and in countries where the biomedical model predominates (OD is now being developed in around 30 countries, with variations according to each context). I think that anyone wishing to develop an OD service will find much inspiration in this book, as well as practical guidance. Of course, the notion of a community response in a time of crisis is nothing new, and in some cultures a community-based response, which naturally adopts a collective view, may well still be the most common practice. In developing dialogical practices/services, we have a lot to learn from each other, and I hope that the opportunities for us to do so will continue to grow in the years to come and that these opportunities will extend the diversity within the approach.

Section 1 of the book introduces the OD approach and its key principles, the history of the development of the approach in Western Lapland and the ways in which the approach can be utilised in working with people/families affected by psychotic experiences. In Section 2 we find several examples of the work, written from a variety of perspectives, including those of service users and family members.[1] Section 3 focuses on OD training and, as well as detailing different training programmes, includes reflections from trainers and training participants. Section 4 highlights work that has been undertaken to develop the approach in a variety of services internationally, including adaptations that have been necessary given current constraints. Section 5 compares OD to a variety of other approaches to people having psychotic experiences. Finally, Section 6 outlines the original research from Finland/Western Lapland and introduces other, mostly ongoing, research projects that are evaluating the introduction of the approach elsewhere.

It has been a privilege to work on this book with my co-editor Brian Martindale, and to collaborate with so many people who are forging much-needed changes. The notion of polyphony (many voices) is at the heart of OD and so it feels very meaningful to have worked on a book that has so many voices in it. Both Brian and I sincerely hope that this book will make a significant contribution to the further development of services in which there are greater possibilities for meaning making in a climate of respect and inclusiveness.

Nick Putman, January 2021

For an up-to-date listing of all places known to be developing OD services, please go to the following webpage: www.open-dialogue.net/compendium

Note

1 In this book a number of service users and family members have wanted their real first names to be used. In other instances, pseudonyms are used, but network members have given their permission for accounts of the work involving them to be included in the book, and in some instances have contributed to these accounts.

References

Haddock, G., Eisner, E., Boone, C., Davies, G., Coogan, C. and Barrowclough, C. (2014) An investigation of the implementation of NICE-recommended CBT interventions for people with schizophrenia. *Journal of Mental Health*, 23(4), p. 162–165. doi.org/10.3109/09638237.2013.869571

Lieberman, J.A., Stroup, T.S., McEvoy, J.P., Swartz, M.S., Rosenheck, R.A., Perkins, D.O., Keefe, R.S., Davis, S.M., Davis, C.E., Lebowitz, B.D., Severe, J. and Hsiao, J.K. (2005) Effectiveness of antipsychotic drugs in patients with chronic schizophrenia. *New England Journal of Medicine*, 353, p. 1209–1223. doi.org/10.1056/NEJMoa051688

Read, J. and Dillon, J. (2013) *Models of madness: Psychological, social and biological approaches to psychosis* (2nd ed.). London: Routledge. doi.org/10.4324/9780203527160

Read, J., van Os, J., Morrison, A.P. and Ross, C.A. (2005) Childhood trauma, psychosis and schizophrenia: A literature review with theoretical and clinical implications. *Acta Psychiatrica Scandinavica*, 112(5), p. 330–350. doi.org/10.1111/j.1600-0447.2005.00634.x

United Nations (2017) *Statement by Mr Dainius Pūras, Special Rapporteur on the right of everyone to the enjoyment of the highest attainable standard of physical and mental health at the 35th session of the Human Rights Council.* [online] Available at: www.ohchr.org/en/NewsEvents/Pages/DisplayNews.aspx?NewsID=22052& LangID=E [Accessed 22 October 2018].

Varese, F., Smeets, F., Drukker, M., Lieverse, R., Lataster, T., Viechtbauer, W., Read, J., van Os J. and Bentall, R.P. (2012) Childhood adversities increase the risk of psychosis: A meta-analysis of patient-control, prospective- and cross-sectional cohort studies. *Schizophrenia Bulletin*, 38(4), p. 661–671. doi.org/10.1093/schbul/sbs050

Section 1

INTRODUCING OPEN DIALOGUE

CONTENTS

1

WHAT IS OPEN DIALOGUE?

Nick Putman
(UK)

The question as to what Open Dialogue (OD) is can be answered in many ways. The most straightforward answer is that OD is a system of mental health care, first developed in Western Lapland, Finland, which has two essential ingredients: a therapeutic and philosophical approach to *being with* people in a time of crisis/need, and a way of organising mental health services that maximises the possibility of being able to respond to people in such a way and in a timely manner. The response is usually to arrange a 'network meeting' in the community, as soon as possible after initial contact with the service, in which the 'person(s) at the centre of concern'[1] and significant members of their social network can participate, along with a professional team of two or more persons.

Although the approach has been in development since the early 1980s, the term 'Open Dialogue' was not used until 1995 (Seikkula et al., 1995), by which time the seven principles that underlie the approach had been formally instituted (these principles are detailed below). The 'Open' in OD refers to the transparent nature of the discourse, i.e. the inclusion of the service user's family/social network in the process of addressing a crisis and all subsequent conversations/decisions, wherever possible/desirable.

Because the OD research in Western Lapland has focused on people diagnosed with psychosis for the first time, some have assumed that it is a specialised approach to those diagnosed with psychosis. In reality, the entire public mental health service in Western Lapland is run according to the seven principles; regardless of the nature of the crisis or problem, the same underlying approach is used. In saying this, it is important to remember that, though network meetings are the most common form of response, there are in fact a variety of ways of responding in the Western Lapland service which is, by design, adapted to the current needs of the individual and network (henceforth called 'need-adapted'). Therefore, the 'same approach' in effect means that the response to each individual, family or network is unique.

The primary focus in this introductory chapter will be on the psychiatric service in Western Lapland, as it remains the only psychiatric service internationally to have comprehensively developed the approach to date (by which

9

I mean that OD is the platform through which all mental health services are provided). Although the approach is now being developed in around 30 countries, with variations according to each context, these developments are more recent and the focus has tended to be on transforming aspects of a service to run more dialogically, rather than the system as a whole – primarily through the use of network meetings, but also by introducing at least some of the seven principles. In my view, the OD approach is likely to be most effective when an entire service is run according to the seven principles; though I think it is also the case that elements of the approach can be developed in a variety of services, to the benefit of those using such services. In the coming years we will learn more about the extent to which it has been possible to transform whole systems of care (the early evidence, as illustrated in a number of accounts in this book, is that it is difficult to do so) and the effect of such transformations on outcomes.

The structure of the Western Lapland service

In some respects, the structure of the Western Lapland service looks much like that of many conventional psychiatric services, with a hospital and outpatient clinics, and a staff team consisting of psychiatrists, psychologists, social workers, rehabilitation workers, peer workers and nurses (who form by far the largest proportion of the staff population). However, as we come to learn more about the seven principles underpinning the OD approach, we will appreciate just how differently the Western Lapland service is organised and conducted.

A distinguishing feature of the Western Lapland service is the degree of collaboration with other statutory agencies. If other professionals or agencies are involved with service users, they are welcome to participate in network meetings, with the consent of the service user/family. This creates a higher degree of collaboration with professionals responsible for, for example, child welfare, teaching and employment, and thus leads to more effective forms of working.

Influences and collaborations

OD did not emerge from nowhere, and many strands of influence can be distinguished. Some of these influences will be detailed in Chapter 2, but worthy of mention here are the practice of Systemic Family Therapy (SFT), Need-Adapted Treatment (NAT) from Turku in the southwest of Finland, the work of Tom Andersen and his colleagues in Tromsø in the north of Norway (Andersen, 1991) and the philosophy of Mikhail Bakhtin (Bakhtin, 1984).

In the 1970s and 1980s there was a growing interest internationally in working with families in mental health services, with different strands of development, of which OD was one. Prior to the development of OD, Yrjö Alanen, Jukka Aaltonen and others had been working to good effect to integrate family therapy with individual psychoanalytic psychotherapy (Alanen, 2009), within a service that aimed to flexibly meet the needs of those affected by psychotic experiences over time. Similarly, Tom Andersen and his team were adapting SFT to their public mental health service, notably by enhancing transparency through the use of reflecting teams (who sat in the same room as the family rather than behind a one-way mirror, as was the practice in SFT), as well as by developing a more philosophical approach (see Chapter 2 for more detail on NAT and the work of Tom Andersen and colleagues).

Some of the early developers of OD had been trained in SFT and started to introduce the approach into the Western Lapland service in the early 1980s. Decisions as to who to invite to family therapy were taken without the family present, in line with traditional hospital practices, and so could only be made on the basis of a perceived problem/pathology in the family. Also, there was a tendency in SFT, as practised at this time, to view the family as an object of treatment, delivered by experts. Before long professionals in the Western Lapland service started to feel uncomfortable with this approach and, quite possibly for similar reasons, few families chose to engage in family therapy, meaning that it was largely an ineffective form of working (personal communication with Jaakko Seikkula).

As the practice changed from the use of SFT to open network meetings, some elements of SFT were retained. These included an attention to the relational context and the use of positive (or logical) connotation and circular questions, though these elements were no longer used as the guiding strategy for family meetings, and therefore had a different emphasis. For instance, positive/logical connotation was no longer used to interpret a symptom of one family member as serving a function for the family system as a whole, but rather as one way of introducing a new perspective, which may further the process of meaning making, and with a greater emphasis on the capabilities of network members.

Though some of the theory underpinning SFT was still relevant, philosophical considerations started to have greater significance, particularly the work of Mikhail Bakhtin. Jaakko Seikkula observed an affinity between Bakhtin's analysis of the characters in Dostoevsky's novels and his experience of network meetings:

> I was astonished that Bakhtin (1984) seemed to describe the same experience in Dostoevsky's novels that we were experiencing in the 'polyphonic' meetings with our clients. There were always many voices present in the network meetings, and as Bakhtin notes, in a polyphonic meeting the position of every participant, especially the author, is changed radically. The only way to proceed is to generate dialogue between all the participants' voices, and in this polyphony no voice can be more important than others.
>
> (Seikkula, 2011, p. 183)

11

The seven principles

By analysing more than a decade of service developments in Western Lapland and comparing these to the earlier traditional psychiatric system, seven main principles illustrating the optimal processes in this new form of community care were identified (Aaltonen et al., 2011):

1 Immediate help
2 Social network perspective
3 Flexibility and mobility
4 Responsibility
5 Psychological continuity
6 Tolerance of uncertainty
7 Dialogism

Though broadly speaking the first five principles are concerned with the structure of the service, and the last two with the form of practice, in reality all of the principles interrelate, and depend upon each other.

Principle 1: immediate help

The Western Lapland service is organised such that, when somebody first contacts the service in a mental health crisis, the person answering the call arranges for a meeting to take place within 24 hours (unless the service user/family request a meeting at a later date). The initial contact with the service can be initiated by a doctor, a professional working for another agency, the person at the centre of concern, or their family (a written referral is not needed). The basic attitude of staff is that there is always a good reason why people call, and thus their concerns should be taken seriously. People's need for support is usually pressing and, if contact is established in a timely and effective manner, a crisis is less likely to escalate, and the need for hospitalisation is also lessened. Where possible, OD teams offer support in the community, and this is more likely to be the case when key members of the social network are willing to participate in network meetings (which is more likely to happen when there is a swift response at the time of initial crisis).

With regards to psychotic experiences, teams working in Western Lapland have found that there is often a fairly brief window of opportunity during a crisis to make contact with the person at the centre of concern in such a way that dialogue about their experiences is possible. If this opportunity is missed, it can be several weeks/months before another opportunity arises.

In the initial conversation following contact with services, time is taken to understand the current situation and the concerns of those involved, as well as to estimate the degree of risk and how rapid the response needs to be. If there is a decision to meet with the family/network, either in someone's home or at an outpatient clinic, there will be a conversation about who should be invited to this meeting, and by whom. A number of people from the network may be involved in this decision, and this should include the person(s) at the centre of concern wherever possible. However, if an individual meeting is preferred, then this will be arranged instead.

At the first meeting, variations on two questions first described by Tom Andersen are asked (Andersen, 1991). The first, 'what is the history of the idea of this meeting?', is designed to enable the family/network to share their understanding of what has led to the crisis in hand and the decision to contact services and participate in the meeting. The second, 'how would you like to use this meeting?', is asked after the first question in the first meeting, and at the start of any further meetings, in order to keep the focus on the issues that are most significant to the network (the content of each meeting is therefore defined by the network, not the professionals). Both questions are addressed to every member of the network, to allow for every voice to be heard, and to create space for different perspectives and opinions on the central issues (though if anyone in the network prefers not to respond, this is respected). There may be different degrees of interest in participating in meetings (Andersen, 1991), and these open questions can help to clarify such differences, which are important to understand in the early stages.

In this chapter a fictitious account of a beneficial OD process (which is based on the experience of practising OD) follows the introduction of each of the seven principles. Such an account cannot convey the complex and varying realities of such processes, including the multitude of contributions from network members and facilitators, but is rather designed to illustrate aspects of the seven principles.

EXAMPLE

Joe, a nurse based in a community team, took a call from a distressed mother, Anne. She was growing increasingly concerned about the erratic behaviour of her 20-year-old son John. John had been isolating himself in his bedroom, shouting, pacing up and down, and complaining that the neighbours were plotting against him. The previous night he had been found by Anne walking barefoot around his neighbourhood, speaking to himself in a non-understandable manner, and her fears for his safety and well-being had increased. Having spoken to Anne for a while, Joe offered to arrange for a team to meet with Anne, John and other significant members of their network later the same day. Anne

---

13

said that she would speak to John about the meeting, as she wasn't sure how he would feel about it. Joe informed Anne that, whilst he hoped John would decide to join the meeting, it could still go ahead even if John didn't wish to do so, as she was clearly very worried, and it felt important to meet with her to listen to and address her concerns. Anne thought that it would be good to invite John's younger sister Sarah, as she was still living at home and was also very concerned. She also explained that she had separated from John's father some years ago, and that he had become rather estranged from the rest of the family. Because of this she felt that it would not be a good idea to invite him, and also didn't want to invite anyone else to the initial meeting. She preferred to meet at the family home, as it might be easier for John to participate in a meeting there.

Having taken the call, Joe was responsible for organising a team to visit the family home. He had an overview of the schedules of all team members, and realised that he had some space in his calendar, as did his colleague Amanda, a psychologist. He contacted the family to confirm the time of the meeting and that he and Amanda would be attending.

Principle 2: social network perspective

As indicated above, key members of the social network of the person at the centre of concern are invited to participate in network meetings, whether these be family members, friends, colleagues or other professionals/agencies who are already involved. There are a number of (potential) advantages to involving the social network in our response to people having psychotic experiences, not least that it reduces the chances of alienation from one's network, which can escalate in such situations.

The OD approach is essentially built on systemic foundations, so veers away from an individualistic understanding of mental health challenges towards the view that, for example, psychotic experiences arise/exist *between* people as well as *in* people. I think that this can be understood in a number of ways. For instance, if I am using the word 'psychotic' to describe someone else's experience, then it is between us because I have chosen to use this word, as opposed to some other word. But, perhaps more significantly, it can also be between people because the family/network have a shared history and it may be that elements of this history are being expressed through the psychotic experiences. Our recognition of this should not lead to the attribution of blame, for this will not prove helpful. However, if issues relating to blame arise, these can be addressed in network meetings, and this may turn out to be an important aspect of the process.

There can be a tendency for any approach that includes the family in the understanding of and response to people having psychotic experiences or other mental health challenges to elicit a backlash from those who feel that the family are being blamed. It was Frieda Fromm-Reichmann who coined the term 'schizophrenogenic mother' (Fromm-Reichmann, 1948) and whatever insights came from her long career working with people having psychotic experiences, the term has (or came to have) a pejorative, and thus unhelpful, tone. The work of people such as Gregory Bateson, in his analysis of 'double-binds' in the communication of families of hospital patients diagnosed with schizophrenia in the 1950s (Bateson et al., 1956) and R.D. Laing, in his analysis of the communication of such families in the 1960s (Laing and Esterson, 1965), can be seen to imply blame, but I don't think that this was their intention. They were actually showing how experiences that are labelled 'psychotic' can be more intelligible when seen in the context of family life. Certain patterns of communication may run through many generations, and so it doesn't make sense to try to identify a root cause. Instead, the focus should be on supporting the family/network to address their issues together. It may be that in recent decades concern about blame has considerably hampered implementing family-based approaches (Martindale, 2017).

The emphasis in OD is not on the 'pathology' of the family, but rather on the resources (or at least potential resources) that there are in the family/network. Network members can share their perspectives on the current crisis and matters of historical significance and may be able to provide a variety of additional forms of support. And where there are historical issues involving family/network members, which have not been previously addressed (to a sufficient extent), the hope is that the network will feel safe enough in network meetings to start to do so (some of the accounts in this book speak to this, i.e. the possibility of family/network members being able to speak about issues that it has not been possible to speak of before).

Usually it is network members who define a situation as a crisis – i.e. at least some in the network recognise that their resources have been exceeded and that they are in need of support. Therefore, if all those who are involved and who have an opinion about the crisis are able to participate in a process which addresses the central issues, such that no one in the network considers there to be a crisis anymore, a positive and sustainable outcome is more likely.

If there is a history of abuse or violence within the family/network, it may be necessary for different team members to meet with different configurations of the network, in order to protect vulnerable members, or because of a sense that it would not be constructive for everyone to meet together. It may however be possible and desirable for the whole network to meet later in the process.

A final point worth making is that, as indicated in the example above, where concerned relatives contact the psychiatric service, a meeting can be arranged even if the person at the centre of concern does not wish to participate. This is because the team is responding directly to the anxieties of the relatives, i.e. it is effectively *they* who are the service users.

EXAMPLE

On arrival at the family home, Joe and Amanda were invited to sit with Anne and Sarah in the living room. John had decided not to join the meeting (though occasionally he could be heard talking in the room above), as he didn't see how it would benefit him.

At the invitation of the team, Anne shared something of her experience and understanding of the recent changes in John's behaviour. She also spoke about his adolescence, difficulties he had experienced at school, including extensive bullying, and her sense of his vulnerability and need for protection. Sarah was invited to share her views and she expressed concern for her mother's well-being and safety, as John had been violent towards her on one occasion. Both felt that a decision needed to be made about how to move forward – something needed to be done, but what? Sarah felt strongly that the situation was unmanageable at home and that John should therefore be hospitalised for a while, whilst Anne wanted him to stay at home, with professional support. The team helped Anne and Sarah to share their concerns and to explore and understand their differences. Joe wondered if, in seeking to protect John, Anne was understating the risk to herself, but Anne felt that the violent incident was isolated.

The team informed the family that they could continue to meet with them in their home, if they wished to do so and the risks seemed manageable at home. Anne hoped that John would engage in future meetings, and even if he didn't, she felt that Sarah and herself would benefit from ongoing support. A decision was made collectively that decisions about hospitalisation or use of medication could be held off until the following day, when the team could return. The team asked Anne and Sarah if they thought that anyone else from their social network should be invited to the next meeting, but they didn't think so.

In the meeting the following day the team heard that, although John was still agitated, he had remained at home since yesterday and the family's distress had been manageable. The team asked the family how they would like to use the meeting. Anne was clearly upset and found it hard to speak. Sarah spoke about how much her mother had suffered in recent years and how the relationship between her parents had deteriorated, becoming increasingly oppressive and violent. At this point John appeared, asking his mother for a cigarette. The team introduced themselves briefly as John went outside to smoke. He then headed back to his bedroom, but later returned to ask for another cigarette, at which point Joe asked him if he could join him whilst he smoked. John replied, "if you like".

John wasn't particularly communicative in the few minutes spent outside with Joe but listened as Joe explained why he and Amanda were visiting the family home. Joe asked John how he saw recent events. John stated that the neighbours had it in for him and were making his life hell. Joe took John's concerns seriously, acknowledging his suffering, and said that he'd like to talk to John more about this. John was noncommittal, but Joe was pleased to have made contact with him. Joe re-joined the others, and a decision was made to meet again the following day.

A few points are worth making here. Firstly, the way in which the team naturally enquired into both Anne and Sarah's experiences and the family history that they shared. As network meetings progress the focus becomes the well-being of all, with less sense of an identified 'service user'. Secondly, the way in which Joe and Amanda helped to slow the pace of the meeting, and specifically the decision-making process. Although sometimes urgent action needs to be taken in a crisis, if network members feel safe enough it can be more beneficial to take time to understand as much as possible about the crisis, discussing issues over multiple meetings before making significant decisions. Thirdly, one aspect of the flexibility in the approach was demonstrated in the way that Joe naturally adapted, leaving the meeting in the living room in an attempt to connect with John, with John's permission. Finally, it is important to note how Joe took John's experiences and concerns relating to the neighbours seriously. He did not attempt to minimise the significance of such experiences or convince him otherwise. In the OD approach we treat experiences that might in other settings be simply labelled as 'psychotic', 'delusional' or 'paranoid' as very significant experiences in the life of the person concerned and seek to understand more. This does not mean that we take such experiences as factual – we do not need to believe that the neighbours are persecuting John in order to take such experiences seriously.

Principle 3: flexibility and mobility

In any dialogical form of practice, there is a natural flexibility and responsiveness inherent in the work. In relation to this third principle, however, flexibility refers specifically to a need-adapted response, i.e. the provision of a variety of forms of response, such that the services provided fit the varying and changing needs of service users (as was the case in Need-Adapted Treatment, as described in Chapter 2). So, whilst the most common form of therapeutic work is the facilitation of network meetings, additional forms can be introduced at any stage, such as individual psychotherapy or trauma work. Practical support may also be offered to address vocational or educational needs or to assist with everyday activities. Decisions about what is needed are made collaboratively with the network during meetings, including the decision as to when to schedule the next network meeting, which is made at the end of each meeting, in order to be as close as possible to the current needs of the network.

Mobility primarily refers to the fact that network meetings take place in the setting that is most suited to the family and the current circumstances. In Western Lapland this is most often the family home, but meetings also take place in outpatient clinics, schools and workplaces (or at Keropudas hospital if it has proved necessary to hospitalise someone). There are a number of advantages to meeting in the family home. It may be challenging for the family to travel to an outpatient clinic at a time of crisis, or the person at the centre of concern may be resistant to travelling, and to engaging in the process at all. Thus, there may be an opportunity to involve more people in meetings if they take place in the family home. For instance, a door to the room in which people are meeting can be left open, and a message can be passed to someone who has chosen not to participate that they are welcome to join at any time if they change their mind. Alternatively, as happened in the example above, if someone passes through the room in which the meeting is taking place, it may be possible to engage them in some way as they do so. Where someone has a change of mind and joins the process at a later stage, it can be helpful to enquire into their motivation for doing so, to check whether this has been a voluntary decision, but also because their reasons for changing their mind could be illuminative.

Another advantage to meeting in the family home is that one gets a richer sense of family life when being with them in their natural habitat. Meetings tend to feel less formal and I think that, in being in someone else's home, away from one's habitual working environment, there is an implicit invitation to professionals to be more humble, which can serve to lessen power imbalances. In Western Lapland the tradition is to take off your shoes when entering the family home, and for this reason, if no other, it is harder to be in an 'expert' position!

EXAMPLE

The team visited the family home on most days over the next two weeks, and John started to participate more, though he continued to be agitated and rarely joined for more than 10 minutes at a time (the team's acceptance of John participating as much or as little as he wished seemed to increase his trust in them).

The team felt that the risks were manageable at home and, as John was starting to engage more, it was decided not to prescribe any neuroleptic medication. However, hearing that his sleep had been limited and erratic for some weeks, a decision was made collectively to prescribe some sleeping tablets.

Towards the end of the first week, Amanda asked John if he would like to invite anyone else to a meeting. Initially John said "no", but this led on to a conversation about his close relationship with a paternal aunt, following which there was a collective decision to invite her. Aunt Jessica started to attend when she could, and shared largely fond memories and stories about her relationship with John stretching back to early childhood, as well as her views on her brother's increasingly erratic behaviour and its negative impact on John and the whole family.

The themes, particularly when John was present, continued to be his experience of being persecuted by neighbours. John spoke more about the forms that this took, mostly him hearing them talking about him through his bedroom wall, and sometimes in the garden. They called him a "rotten apple" and shared opinions on almost anything that John found himself thinking about, almost always portraying him in a bad light. John would sometimes try to drown out his neighbours' voices by listening to music on headphones, with varying degrees of success.

John responded well to his aunt's presence in meetings and to the stories she shared – in this way it became possible to speak about topics other than the neighbours. Initially he was protective of his father when others criticised him, but gradually he acknowledged ways in which his father's behaviour had been difficult for him and for the family. Towards the end of the first month of meeting with the team (by which time meetings were happening around twice a week), John broke down as he recounted an incident in which his father physically attacked him after a row about his school performance.

Here I would like to make a brief comment about the use of medication in an OD service. In Western Lapland medication is sometimes used with people having psychotic experiences. Tranquillisers such as benzodiazepines may be used initially to improve sleep and for severe anxiety (as in the example above). Neuroleptics are not considered to be the primary treatment modality, but are prescribed sparingly (and where possible only for a short duration) for less than half of those diagnosed with psychosis. The excessive and especially long-term use of neuroleptics can affect an individual's capacity to be in touch with their thoughts, emotions and experiences (and thus the possibilities for finding meaning), though a modest dose may help some to feel more connected in this way, and thus to engage in dialogue (Hulkko et al., 2017). In Western Lapland, teams will generally look for every opportunity for dialogue before considering prescribing neuroleptics and, if dialogue proves possible, it is less likely that neuroleptics will be used. But if any network members/professionals feel that the use of neuroleptics may be advisable, the possibility of doing so will be discussed at some length, typically over at least three meetings (Seikkula et al., 2003), before a decision is taken.

Principle 4: responsibility

If a team member answers a phone call from a family in crisis in the Western Lapland psychiatric service, then it is their responsibility to arrange the first meeting, as was the case with Joe above. Usually an experienced member of nursing staff is responsible for answering the phone. So, right from the start, the family have access to an experienced mental health professional who can offer some initial support. Once a team is formed, team members then share the responsibility for the entire process, including the facilitation of network meetings. It is rare that they need to refer to an outside authority in order to make decisions about how to proceed, as they are trusted by senior clinicians to carry out their work to a high standard. However, if it seems advisable to invite someone with specific expertise to a meeting (such as on the use of medication), then this will be organised.

More broadly, the notion of responsibility is at the core of OD, which is based on a timely responsiveness, grounded in the needs and the communication of the family. OD practitioners seek to be non-defensive, taking responsibility for their contributions and the ways in which these may affect others in meetings, with a willingness to be changed by the experience. As Kari Valtanen, a psychiatrist in the Western Lapland service, puts it in Daniel Mackler's film about the OD approach, "I risk myself when I enter into a conversation" (*Open Dialogue: An Alternative Finnish Approach to Healing Psychosis*, 2011, 03:19–03:22). The subjectivity of team members is a necessary part of dialogical work, sitting alongside the ethical responsibility to respect the otherness of those in the network.

EXAMPLE

Returning briefly to Anne's decision to first contact services, at a time when she felt desperate. She had done all that she could to manage the situation at home with support from Sarah, and a couple of close friends, but now needed more support, and a professional opinion on John's behaviour. She felt reassured by the initial conversation with Joe

---

who, through his calm manner, and the quality of his listening, helped her to feel safe enough until the meeting later the same day. Joe, as the person first contacted, was responsible for putting together the team. He had worked with Amanda several times before and felt confident that they could form a strong team, due to the trust that had built up between them over the years.

In the first meeting with the family the team were clear that there were risks associated with John remaining at home, but they also became aware of a resourcefulness in the family which led them to believe that, with sufficient support in the form of regular network meetings, they could manage the situation in this way. John was troubled by the neighbours, which might have been an indication to move him to another setting, but the team were hopeful that they could address this issue in situ. Joe and Amanda recognised their responsibility in working in this way in the family home, but were concerned not to disempower the family, and diminish their capacity to take responsibility for their own lives, with the necessary support. At times Joe and Amanda shared differing views on how to proceed, mostly when reflecting (see below for more on reflections), but always encouraged family members to add their views to any thoughts they shared, in the hope that the family's sense of their own agency and resourcefulness would increase.

Principle 5: psychological continuity

Once a team is established for a family/network, the same team will work with them for as long as support is needed. Even if the work ends, but later the family/network need further support, it will be the same team who respond (provided they are still working in the service). Although the approach is designed to strengthen the resources in the social network and thereby lessen service dependency, the psychological continuity with team members is important. For, whatever the particular skills that practitioners bring to the facilitation of the process, human relations are at the heart of this way of working.

An important feature of this continuity is that the same team works with the network regardless of whether the person at the centre of concern is in the community or in hospital (i.e. professionals who are based in the community can attend network meetings on the ward and vice versa). I think that this blurring of the boundaries between inpatient and outpatient services is crucial as, in my experience, the value of work already done can be lessened or lost when people are passed between different teams/services.

Just as the same team members participate throughout the process, members of the social network are also invited to do so. Due to other commitments, it can be difficult for everyone to always attend, but the hope is that network members will attend whenever possible, and at any stage there may be a decision to invite additional members.

Where individual psychotherapeutic work with one member of the network is indicated, one of the team working with the family is likely to undertake this work if they have the necessary training. This ensures psychological continuity between the individual work and the network meetings, an arrangement which raises questions about confidentiality, but which can, if handled sensitively, prove advantageous.

EXAMPLE

Joe and Amanda continued to meet with the family for several months. Gradually the frequency of meetings reduced, so that by six months they were taking place fortnightly. The dialogue in these meetings ranged widely, though naturally John's concerns were central. He still felt tormented by the neighbours, and this continued to be discussed and taken seriously. However, largely through the contributions of Anne and Sarah, the topic of John's relationship with his father featured more. John's willingness to discuss this fluctuated. At times he could be rather hostile to others in the meeting, and suspicious of the motives of the team. However, on other occasions he seemed more connected to the team and particularly to Joe. As the work progressed, he started to anticipate meetings, and to talk more about his experiences of being abused at school and by his father. Joe and Amanda were moved by his stories, which were characterised by violence, confusion and a profound sense of inferiority and loneliness. Sometimes the main focus was Anne's relationship with John's father, and also her difficult relationship with her own father, which was distant, and occasionally violent. John became animated and angry as Anne spoke of her own experiences of paternal abuse, showing some empathy for and protectiveness towards her. As he later recalled the one occasion where he had hit his mother, he berated himself for having done so, and for about a week the family were concerned about his state of mind, and whether he might harm himself. The team, aware of the risk, were careful at this point to express appreciation for John's empathy and protective instinct, and also his courage to address his own behaviour and his feelings about this. Anne was keen to point out that John had in his life been the victim of violence far more than the perpetrator.

In the above example the family started to trust the team more, and the continuity of the team was a significant factor in this respect. As with any therapeutic process, the consistency of professionals and meetings is central. As an alternative to 'psychological continuity', we could also use 'emotional continuity'. The task for the team is to be emotionally available and connected (they effectively become part of the network), whilst retaining the capacity to reflect in a helpful way.

Principle 6: tolerance of uncertainty

In the Western Lapland service, staff recognise that every crisis is unique, and that it is therefore necessary to tolerate a good deal of uncertainty in their work. The word 'tolerate' suggests that uncertainty is burdensome and indeed, in a time of crisis, with heightened risk and emotion, being with the uncertainty of what has happened, what is unfolding, and what is needed, is not easy. Network members may well have a very understandable desire for something to be done, to be fixed. At other times though, it may feel more possible to embrace the uncertainty – to have a different relation to the unknown, which is full of possibility.

Tolerance of uncertainty is the bedfellow of 'not knowing', a philosophical stance that transcends the centuries, but is most often traced back to Keats' notion of negative capability:

> [T]hat is when man is capable of being in uncertainties, mysteries, doubts, without any irritable reaching after fact and reason.
>
> (Keats, 1899, p. 277)

This notion of negative capability came to OD via Wilfred Bion's elaboration of it in *Attention and Interpretation* (Bion, 1970), where he advocated for a state of mind in the analyst which he termed 'patience', which "should be retained, without 'irritable reaching after fact and reason' until a pattern evolves" (p. 124). This is related to his notion of analysts being without memory and desire (Bion, 1967), which is only possible if they can bear the pain and confusion of not knowing.

Another version of 'not knowing' commonly referred to in the OD literature is that proposed by Harlene Anderson and Harry Goolishian (1992) – a more humble, flexible, curious and collaborative way of being with the people we work with, in which practitioners stand to be as affected by the encounter as service users/family members. Not unrelated is their caution against understanding too quickly, for this runs the risk of blocking the development of new meaning.

One of the things that struck me when I visited Western Lapland for the first time was the quality of the presence of team members in network meetings.

Here it is important to distinguish between a strong presence grounded in deep listening (that creates space) and a strong presence that is directive (that takes up space). In Western Lapland you will find the former, and it is this that helps people to feel safe enough to engage and trust in the process. Practitioners slow down the pace so that everyone's experiences and ways of understanding the current situation can be heard. Premature conclusions are avoided, and the pressing need for answers or decisions starts to lessen. As the process unfolds, answers (or perhaps, more accurately, meanings) emerge naturally from the collective dialogue, rather than being or feeling forced, and then, where necessary, decisions can be made.

We can't know at the start how long this process will take and, in the early stages of a crisis, particularly a psychotic crisis, it may well be important to meet every day for a week or two, in order for those participating to feel safe enough. At the conclusion of initial meetings that take place following a crisis, there may still be considerable uncertainty, with anxieties running high. In such circumstances it can be reassuring to hear the team acknowledge this and think with the network about their capacity to manage until a meeting the following day. If this doesn't feel possible, a nurse could stay overnight with the family until the next meeting.

Teamwork is at the heart of the OD approach, and network meetings are thus facilitated by a team of two or three practitioners. One important advantage is that co-facilitation helps practitioners to tolerate the uncertainty and to avoid making premature decisions. As a team we are likely to notice more in network meetings, and in our responses to and reflections on what we hear and see, we add to the polyphony and help the network to be with their uncertainty, to feel safer. We do not have the answers, but as we listen carefully and take the communication of all present seriously, network members usually have the experience that something is actually being done.

In the Western Lapland service they speak of a culture of 'non-assessment'. In their view, structured assessments can interfere with the capacity to *be with* people, and so the emphasis is on a more open and spontaneous exchange. Though not completing risk assessment forms, team members are judging the degree of risk in any situation and would probably argue that their capacity to do so is enhanced if they have a good connection with network members, such that risks can be discussed more openly.

EXAMPLE

Though there had been a collective decision to manage the crisis at home, there was uncertainty as to whether this would be sustainable, and it was necessary for the team, as well as the family, to manage considerable anxiety. The trust established between Joe and Amanda in

---

working together in similar crisis situations helped, as did the consistency of network meetings. It was reassuring to the family to know that they could call the service 24 hours a day. It was also important to Anne to be able to express herself freely, including being honest about daily challenges and difficulties, without being judged and without the fear that professionals would rush to intervene in a directive way.

Although it was initially difficult to make sense of John's experience of the neighbours, the Western Lapland teams have found that usually such experiences start to make sense when there is enough time and space for everyone to express themselves, as turned out to be the case here.

Principle 7: dialogism

Dialogue is both the process and the goal in OD. In a crisis, network members will often have strong feelings and opinions about the current situation, which they need to express. Thus, their communication may be monological at first, and there needs to be space for this. However, the likelihood is that, as network members are increasingly able to express themselves in the space provided, a space in which their concerns are listened to carefully, taken seriously, and responded to, the opportunities for dialogue increase. The teamwork is crucial here – having two or more facilitators in a meeting at a time of crisis increases the possibility of everyone being and feeling heard. In addition the capacity of team members to be in dialogue with each other, listening carefully to each other whilst allowing for differences between them, helps to create an atmosphere in which dialogue is more likely to develop. If there are unresolved and unspoken issues between team members, whether these be more related to personality, power or values, it is likely to adversely affect the process.

Responsive listening

In dialogical practice we *follow* the themes, the language, and the practical needs of those we work with, in our interactions and in our reflections (see page 30 below for more on reflecting). In this way we hope to connect to what is most significant for the network. The primary focus is not on assessing symptoms and determining diagnosis, but on exploring the network's ways of understanding whatever challenges they are experiencing and their ideas about what a good outcome would look like, perhaps letting go of what we as practitioners think would be a good development. This can sometimes be achieved by simply repeating words or phrases that seem particularly significant. Such repetition may lead network members to reflect on their words and experiences more fully, and to elaborate further. When words are repeated it is never an exact repetition, for there will be a different intonation. Bakhtin's concept of the "penetrated word" (1984, p. 241–242) seems significant here – a word penetrated by the tone of another when repeated, such that the original speaker can find their own voice more readily. The repeating (sameness) shows the speaker that they have been heard and taken seriously, whilst the differing tone (difference) emphasises the experience of being heard by *another*, and possibly opens up a different perspective.

OD practitioners engage in a responsive form of listening, where their responses to verbal and non-verbal communication show network members that their utterances are significant, helping to create an atmosphere in which they feel recognised and safe enough to start to share more intimate aspects of their experience. There is a strong emphasis on the present moment in dialogical practice, on the ways in which network members are moved, moment-to-moment, as they share significant narratives. So, we can extend the notion of the uniqueness of each crisis to the uniqueness of each moment, or what Bakhtin called the "once-occurrent event of being" (1993, p. 2).

Agency

In an analysis of network meetings with families affected by psychotic experiences, Jaakko Seikkula showed that good outcomes were associated with network members contributing more to the dialogue than clinicians:

> The patient and the family had more possibilities for control over initiatives and responses in new topics of discussion. This could be interpreted as a sign of greater possibilities to become an agent in relation to the story of their lives that was narrated in the crisis meeting.
> (Seikkula, 2002, p. 269)

Thus, one of the desirable consequences of the practice of OD is that the social network's sense of their own agency increases as they find themselves addressing their issues together. Where network members are able to address their issues in this way, practitioners will naturally leave space for them to do so.

'Witness' and 'aboutness'

John Shotter's distinction between 'witness' and 'aboutness' thinking helps us to understand something of the quality of presence needed in the facilitation of network meetings (Shotter, 2004). Rather than separating themselves off, through a clinical gaze, sealed in a position of expertise ('aboutness' thinking), practitioners join with the network, using ordinary language ('witness' thinking). One consequence of 'witness' practice is that professionals bring themselves into their work more, and therefore it is particularly important that

WHAT IS OPEN DIALOGUE?

they are mindful of their own emotional responses, for a variety of reasons. For instance, such responses may indicate that the dialogue is resonating in some way with their own life story and, if this is the case, it is important to be aware of this. They may also help to illuminate how others in the meeting are feeling. It is part of the skill of the practitioner to judge if, when and how to share such emotional responses.

Authenticity and creativity

In OD, practitioners support network members to find their voice in relation to each other, to express themselves as authentically as possible, i.e. to speak *their* truth. The notion of authenticity is not straightforward, however, in postmodern thought. Bakhtin described the self as "unfinalisable", polyphonic and mutable (1984). In other words, we are socially constructed, from a multitude of influences which can continue to (in)form us throughout our lives. Thus, to speak is to "appropriate the words of others and populate them with one's own intention" (Wertsch, 1998, p. 78). The OD approach, and network meetings in particular, supports this process. As Seikkula and Olson (2003) state:

> The Bakhtinian idea of dialogue and its adaptation to the psychotic situation derive from a tradition that sees language and communication as primarily constitutive of social reality. Constructing words and establishing symbolic communication is a voice-making, identity-making, agentic activity occurring jointly 'between people' (Gergen, 1999). The crisis becomes the opportunity to make and remake the fabric of stories, identities, and relationships that construct the self and a social world.
>
> (Seikkula and Olson, 2003, p. 409)

There is then an inherent creativity in an OD process. New understandings emerge in the space between people, and words can be found for experiences which did not previously have words. The emphasis here is not on representational knowledge, i.e. on pre-existing facts – but rather on practical knowledge or, as Wittgenstein put it, with "knowing how to go on" (1980, cited in Shotter, 1996, p. 399) together.

EXAMPLE

In keeping with the principle of dialogism, Amanda and Joe were careful to create (or leave) space for network members to tell *their* stories. The emphasis was not on diagnosis, but rather on network members'

---

lived experience and everyone having the opportunity to share their perspectives on current and historical issues. Through responding to John's experience of feeling persecuted by the neighbours, but not getting fixated on this or trying to challenge his beliefs, a space gradually started to open for John and others to address other significant experiences which, in certain respects, paralleled his experience of the neighbours, such as his experiences of being bullied at school and criticised and abused by his father. It was the team's impression that, as John was able to speak of these historical experiences, and to be more connected emotionally to others in meetings, the intensity of his experience of being persecuted by neighbours decreased.

Whilst Amanda and Joe shared different viewpoints at times during network meetings, usually in the form of reflections, they were careful to do so tentatively and subjectively, acknowledging that there are always other ways of seeing/understanding. They did not offer interpretations because, in the OD tradition, these are seen to suggest a position of expertise, and thus to close down possibilities for dialogue. In their reflections, they were careful to acknowledge each network member present, which had a positive impact on the network members' sense of their own value and their engagement in the process. On occasion Joe reflected to himself that some of John's experiences resonated with violent aspects of his own relationship with his father and he wondered whether it would be helpful to share anything of this experience in his reflections, but decided against doing so. It was important that he was aware of this resonance, of both its potential for facilitating understanding, but also the possibility of it blinding him to the ways in which John's experiences were different from his own.

John's expression of concern for Anne, as she recounted being abused by her father, seemed particularly significant, and Amanda sensed an emotional shift in John as his mother spoke. She didn't want to interrupt Anne's account, but felt that it was also important to attend to what was arising at that moment for John, so she enquired about this soon after. As John found words for his feelings and thoughts about his mother's experience, he became more animated, and seemingly more empowered. He was clearly concerned about his mother, but there was also an increasing sense of his capacity to comfort her and his desire to protect her. He was not just 'the patient' – he was also a capable young man of 20 years, a concerned son. Soon his emotions shifted as he likened himself to his father and his grandfather, precipitating a precarious few days in which everyone was worried about him. The frequency of network meetings therefore increased during this period and, as a consequence of the ongoing dialogue and reflections about his experience, John started to be able to take responsibility for his actions and in time to be less harsh on himself. His taking responsibility, and his growing capacity to understand his behaviour and experience in the context of family history, signified a radical shift from what had been possible for his father and grandfather.

We leave this fictionalised account here, with it having served its purpose in illustrating many aspects of OD's seven principles. If we were to wind the story forward we may well find another stage in the process, in which John is supported to take steps to engage in activities that are meaningful and beneficial to him, whether that be study, an occupation, or something else. This may involve inviting a professional from a vocational support service to a network meeting or, if he had previously been working or studying, a previous employer or tutor. If friendships had broken down due to John's difficulties, another option would be to invite one or more of his friends to a network meeting. Or perhaps John would develop an interest in pursuing individual psychotherapeutic work, in addition to or instead of ongoing network meetings.

Other principles/values

I think it is worth highlighting additional principles/values that are not inscribed directly into the seven core principles, but which are central to the OD approach, namely: (i) equality, democracy and respect, (ii) transparency, and (iii) a process orientation.

Equality, democracy and respect

Within OD there is a deep respect for the lived experience of all those participating. We are not seeking consensus, but rather the juxtaposition and creative exchange of multiple viewpoints and voices, even if they are in tension between people ('outer polyphony') or within a person ('inner polyphony'). Bakhtin argued that dialogical conversations can be characterised as being "without rank" (1986, p. 97). In other words, all voices are treated equally in network meetings, and the professional team does not seek to impose their views. Democracy is an important ethic in Finnish culture, and naturally imbues the work in the Western Lapland service. Sometimes decisions need to be made in network meetings as to how to proceed in relation to a specific issue, and there may be opposing views between network members (or even team members). If it proves difficult/impossible to come to a decision, one option is to invite another practitioner or network member to participate, to add their perspective(s), as this may bring some momentum to the process.

Transparency (and reflecting)

In an OD service, professionals do not have conversations about the network in their absence. This is not only out of respect for the network but also because the process is strengthened when conversations are contained within network meetings – when professionals have to find a way to skilfully and respectfully speak about difficult matters, rather than take them elsewhere. Whilst team members can talk about their work in supervision sessions, the emphasis here will be on their *own* experiences in network meetings that *they* are struggling with or need to understand more fully, rather than on family/network issues.

The reflecting process in network meetings is one form of transparency. On at least one occasion per meeting team members will turn to each other to share their thoughts, feelings or associations on what they have experienced so far in the meeting. In some ways their reflections may resemble a conversation that would, in other services, take place in a team meeting between professionals without the family present (or perhaps behind a one-way mirror, as in some forms of family therapy). Those developing OD in Western Lapland considered it more respectful to have such conversations in the family's presence and to be sensitive about the ways in which they spoke when they did so.

Reflections may flow from the conversation, with team members spontaneously turning to each other to reflect, or they may be more formally introduced, with the family's permission being sought for the sharing of reflections. There are many reasons why a team might be moved to reflect, including times when there is a high degree of conflict in the room, when network members are frightened/troubled by aspects of their experience, when the team or network members are struggling to make sense of something, when the team find it easier/preferable to share or explore a particular issue with each other rather than directly with the family, or simply when a significant period of time has passed without any reflections.

In reflections team members share their thoughts, feelings and associations in a speculative manner, using ordinary language, in order to add to the polyphony and the network's possibilities for making sense of their experiences. Usually the network like to hear what the team has to say – it is an opportunity for them to just listen, in a different way than if they were engaged in free-flowing conversation (where they may feel moved to respond at any moment). After each reflective sequence, network members are invited to respond to any of the reflections they have heard.

Process-oriented practice

OD practitioners speak of 'trust in the process', by which they largely mean two things. Firstly, their work is process oriented, rather than goal oriented.

It is the experience of being in network meetings over a course of time, of attempting to address pertinent issues together in various ways, that is particularly significant. Secondly, they are referring to their experience that, when social networks and professionals are both committed to engaging in ongoing network meetings, organised according to the seven principles, it is usually possible to address the most significant issues, such that a positive outcome is likely.

It is hard to generalise about processes in different crises, but a common experience is the shift from monological to dialogical communication. Gradually, given the opportunity to express oneself and to be responded to in the ways outlined above, the possibilities for dialogue, for furthering meaning and understanding, start to emerge. The experience of being in a democratic process, with possibilities for genuine dialogue, seems to be at least as significant as the specific issues addressed in the meetings. Furthermore, the more network members can bear intense emotions and give voice to these during network meetings, the more favourable the outcome seems to be – an outcome that may be determined more by embodied experience (in other words, the ways in which network members come to feel different in themselves and in their relations and behave/respond differently) than by explanations offered or decisions reached.

Conclusion

OD has the potential to transform public mental health services into systems that are responsive, empowering and inclusive. In such services people would be supported to find and integrate the meaning in their experiences, such that they can move forward with their lives. It represents a paradigm shift, from top-down expertise to skilful collaboration, from an emphasis on biological basis to an emphasis on social construction, from a focus on causes to an exploration of reasons.

Those of us who have been working with people having psychotic experiences for some time know only too well how prevalent the 'revolving door syndrome' is, i.e. repeated admissions to hospital. In my view, to a significant extent, this reflects a limitation in the current state of much service provision, and notable in this regard are the lack of psychotherapeutic support and psychological continuity, the minimal attention to social factors/relations, and the complications that can be a feature of (long-term) medication use. Given the careful attention to these factors in the OD service in Western Lapland, it is no surprise to me that their relapse rates are low. The research from Western Lapland, which has focused on those experiencing a psychotic crisis for the first time, shows that only 17–28% relapse within the first two years and 19–32% within the first five years (see Section 6 of this book for more detail).

It is often a struggle to finance mental health service development, and yet if the outcome statistics from Western Lapland are repeated elsewhere (lower use of hospital and medications, lower relapse rates, and a high proportion of people working or studying) there could be considerable cost savings from investment in developing OD services. Notwithstanding financial concerns, this approach seems widely valued by service users and their families, who report positively on the quality of listening, relating and collaborating. Furthermore, professionals who have the opportunity to develop the approach in their service often speak of a positive shift in their work culture, and a resonance with the values that led them to embark on their mental health career, such as the necessity of building relationships and finding meaning. Clearly more research is needed to evaluate the development of OD internationally and its adaptability to different contexts. Early indications, such as those reported in this book, are that the use of network meetings translates well.

The shift to community care began half a century ago, and whilst many such developments have helped to reduce some of the adverse effects of long-term care in hospitals and other institutions, it can be argued that there are still significant limitations in community services. And here the OD approach holds great promise, for it supports the development of community and social capital (see Chapter 37) and helps to reduce alienation and stigmatisation. In these ways it addresses some of the societal issues of our time directly.

Note

1 This term is included in single quotes here to signify that, whilst there is typically one person at the centre of concern on initial contact with services, i.e. one person who family members or others are particularly concerned about, it usually turns out to be the case that other members of the network are deeply affected/suffering too, and the focus from the start in the OD approach is on the whole network rather than one individual. Further uses of the term 'person at the centre of concern' in the book will not include these quotes, but the reader is invited to keep this use of the term in mind.

References

Aaltonen, J., Seikkula, J. and Lehtinen, K. (2011) The comprehensive Open-Dialogue approach in Western Lapland: I. The incidence of non-affective psychosis and prodromal states. *Psychosis*, 3(3), p. 179–191. doi.org/10.1080/17522439.2011.601750

Alanen, Y.O. (2009) Towards a more humanistic psychiatry: Development of need-adapted treatment of schizophrenia group psychoses. *Psychosis*, 1(2), p. 156–166. doi.org/10.1080/17522430902795667

Andersen, T. (ed.) (1991) *The reflecting team: Dialogues and dialogues about the dialogues.* New York: W.W. Norton.

Anderson, H. and Goolishian, H. (1992) 'The client is the expert: A not-knowing approach to therapy' in S. McNamee and K. Gergen (eds.) *Therapy as social construction.* London: SAGE, p. 25–39.

Bakhtin, M.M. (1984) *Problems of Dostoevsky's Poetics*, ed. C. Emerson. Minneapolis, MN: University of Minnesota Press. doi.org/10.5749/j.ctt22727z1

Bakhtin, M.M. (1986) *Speech genres and other late essays*, trans. V.W. McGee. Austin, TX: University of Texas Press.

Bakhtin, M.M. (1993) *Toward a Philosophy of the Act*, trans. V. Liapunov, ed. V. Liapunov and M. Holquist. Austin, TX: University of Texas Press.

Bateson, G., Jackson, D.D., Haley, J. and Weakland, J. (1956) Toward a theory of schizophrenia. *Behavioral Science*, 1(4), p. 251–264. doi.org/10.1002/bs.3830010402

Bion, W.R. (1967) Notes on memory and desire. *Psychoanalytic Forum*, 2, p. 271–286.

Bion, W.R. (1970) *Attention and interpretation: A scientific approach to insight in psycho-analysis and groups*. London: Tavistock Publications.

Fromm-Reichmann, F. (1948) Notes on the development of treatment of schizophrenics by psychoanalytic psychotherapy. *Psychiatry*, 11(3), p. 263–273. doi.org/10.1080/00332747.1948.11022688

Hulkko, A.P., Murray, G.K., Moilanen, J., Haapea, M., Rannikko, I., Jones, P.B., Barnett, J.H., Huhtaniska, S., Isohanni, M.K., Koponen, H., Jääskeläinen, E. and Miettunen, J. (2017) Lifetime use of psychiatric medications and cognition at 43 years of age in schizophrenia in the Northern Finland Birth Cohort 1966. *European Psychiatry*, 45, p. 50–58. doi.org/10.1016/j.eurpsy.2017.06.004

Keats, J. (1899) *The complete poetical works and letters of John Keats, Cambridge Edition*. Boston, MA: Houghton Mifflin and Company.

Laing, R.D. and Esterson, A. (1965) *Sanity, madness and the family*. London: Routledge.

Martindale, B.V. (2017) A psychoanalytic contribution to understanding the lack of professional involvement in psychotherapeutic work with families where there is psychosis. *British Journal of Psychotherapy*, 33(2), p. 224–238. doi.org/10.1111/bjp.12290

Open Dialogue: An Alternative Finnish Approach to Healing Psychosis (2011) Directed by D. Mackler [DVD]. A Truthtraveler Production.

Seikkula, J. (2002) Open dialogues with good and poor outcomes for psychotic crises: Examples from families with violence. *Journal of Marital and Family Therapy*, 28(3), p. 263–274. doi.org/10.1111/j.1752-0606.2002.tb01183.x

Seikkula, J. (2011) Becoming dialogical: Psychotherapy or a way of life? *Australian and New Zealand Journal of Family Therapy (ANZJFT)*, 32(3), p. 179–193. doi.org/10.1375/anft.32.3.179

Seikkula, J. and Olson, M.E. (2003) The open dialogue approach to acute psychosis: Its poetics and micropolitics. *Family Process*, 42(3), p. 403–418. doi.org/10.1111/j.1545-5300.2003.00403.x

Seikkula, J., Aaltonen, J., Alakare, B., Haarakangas, K., Keränen, J. and Sutela, M. (1995) 'Treating psychosis by means of open dialogue' in S. Friedman (ed.) *The reflecting team in action: Collaborative practice in family therapy*. New York: Guilford Press, p. 62–80.

Seikkula, J., Alakare, B., Aaltonen, J., Holma, J., Rasinkangas, A. and Lehtinen, V. (2003) Open Dialogue approach: Treatment principles and preliminary results of a two-year follow-up on first episode schizophrenia. *Ethical Human Sciences and Services*, 5(3), p. 163–182.

Shotter, J. (1996) Now I can go on: Wittgenstein and our embodied embeddedness in the 'hurly-burly' of life. *Human Studies*, 19(4), p. 385–407.

Shotter, J. (2004) *On the edge of social constructionism: 'Withness-thinking' versus 'aboutness-thinking'*. London: KCC Foundation.

Wertsch, J.V. (1998) *Mind in action*. Oxford: Oxford University Press.

Wittgenstein, L. (1980) *Remarks on the philosophy of psychology. Vols. 1 and 2*. Oxford: Blackwell.

2

THE HISTORICAL DEVELOPMENT OF OPEN DIALOGUE IN WESTERN LAPLAND

Birgitta Alakare and Jaakko Seikkula
(Finland)

In this chapter we will outline the historical development of Open Dialogue (OD) in Western Lapland, by introducing the context in which we first started to develop the approach, the initial steps to include families more in our work and to introduce network meetings, both in the hospital and community settings, and significant people who influenced our thinking during these developments.[1] We go on to describe changes in the ways we understood psychosis, the development of our training programmes and research projects and the importance of teamwork in our service.

The OD approach has been developed in Western Lapland over many years, since the beginning of 1980. Step by step, we have developed principles to organise our work so as to help the people using our service in a quicker, more flexible and dialogical way. The seven principles of OD, introduced in Chapter 1, came out of our research (Aaltonen et al., 2011; Seikkula et al., 1995) as well as our clinical experiences.

We consider the OD approach to be a way of organising a system of psychiatric care and therefore not a single therapeutic method. As we were first developing the approach in Western Lapland, we found that certain practical guidelines for the whole treatment process were particularly beneficial, as these helped to generate dialogue more easily. As described in Chapter 1, the network meeting (also referred to as 'treatment meeting') is the basic therapeutic event in the Western Lapland service, and is the forum for open dialogue. This book focuses on OD for psychosis; however, in Western Lapland, a person with any mental health difficulty will be offered help within the approach. Specific considerations for those experiencing psychosis are addressed in Chapter 3.

Background

The health care district area of Länsi-Pohja (Western Lapland) lies to the north of the Gulf of Bothnia and shares its western border with Sweden.

The geographical region is small, as well as the population, which stands at 63,000 nowadays. At the beginning of the 1980s the population was 72,000. During recent decades more young people have been moving away to study and work. In Western Lapland unemployment stands at over 15%, whilst the figure nationally is nearer 8%.

Over 80% of the population live within 30 kilometres of Keropudas psychiatric hospital, situated in Tornio. It is a part of the central hospital of Western Lapland and all psychiatric beds are there. At the beginning of the 1980s we had 160 psychiatric beds at Keropudas and another 160 beds in Rovaniemi just for our district. So, in our region, we had 4.2 psychiatric beds per 1,000 inhabitants at this time, while the mean ratio in Finland at that time was 4.1 per 1,000 (Tuori et al., 1998). Gradually it has been possible to decrease the number of beds, such that, in 2019, our psychiatric unit has 22 beds (0.37 per 1000 inhabitants), and only around 10–20 beds are in daily use.

One specific element of Western Lapland is the history of a high incidence of diagnoses of schizophrenia. In the late 1980s the mean incidence over five years was 30.3 new people diagnosed with schizophrenia per 100,000 inhabitants per year. By the early 1990s the mean incidence over five years had declined to 17.1 per 100,000 per year (Aaltonen et al., 1997, 2011). In the same time period, the incidence of brief psychotic episodes increased from 1.2 to 6.7 per 100,000 inhabitants (Aaltonen et al., 2011). By 1994, the incidence of people diagnosed with schizophrenia had dropped to 7 per 100,000 inhabitants per year, a decline which continued over the next 10-year period, as noted in the study by Seikkula et al. (2011), in which the annual incidence reported was 2 per 100,000 inhabitants. As we developed our psychiatric service, we were able to make it more easily accessible, in that a person or a family could access the service without a referral. More of the population became aware that they could get help with any mental health difficulty and so they came to treatment much earlier. For instance, the duration of untreated psychosis declined from 3.5 months in 1995 to just three weeks in 2003 (Seikkula et al., 2011). In the past, psychotic symptoms could continue for a long time before people contacted our service. Our hypothesis is that the shorter duration of untreated psychosis was the main factor in the reduction in the incidence of schizophrenia and increase in brief psychotic episodes, though other changes to our service, such as the nature of our dialogical work with families/networks, were probably also significant.

Up until 1979 Keropudas hospital was a 'B-hospital', which meant that everyone staying in the hospital was diagnosed as being chronically ill and considered likely to spend the rest of their lives in the hospital (this contrasts with an 'A-hospital', which is an acute hospital where people stay for a shorter period of time). Almost everyone had a diagnosis of schizophrenia and was taking medication – usually a high dose of neuroleptics and often several different ones at the same time. Therefore, most of the service users experienced many side effects and took medication for these also!

There were, however, also many positive aspects to the hospital. It had land for agriculture and forests. Service users could grow potatoes and undertake forestry work, so they had quite a lot of structured activity during the day. The staff members and service users were very familiar with each other and they did many things together, e.g. almost everyone (including ourselves) were out in the field, sharing tasks such as digging up potatoes.

The law in Finland changed in 1979 so that all mental hospitals could be changed to acute hospitals, and the local politicians wanted to have an acute psychiatric hospital within our district. This presented a new possibility to us – Keropudas could be developed into a hospital with acute psychiatric services, whilst continuing to house some people in need of long-term support.

At the beginning of the 1980s many new professionals came to work at Keropudas hospital, in part because of the restructuring of the service. Psychiatrist Jyrki Keränen was appointed as chief psychiatrist of the hospital in 1980. Also, Jaakko Seikkula came to work as a clinical psychologist in 1981, and Birgitta Alakare started in the hospital in 1982, later specialising in psychiatry. Birgitta worked as the chief psychiatrist in the health care district from 1995, following Jyrki Keränen, until 2014 when she retired. Many other key members of the staff team, such as psychologist Markku Sutela, psychologist Kauko Haarakangas, and psychiatrist Pirjo Saastamoinen, amongst others, arrived in the middle of the 1980s. And there were many other enthusiastic people working both in the hospital and also the outpatient clinics. The whole staff team was very eager to develop new ideas for treatment and to transform Keropudas into a modern psychiatric hospital.

Birgitta, one of the authors of this chapter, writes of her personal experience:

When I started working at Keropudas hospital in 1982 my plan was to work there for just six months. My aim was to specialise in geriatric medicine. From the first day though I was inspired by how the staff worked together – teamwork became important to me and I never met service users alone, except later when doing individual psychotherapy. Jyrki Keränen supported teamwork. I could ask experienced nurses for advice about treatment and medication, and our psychologists were present on the ward. In my opinion the most important work psychiatrists, psychologists and other specialists can do is to be present on the ward and work together with other personnel, supporting a psychotherapeutic attitude in every aspect. Everyone's presence is important when you are developing the system (see 'Teamwork' section below for more on teamwork).

Families in the treatment

Professor Jukka Aaltonen was invited to visit Keropudas hospital as a supervisor and teacher in 1981. He ran two-day workshops twice a year for decades. In the beginning the workshops were open to all personnel, including the cleaners of the hospital if they were interested in participating. He taught us the basics of family therapy. In 1983 psychologists Jaakko Seikkula and Markku Sutela began their family therapy training in Oulu and in 1986 started the first family therapy training in Tornio. Professor Jukka Aaltonen had worked for years in the team led by Professor Yrjö Alanen in Turku in the south-west of Finland. Since the late 1960s their team had developed Need-Adapted Treatment (NAT). The principles of NAT became familiar to us and are the basis of the OD approach.

Need-Adapted Treatment[2]

Need-Adapted Treatment (NAT) was developed by Professor Yrjö Alanen and his colleagues in Turku, with its roots stretching back to the 1960s. Its principles were part of the National Schizophrenia Project (1981–1987), led by Professor Alanen, an initiative aiming to develop a more psychotherapeutic and humanistic approach to people having psychotic experiences. Alanen trained originally as a psychiatrist and then undertook additional training as a psychoanalyst.

The primary emphasis in NAT lay on the following (Alanen, 1997):

1 Therapeutic activities are planned and carried out flexibly and individually in each case.
2 Assessment and treatment are dominated by a psychotherapeutic attitude.
3 Different therapeutic approaches should supplement each other rather than constituting an 'either/or' approach.
4 Treatment should attain and maintain the quality of a continuous process.
5 There should be a follow-up of individual service users and the efficacy of the treatment methods (an additional element added later by Lehtinen, 1993).

Alanen was particularly interested in the role of family dynamics and communication in the development of psychosis, and so started to advocate for the inclusion of families in therapeutic work and the development of skills to facilitate this. The integration of family meetings with individual psychoanalytic-orientated therapy primarily reflected Alanen's view that family work was often necessary before individual work could prove effective, i.e. that there are often symbiotic attachments (merged/enmeshed aspects in relationships) which need to be addressed before people can work towards greater individuation. Ultimately, however, the approach was flexible, with a recognition that psychotic experiences can develop for a variety of reasons and that a variety of ways of responding to the changing needs of clients and those in their immediate network are necessary (hence the term 'need-adapted').

The OD approach can essentially be seen as a form (and thus an extension) of NAT, and it is therefore no surprise to find many parallels between the services in Turku at that time and those developed in Western Lapland. In particular the OD principles of 'flexibility and mobility' and 'psychological continuity' follow closely from the core aspects of NAT.

Alanen and Jukka Aaltonen, who later worked closely together in the development of NAT, were keen to create training and practices which involved multi-professional collaboration, and this can be seen to be a precursor to the importance placed in OD on professionals of all disciplines having access to a common three/four-year training programme, i.e. to the democratic ethic in the approach. More broadly Alanen and Aaltonen believed that cross fertilisation between a variety of therapeutic approaches in a service is likely to lead to a deeper understanding of the kinds of difficulties that people present with and what is needed by way of a response (Aaltonen et al., 2002), which is similar to the value attributed to 'polyphony' in the OD approach.

As a consequence of their clinical experience and also their research (see Chapter 37 for outcome studies on NAT), Alanen and his colleagues came to realise that psychotic experiences are usually related to people's life history, and that a "psychotherapeutic attitude" (Alanen et al., 1991, p. 367) is therefore needed, i.e. an attempt to understand more about what has happened and is happening in the lives of those involved. The involvement of family members generally helps in such a process of developing understanding, and they may well also be in need of support in a time of crisis. The person having psychotic experiences was invited to play an active role in the dialogue in family meetings:

A crucial part of their therapeutic impact is obviously attributable to the support offered to the patient's self-esteem by giving each patient a chance to take part in discussing the situation and in planning his or her care on an equal footing with the others.

(Alanen, 2009, p. 161)

In appealing to the capability of the person having psychotic experiences, professionals hoped to avert or reverse any regressive/passive tendencies to see all expertise as outside of oneself, and a similar intention can be found in the OD approach. Another similarity is an emphasis on the use of ordinary everyday language, a necessary condition for the possibility of an inclusive dialogue.

Alanen and his colleagues believed that improved family relations were one of the most crucial factors in determining outcome, and so, as well as the potential short-term gains in involving family members in the treatment process, the hope was that such interaction/engagement would generalise to better communication/relations in the long term.

There are some differences in emphasis between NAT and OD, or at least, as the service in Western Lapland developed. In Western Lapland they talk of a culture of non-assessment – in other words they are not looking to determine the dynamics in the family, as would have been the case in systemic family therapy and, to some extent, in NAT too, which retained a stronger psychoanalytic/systemic influence in its core thinking. There were also some planning discussions by clinical staff separate from the service user and their family in NAT, which is not the case with OD, where all conversations about the family/network take place in their presence.

In the early 1980s we started to invite family members to talk with us at Keropudas hospital, both in relation to acute admissions and in situations where there was a history of long-term hospitalisation. We were moved by the desire of family members to be involved in the treatment process, even though their relative may have been in hospital for years, and in some cases over thirty years. Family members wanted to talk about their family experiences in depth, and it seemed that they had not been heard before (see Chapter 3 for more detail on our early experiences of meeting with the families of people with long-term psychotic experiences).

With the support of Jukka Aaltonen and several team members we came up with the idea of building a family-centred system. We had the opportunity to plan the whole treatment process for people new to our service and could thus initiate new practices and ensure their continuation. The administration of the hospital understood the need for educating staff and supported it at that time.

We felt that we had to change our behaviour in family meetings. In applying the ideas of systemic family therapy, we had thought previously that we as therapists needed to follow specific guidelines for interviewing and to plan specific systemic interventions for making change possible in the family. However, as we reflected on our work, we realised that we could no longer interview families and plan interventions, but instead needed to learn to listen more carefully to the families – to listen to *their* stories, *their* understanding and what *they* felt was needed. We tried to make network meetings comfortable and safe for service users and family members, so that they could talk freely about their feelings and experiences.

Understandings of psychosis

As we have mentioned already, at the beginning of the 1980s all of the service users in Keropudas Hospital were diagnosed as chronically ill, and the vast majority were suffering from psychotic experiences. We wanted to understand more about their experiences and therefore it was natural that we started to study the psychotherapy of schizophrenia. We organised summer schools on this topic, inviting the most prominent psychotherapists in Finland working with individuals experiencing psychosis, for example, the psychoanalysts Martti Siirala and Pirkko Siltala, as well as Antero Toskala, a cognitive therapist. They all taught us that it is important to take the content of hallucinations seriously.

Although we now know that many authors over decades have recognised that the experience of psychosis may well relate to prior life experiences, we found it especially useful and important to read the texts of psychoanalyst Bertram Karon (Karon and Vandenbos, 1981) and we had the opportunity to invite him to visit Tornio. The influence of his book and the visit were enormous and important in that we learned to listen to what service users said about their hallucinations and other psychotic symptoms more carefully, without challenging these experiences. According to Karon and Vandenbos (1981), the content of hallucinations are shaped in some way by real incidents in the person's life. We therefore became more interested in understanding people's psychotic experiences and the meaning they themselves gave to these experiences. We think that learning more about individual psychotherapy helped us to listen to every person more carefully and to become more dialogical.

In his work Bertram Karon only offered individual psychoanalytic psychotherapy to psychotic persons if the use of neuroleptic medication was stopped. He did not actively include families in the therapy, whereas our approach became strongly focused on including them. When we invited Bertram Karon to visit Tornio in the summer of 1994, there was a creative tension between the two approaches. Bertram Karon said that he was impressed by our way of including families, and since this meeting our two approaches have mutually influenced each other (further detail of the influ-ence of Karon's thinking on our work with those experiencing psychosis can be found in Chapter 3).

Open Dialogue as a form of Need-Adapted Treatment

The new approach did not emerge automatically from one decision. There were many different phases in the process of developing open dialogues. The important critical steps were as follows:

1   In 1984 open family network meetings began to take the place of sys-temic family therapy after someone was admitted to hospital. A team from Turku (Viljo Räkköläinen and others) had told us about their work and their meetings with family members. They called these meetings 'treatment meetings', and also spoke about 'admission meetings', which took place before hospitalisation, and in which a decision could be made to work with people in the community instead of admitting them to hospital. After this seminar we decided that, in our service in Western Lapland, we should no longer talk about the service user or the family without them being present. Prior to this we were accustomed to talking about the service user and planning the treatment before we met them and their family, and then, on meeting them, telling them what the plan was.

The decision to work more transparently had a profound impact on our practice. We had to learn to talk with people in a different way to how we had previously. Also, we came to realise that family therapy is only one possible treatment method, and it became important to us to listen to what the family wanted and then decide together what was needed.

2   In late 1986 we decided that the first network meeting would take place at the hospital but *before* deciding whether hospital treatment was necessary. Prior to this every person referred had been admitted to the hospital and the network meeting took place on the next day. However, in around a third of cases it was decided in this meeting that the person concerned could leave the hospital, as hospitalisation was unnecessary. Realising this, we wanted to change our system, such that in the initial network meeting (the so called 'admission meeting') we could decide together with the service user and their family whether hospitalisation was needed or not. If it was not necessary, we had to offer something else instead, and so a crisis clinic was formed in order to organise teams to work with specific families in the community (which we called 'case-specific teams'). At the same time, we began to arrange home visits. This led to a decrease in admission rates by 30%, as had happened in Turku (as reported further in Chapters 36 and 37).

3   In 1990 all of the mental health outpatient clinics in Western Lapland started to organise mobile crisis intervention teams, meaning that the entire psychiatric system in the small Länsi-Pohja province has followed

the OD approach since the early 1990s. We could say that we have as many teams as we have service users, as every team is organised differently, according to the needs of the service user and their family, and anyone from the entire personnel can be a member of a team. These case-specific teams do not only work with the service user/family in the crisis phase, but rather take responsibility for the whole treatment process.

Training

We organised summer schools every year from the early 1980s. These five-day training sessions were open to every staff member. Jaakko invited many key people in the family therapy and psychosis field to Tornio, such as Harry Goolishian and Harlene Anderson, who developed collaborative therapy in their work with families (Anderson, 1997; Anderson and Goolishian, 1998, 1992), Lynn Hoffman, a family therapist with a postmodern approach,[3] Bertram Karon, Yrjö Alanen and his team, and many others who have been mentioned above. The Swedish group of Johan Klefbeck and colleagues taught us about special structured 'spiral' network meetings, which were based on the work of Ross Speck and Carolyn Attneave in the US (Klefbeck et al., 1988). Spiral meetings are organised in very serious situations, such as when a child is at such a high degree of risk that professionals are considering whether to remove them from the family home into public care, and could engage as many as 20–30 members of the family's social network in a creative process to address the issues at hand.

In the late 1980s we got to know Tom Andersen and his work, and after this Tom visited our hospital many times. Tom and the team in Tromsø, Norway, had developed a reflective practice in family meetings (Andersen, 1991). They used a separate team to reflect on what had been said during meetings. The idea of the reflecting team influenced our network meetings. At first, we tried to use a separate reflecting team also, but we found it uncomfortable. Instead the same team members who were facilitating the network meetings took the reflective position for a while during the course of each meeting. We started to talk about our own feelings and ideas more openly, in a reflective manner. It made our meetings more dialogical.

Tom Andersen[4]

Tom Andersen, a Norwegian psychiatrist from Tromsø, was an important influence on the development of OD from the 1980s. In the early to mid 1980s he was reflecting on the practice of family therapy in the psychiatric service in Tromsø, noticing feelings of discomfort at

---

certain aspects of the practice – notably the way in which the therapy team behind the one-way mirror spoke about the family during family meetings, hypothesising about family dynamics and potential interventions. Andersen encouraged the team behind the screen to just listen instead, and to limit their communication to the sharing of reflections at specific points in the meeting. In these reflections each team member could share their own thoughts, feelings and associations independently. Different points of view were welcome, adding to an inexorable polyphony. Our picture/experience of the world is necessarily subjective and, therefore, Andersen argued, we need to shift from an 'either/or' to a 'both/and' perspective. As professionals we do not have the answers, but we can add new perspectives that may help to open up new possibilities:

> I am not occupied with finding a new story or finding a new solution. All that comes by itself when people are given the chance to search through their own words and own expressions. I am neither occupied with causes, nor explanations.
>
> (Andersen, 2007, p. 35)

Andersen emphasised that we cannot instruct social systems to change. Instead we need to work to develop a space in which family/network members can express themselves and relate to each other. This may be challenging work, involving a good deal of skilful facilitation, but it offers greater promise.

Andersen and colleagues decided to make the reflecting process in family meetings transparent. On noticing one day that there was a microphone in the room in which the therapy team was sitting, he and his team decided to switch it on so that the family could hear the team's reflections. In this way the therapy team became the 'reflecting team', who would ultimately come to sit in the same room as the family (outside the main circle created for the meeting), when the use of the one-way mirror was dropped. Andersen's initial fears about the reflecting team upsetting the family in some way, by the ways in which they spoke about them (i.e. the use of technical or judgemental language), proved to be unfounded, as practitioners naturally adopted a respectful tone in their reflections and used more ordinary language. Sharing reflections transparently in this way was not just a matter of being respectful, though. Andersen and his team thought that the family might benefit from hearing the team's deliberations/process.

Andersen emphasised the importance of practice coming first and theory later and, in another break from systemic family therapy as traditionally practised, it was decided that the team would not discuss, plan, or generate hypotheses for meetings beforehand. Instead family/ network members were asked to define the important topics at the start of each meeting.

Andersen also focused on the significance of the present moment, the value in bringing attention to subtle and not so subtle shifts in thought, feeling and behaviour that occur in the course of a meeting. For it is in these moments that new possibilities or openings can arise (here he recognised the need to be sensitive to someone's readiness to speak about something). He was particularly interested in language, in words that seemed to carry particular significance for an individual, and in finding words for non-verbal actions/behaviour. He stressed that language/expression is not just informative – it is also formative. He also spoke about the value of team members matching the rhythm of the network, or in other words becoming attuned to the pacing, bodily movements and tone of network members, and allowing themselves to be affected/moved by this, in such a way that enhances connection and the communicative flow. He also stressed the importance of proceeding slowly enough such that all those present could be aware of their inner dialogue.

Harlene Anderson and Harry Goolishian were an important influence on Andersen's thinking. "Listen to what they say!" Goolishian would exclaim (Andersen, 1992, p. 90). Or, in other words, respond to what the family are actually saying, rather than what *you think* they are saying. In this way, Andersen's work was essentially phenomenological in nature, and OD continues in this tradition.

It is clear that Andersen's influence on OD was significant, but it's also true that the work of the teams in Tromsø and Western Lapland have developed in parallel, with some of the influences being reciprocal. The outer reflecting team is used in training programmes in Western Lapland, but not in the practice with families/networks, where all team members sit in the same circle as the family/network, and share responsibility for both facilitating and reflecting.

Family therapy training

In the Western Lapland psychiatric service any staff member can be called on to participate in case-specific teams, according to the needs of an individual or family. It was therefore necessary to provide further training for all staff members, as we felt that there was not enough emphasis on community-based and family-centred practice in their original training (they were too focused on individual treatment). Thus, since 1989, every staff member from both inpatient and outpatient services (including doctors, psychologists, nurses and social workers – a total of around 120 professionals) has been offered the opportunity to participate in a three-year family therapy training programme, such that, by the early 2000s, almost 90% of staff members in our service had obtained a qualification as a psychotherapist in family therapy according to Finnish law (the number of family therapists per capita in this area was the highest in Finland). However, more recently the proportion of staff qualified to this level has reduced to about 60%, as many trained persons have retired, and new people have come to work here.

We planned the training so that it meets national psychotherapy standards, but also with a particular focus on the treatment of severe crisis situations. The training increases trainees' self-confidence and courage, so that they can safely listen to people's difficult or traumatic stories and experiences without trying to solve things quickly – i.e. trainees learn to tolerate anxiety. They also learn to talk openly about their thoughts and feelings while listening carefully to what people are saying. The training helps people to build trust in their co-workers and in the resources of the family/network. It helps them to trust that the dialogue really helps in difficult situations.

From 2000, the training of staff in Western Lapland consisted of a one-year foundation training followed by the three-year family therapy programme (Aaltonen et al., 2011). In addition, staff members have been encouraged to undergo other shorter forms of psychotherapy training, such as a two-year training in individual psychodynamic therapy or a one-year training in trauma therapy.

More recently the law in Finland has changed, meaning that all training to the level of qualified psychotherapist has to be organised by universities and run over four years. In addition, if you do not have an academic qualification as a psychologist, social worker or medical doctor, you have to have a basic training in psychotherapy before you can enter the four-year training, and this usually takes one and a half years – so it became a very long (and expensive) process for some. Furthermore, nurses without an education at a University of Applied Sciences are now not able to participate in psychotherapy training at all. These changes created a big problem in our hospital, because many nurses there have no academic qualification, and as a psychotherapeutic community every staff member needs psychotherapeutic training. Therefore, in order to maintain the quality of the work in our service, we are now planning to run our own in-house four-year training, which unfortunately means that those participating will not be able to get the title of certified psychotherapist and some people would like to have this.

Further detail about OD training programmes, which are now run internationally as well as in Western Lapland, can be found in Section 3.

Research

Although OD research in Western Lapland is reported in Chapter 37, we include a sample of the research here in order to emphasise how important it has been in providing feedback on changes to our therapeutic processes, and thereby facilitating the stepwise development of OD in Western Lapland. It is worth repeating that the seven principles of OD came out of our research (as well as clinical experience) and were not principles planned before and then followed.

Our early research confirmed that immediate help, with the flexible involvement of the service user and their network, along with psychological continuity, were key factors in reducing the need for hospitalisation (Seikkula, 1991) and later on the incidence of schizophrenia (Aaltonen et al., 2011; Seikkula et al., 2011). We understood the importance of creating unique 'systems of care' around each service user/network, the decision making about whether hospitalisation is needed, and the involvement of the family/network in this decision making (Keränen, 1992; Seikkula, 1991). A later qualitative study in Western Lapland underscored the importance of developing ways of listening to all those present and facilitating dialogue and polyphony (Haarakangas, 1997).

Our involvement in the national Acute Psychosis Integration (API) project was very important in confirming the benefits of our approach, i.e. that, in many instances, a person with psychotic symptoms can be treated at home without medication and can recover (Seikkula et al., 2011). This project is discussed in more detail in the research section of this book, but here we would like to emphasise the usefulness of conducting research some years later on a new cohort of people with psychotic symptoms, using the same methodology as in the API project. The outcomes for this additional cohort demonstrated the ongoing stability of our good results, implying that the earlier outcomes could not be attributed to unique factors in the early development of our approach, such as initial enthusiasm. Particular features of our research outcomes have been our very low use of hospital beds, the low use of neuroleptics and the high rate of return to education or employment.

Our participation in a national randomised control trial of depression, involving the addition of couple therapy to treatment as usual, demonstrated the usefulness of a dialogic approach in other severe conditions (Seikkula et al., 2013). The outcomes were good, in that people got better sooner and the total number of meetings were fewer than in the control group (people receiving treatment as usual). In addition, in Western Lapland the work was undertaken by a crisis intervention team so that the service users' therapeutic treatment started immediately, whilst in the other two districts they had to wait longer for treatment by a specialised depression team. We remind readers here that OD is the basic platform for all psychiatric referrals in Western Lapland, even though psychosis has been the focus of most of the research.

Teamwork

Teamwork is essential to the OD approach. Every service user/family has a team of two or more professionals organised according to their particular needs. Broadly the idea in the Western Lapland service is that a team can be formed of any two or three members of staff (given that all have had some training in facilitating network meetings). However, there may also be some consideration of which staff members could be well suited to a specific network because of their particular skills and professional roles. Most commonly there are two nurses or a nurse and a psychologist, but other professionals may also join a team. The presence of a team, as opposed to a single professional, seems to enhance the family's sense of safety. It also helps to generate polyphony and more ideas, as well as to enhance the team's capacity to tolerate uncertainty and thereby avoid reaching for solutions or premature decisions (as staff members feel safer when working as a team). This was seen in the study of Jyrki Keränen (1992) when he compared admission interviews conducted by a single psychiatrist with admission meetings facilitated by a team. It was only possible to focus on the broader social life of the network in the meetings with the team. In contrast, the interviews with the psychiatrist focused on clarifying symptoms and action points.

In treating psychosis, we have found that a team of three members is often helpful (for instance a psychiatrist from the crisis clinic, a psychologist from the service user's local outpatient clinic and a nurse from the ward of the hospital). It is important to have at least one member from the outpatient clinic, someone who has experience of the treatment of psychosis in outpatient settings. Three team members help to tolerate more uncertainty and to generate more perspectives on how to proceed in the current crisis.

One of us (Birgitta Alakare) worked as a psychiatrist in the Western Lapland service for 32 years. She felt comfortable being one equal member of a team, as opposed to just being a psychiatrist prescribing medication and sick leave. She appreciated it when every team member asked questions and offered their opinions concerning the treatment. Her reflections about prescribing medication or hospital admission would be discussed in the meeting as one opinion, rather than unquestionably given as a prescription. Birgitta now feels that psychiatrists should not meet any service user without another team member. The only exception here would be when the psychiatrist is conducting individual psychotherapy (should a need for psychotherapy be identified and a psychiatrist in the team is in a position to offer this). If the psychiatrist meets the service user alone, the pressure to find quick solutions is too great, with medication often being the solution that is turned to. It is not easy to tolerate uncertainty if you are alone.

48

Concluding comments

OD is not a model or a manual for care; it is more a way of organising services and meeting others respectfully and in dialogue. We are actually against the idea of implementing generalised models for psychiatric treatment and would argue instead that each service should develop in response and according to local needs/conditions (as exemplified in the contributions to Section 4 in this book). Any treatment process with a service user is always a unique process, and the treatment system should also be unique. However, a dialogical and respectful attitude should be maintained in every meeting. When developing this kind of approach, it is important that the whole organisation is as non-hierarchical as possible, for network meetings are not dialogical if it is not possible for every voice to be genuinely heard.

Since the early 1980s we have been developing our work towards open dialogue. As Kauko Haarakangas put it, from 'experts' we have to become 'dialogicians', such that we can be more relaxed in our work, and find more perspectives on service users' situations jointly with them. The service user and family have been transformed from objects of our treatment methods to co-workers, and we have become active listeners. In the Finnish language, we describe this situation of working and supporting the family in difficult times as "walking together".

Notes

1 In this chapter a number of people are mentioned who remain of considerable importance to those who developed OD in Finland but who will not be known outside of Finland. They are included for the historical record.
2 This section was written by Nick Putman.
3 Postmodern therapeutic practices are characterised by a collaborative and intersubjective approach in which there is a close attention to language and deconstructing commonly assumed 'givens', such that the service user/network can evaluate the value of such givens for themselves.
4 This section was written by Nick Putman.

References

Aaltonen, J., Alanen, Y.O., Keinänen, M. and Räkköläinen, V. (2002) An advanced specialist-level training programme in psychodynamic individual psychotherapy of psychotic and borderline patients: The Finnish approach. *European Journal of Psychotherapy, Counselling & Health*, 5(1), p. 13–30. doi.org/10.1080/13642530210159215

Aaltonen, J., Seikkula, J., Alakare, B., Haarakangas, K., Keränen, J. and Sutela, M. (1997) Western Lapland project: A comprehensive family- and network-centered community psychiatric project. *ISPS Abstracts and Lectures 12–16 October 1997.* London.

Aaltonen, J., Seikkula, J. and Lehtinen, K. (2011) The comprehensive Open Dialogue approach in Western Lapland: I. The incidence of non-affective psychosis and pro-dromal states. *Psychosis*, 3(3), p. 179–191. doi.org/10.1080/17522439.2011.601750

Alanen, Y.O. (1997) *Schizophrenia: Its origins and need-adapted treatment.* London: Karnac.

Alanen, Y.O. (2009) Towards a more humanistic psychiatry: Development of need-adapted treatment of schizophrenia group psychoses. *Psychosis*, 1(2), 156–166. doi. org/10.1080/17522430902795667

Alanen, Y., Lehtinen, K., Räkköläinen, V. and Aaltonen, J. (1991) Need-adapted treatment of new schizophrenic patients: Experiences and results of the Turku Project. *Acta Psychiatrica Scandinavica*, 83(5), p. 363–372. doi.org/10.1111/j.1600-0447.1991.tb05557.x

Andersen, T. (1991) *The reflecting team: Dialogues and dialogues about the dialogues.* New York: Norton.

Andersen, T. (1992) Relationship, language and pre-understanding in the reflecting processes. *Australian and New Zealand Journal of Family Therapy*, 13(2), p. 87–91. doi.org/10.1002/j.1467-8438.1992.tb00896.x

Andersen, T. (2007) Reflecting talks may have many versions: Here is mine. *International Journal of Psychotherapy*, 11(2), p. 27–44.

Anderson, H. (1997) *Conversation, language and possibilities. A postmodern approach to therapy.* New York: Basic Books.

Anderson, H. and Goolishian, H. (1988) Human systems as linguistic systems: Preliminary and evolving ideas about the implications for clinical theory. *Family Process*, 27(4), p. 371–393. doi.org/10.1111/j.1545-5300.1988.00371.x

Anderson, H. and Goolishian, H. (1992) 'The client is the expert: A not-knowing approach to therapy' in S. McNamee and K. Gergen (eds.) *Therapy as social construction.* London: SAGE, p. 25–39.

Haarakangas, K. (1997) The voices in the treatment meeting: A dialogical analysis of treatment meeting conversations in a family-centred psychiatric treatment process in regard to the team activity. Diss. English Summary. *Jyväskylä Studies in Education, Psychology and Social Research, 130.*

Karon, B. and Vandenbos, G. (1981) *Psychotherapy of schizophrenia: The treatment of choice.* Lanham, MD: Rowman & Littlefield Publishers, Inc.

Keränen, J. (1992) The choice between outpatient and inpatient treatment in a family centred psychiatric treatment system. English summary. *Jyväskylä Studies in Education, Psychology and Social Research, 93.*

Klefbeck, J., Bergerhed, E., Forsberg, G., Hultkranz-Jeppson, A. and Marklund, K. (1988) *Nä tverksarbete i multiproblemfamiljer [Networking in multi-problem families].* Botkyrka: Botkyrka kommun.

Lehtinen, K. (1993) Need-adapted treatment of schizophrenia: A five-year follow-up study from the Turku project. *Acta Psychiatrica Scandinavica*, 87(2), p. 96–101. doi. org/10.1111/j.1600-0447.1993.tb03337.x

Seikkula, J. (1991) Family-hospital boundary system in the social network. English summary. *Jyväskylä Studies in Education, Psychology and Social Research, 80.*

Seikkula, J., Aaltonen, J., Alakare, B., Haarakangas, K., Keränen, J. and Sutela, M. (1995) 'Treating psychosis by means of open dialogue' in S. Friedman (ed.) *The reflecting team in action: Collaborative practice in family therapy.* New York: Guilford Press, p 62–80.

Seikkula, J., Aaltonen, J., Kalla, O., Saarinen, P. and Tolvanen, A. (2013) Couple therapy for depression in a naturalistic setting in Finland: A 2-year randomized trial. *Journal of Family Therapy*, 35(3), p. 281–302. doi.org/10.1111/j.1467-6427.2012.00592.x

Seikkula, J., Alakare, B. and Aaltonen, J. (2011) The comprehensive Open-Dialogue approach in Western Lapland: II. Long-term stability of acute psychosis outcomes in advanced community care. *Psychosis* 3(3), p. 192–204. doi.org/10.1080/17522439.2011.595819

Tuori, T., Lehtinen, V., Hakkarainen, A., Jaaskelainen, J., Kokkola, A., Ojanen, M. Pylkkanen, K., Salokangas, R.K.R., Solantaus, J. and Alanen, Y.O. (1998) The Finnish National Schizophrenia Project 1981–1987: 10-year evaluation of its results. *Acta Psychiatrica Scandinavica*, 97(1), p. 10–17. doi.org/10.1111/j.1600-0447.1998.tb09956.x

3

PSYCHOSIS IS NOT AN ILLNESS BUT A RESPONSE TO EXTREME STRESS – DIALOGUE IS A CURE FOR IT[1]

Jaakko Seikkula
(Finland)

Introduction

This chapter describes how psychosis can be seen as an active psychological response to extreme/traumatic experiences, when it has not been possible to process the affects aroused by such experiences through language. If the Open Dialogue (OD) network manages to generate a deliberating atmosphere, allowing different, even contradictory, voices to be heard, including the voice of the person experiencing psychosis, then there is the possibility of constructing narratives of restitution and reparation, even many years after the psychosis first manifested. A number of key points about the practice of facilitating network meetings with someone experiencing psychosis and their network are highlighted.

Psychosis, the body, trauma and extreme stress

There are many ways of understanding psychotic problems. In the literature psychosis is mostly seen as a pathological state, which needs to be cured. However, the basis of the dialogical perspective on human life is to emphasise respecting the Other with his/her view of life, without conditions. Thus, it is important to see psychotic behaviour from the point of view of the unique life of the person at the centre of concern, without pathologising it. From the dialogical point of view psychotic experience can be seen as one way of dealing with terrifying experiences in one's life. Several authors have already contributed to the literature on the dialogical approach to understanding psychotic behaviour (Dilks, 2013; Lysaker and Lysaker, 2001; Seikkula et al., 2001).

In OD psychotic behaviour is not regarded as a distinct set of categorical phenomena, as in an illness. Instead such behaviour is seen to be the result of an active attempt of an embodied mind to cope with experiences that are so 'heavy' that it has been impossible to construct a rational spoken narrative about them. For example, most people diagnosed with psychosis have experienced physical or sexual abuse, either as a child or as an adult (Aas et al., 2019; Goodman et al., 1997).

Sometimes present-day stressful situations, that resemble earlier stressful/traumatic experiences in some respects, can evoke affects related to these earlier experiences. Affects, in general, can be seen as a bodily reaction, an attempt to recover the homeostasis that has been threatened by something that has occurred outside or inside the body. When dealing with huge affective arousal relating to past trauma, our embodied mind can generate hallucinations or delusions, instead of a clear narrative memory of these experiences. One could say that in psychotic behaviour the body talks through metaphor, 'narrating' and enacting the person's experiences. We need words in order to make sense of, and thereby cope with, intense affect/trauma, and in the absence of a clear narrative, psychotic experiences may appear. Some have called this the pre-narrative quality of psychotic experience (Holma and Aaltonen, 1997).

In therapeutic conversations it seems to be important to avoid identifying the traumatic experience as the reason for the psychosis, because psychotic experiences are not caused by the traumatic incidents alone, but rather are responses to *current* affective experiences which stem from the earlier experiences, as in the example below. Furthermore, psychotic phenomena can also be a response to biological changes, illicit drug use or organic brain damage.

To illustrate my main point, I would like to share the story of a woman who developed psychosis, fearing that her husband was under the influence of drugs and would come and kill her.[2] During the meeting with the family, it was discovered that 16 years earlier she had been living with a man who was a heavy drug abuser. While under the influence of drugs he had repeatedly beaten her, a fact that she had never disclosed to anyone else. A couple of months before her first psychotic episode, the man had phoned her for the first time in 16 years. On hearing his voice, she could not say anything, but her body shook, remembering the terror of dying that she had experienced while living with the threat of violence from him. The fear she felt towards her husband was a psychotic one; it was not him who was coming to kill her. At the same time, however, she was referring to something she had really experienced, that is, violence at the hands of her former partner. Such experiences of severe victimisation are not stored in the mind in such a way that they are recorded in language and can therefore be reflected upon (i.e. they are not stored in explicit memory), but instead remain 'locked' in the mind, which records terrors in a timeless way in implicit memory (Van der Kolk and Fisher, 1995).

In the tradition of OD, a psychotherapeutic approach has been developed which is based on the idea of seeing hallucinations and delusions as a part of psychological functioning in crises, as being related to overwhelming affects.

In clinical practice it is unhelpful to see these as pathology in the sense of being a physical illness, rather than a psychological reaction. As a fruitful hypothesis for helping people in their psychotic crises, we could see hallucinations and delusions as one form of affect. Emotional states – such as feeling anxious, having panic attacks, or being in a depressed mood – belong to life as natural responses to different circumstances. When extreme, they can become problematic and prohibit or inhibit constructive responses to the stressors in our everyday lives. We may then be diagnosed as suffering from anxiety, or panic disorder, or depression. As I see it, these phenomena arise in a similar way to hallucinations and delusions, as hallucinations are also reactions of our embodied mind to extreme stress – usually there are several stressors at the same time.

By way of example, let's say a person hears the voice of a loved one who died suddenly. It is not difficult for this person to understand such an experience as their emotions trying to re-establish homeostasis and save him/her from the pain of loss. However, at some point, if the pain remains unbearable, this person may lose the capacity to understand in this way, i.e. to accept that the person is no longer alive and that there is therefore no voice coming from the external world. In psychotic experience an individual loses the understanding of how affective experiences relate to their lives. Hearing hallucinatory voices is not the criteria for the diagnosis of psychosis – rather it is not having the capability to test reality (Cullberg, 2000).

Bertram P. Karon carried out ground-breaking work in developing individual psychotherapy for people experiencing psychosis. In the book he wrote with Gary Vandenbos (Karon and Vandenbos, 1981) they show, using several case examples, how psychotic phenomena can be understood as a response to real and terrifying experiences. For instance, in one situation a young man started to speak Latin. Instead of seeing this as something random and meaningless, the therapist wondered if the young man had had an experience within the church. It transpired that he had been sexually abused by a priest when he was in the church choir. In psychotic problems, Karon and Vandenbos see affective reactions as primary and only think about problems in reasoning and thinking as a secondary process. In their view people experiencing psychosis are living in a state of terror and because of that their reasoning may be affected. They think that psychotic behaviour serves as an active defence against something more terrible, death. In their reasoning, psychotic experiences relate to the terror of dying. Hallucinations and delusions are understood to be ways of dealing with the terrifying experiences in a non-direct, metaphorical way.

As a starting point for a successful therapeutic relationship, Karon and Vandenbos (1981) propose that the psychotherapist should take a strong position by supporting the person they are working with in their defence against death, by promising not to let anyone harm them. And then, from a dialogical point of view, their descriptions of the link between psychotic experiences and real-life incidents are very helpful in contributing to our understanding of the inner/vertical dialogues in psychotherapy (i.e. our relationship to past experiences). Unfortunately, they give a rather linear description about the role of the mother – and the family – as causing psychotic problems. In making this assumption, they were not able to collaborate with the family of the person experiencing psychosis, but instead proposed that the family should be met by someone outside the therapeutic process, and that the psychotherapist should not participate in these family sessions. In OD the family is not seen as pathological, as needing to be changed, but instead everyone is recognised and respected in the dialogue.

Generating dialogue is the response to psychotic experiences

In OD, the verbalisation of hallucinations or delusions is helpful in beginning the process of constructing a spoken narrative of prior terrifying experiences. The hope is that what was previously unbearable and unthinkable can become more bearable. A major aim in this process is to help the person experiencing psychosis to develop a fuller understanding of their reactions and to see how these are connected to their current and past experiences.

The role of the team in network meetings is to allow the person experiencing psychosis, and their network, to take the lead in determining the content of the meeting. The starting point for treatment is the language of the family – that is, how each family has, in their own language, named or understood the problem. The treatment team adapts its language according to the unique needs of the person experiencing psychosis and their family. Every conversation creates a new language (Bakhtin, 1984). Each person present speaks in their own voice and, as Anderson (1997) notes, listening becomes more important than the manner of interviewing.

When a professional first hears about someone's hallucinations or delusions, they may seem almost impossible to follow and understand. It is important, however, to accept hallucinations or delusions as one voice amongst others. In the beginning, these are not challenged, but the person is asked to say more about their experiences. The main task for team members is to ensure a response to the utterances of family members in a dialogical way, in order to promote new understandings among the different participants (Bakhtin, 1984). Team members can respond to what they have heard in a reflective discussion, while the family/network listen (as described in Chapter 1), and usually the family/network listen very carefully to what the professionals have to say about their situation.

Although it is not the case that every person experiencing psychosis has been a victim of physical or sexual abuse, this notion can help professionals to orientate more towards real events that have taken place, in their attempt to understand psychotic experiences through dialogue with the person's social network. And though our professional experience tells us that psychosis is usually the consequence of extreme life experiences, in the OD approach there is no pre-planned agenda or assumption as to what these experiences might be for any given person. They could have been of any kind and could have happened at any time. Furthermore, the aim in the dialogue is not to find out the exact original experience(s), but rather to support discussions about many different issues, as these can open paths for healing. The important issue is for practitioners to take extremely seriously everything that people in crises are saying – especially 'psychotic' utterances – instead of seeing them as meaningless or impossible to understand.

As hallucinations and delusions often relate to real incidents from earlier in a person's life, it is important to take time to discuss them (see section below: 'Some simple guidelines for dialogues with people having psychotic experiences'). For example, a team member could ask: "Did I hear you correctly when you said that you have control of your neighbour's thoughts? Could you tell me more about that?" The other network members could then be asked: "What do others think of this? How do you understand what M is saying?" The purpose of such questioning is to allow different voices to be heard concerning the themes under discussion, including the 'psychotic' voice(s). If the team manages to generate a deliberating atmosphere, allowing different, even contradictory, voices to be heard, the network has the possibility of constructing narratives of restitution or reparation (Stern et al., 1999). And, as Trimble (2000) puts it, "restoration of trust in soothing interpersonal emotional regulation makes it possible to allow others to affect us in dialogic relationships" (p. 15). To be open to each other's views and experiences is necessary for the person experiencing psychosis and the social network to begin to construct new words for their problems.

Once a young man asked for OD meetings.[3] He and his family were very disappointed by the family meeting in a traditional psychiatric hospital that they had had when he had been hospitalised because of psychotic episodes. He said that his parents were willing to come to the meeting even though they had separated a long time ago and no longer had any contact with each other. He also informed us that his parents had had considerable difficulties in communicating with each other and that this was the reason they had separated. In the first meeting we met with the son, his younger brother and their mother, in the second with the two young men and their father, and in the third with all four family members together. The third meeting was loaded with extreme tension. The younger brother started by saying that this meeting should have taken place 20 years ago, and after a while the mother said the same. Difficult issues were taken up from family life when they had all been together in the past, such as the problems the parents had had in dealing with each other and taking care of the children when they were small. The father was very rigid in his attitude in the meeting, even in the way he was sitting, but he listened to the criticism from his children. When asked what he thought about their critical comments he said that he felt bad and that it was not his intention to harm his children in any way.

Towards the end of the 90-minute meeting the atmosphere became more relaxed and the family even made some jokes about their history and laughed together. When asked at the end of the meeting how they had found the meeting, all of them said that they were surprised by how different it was to the meeting in the hospital. They said that in the hospital the doctor in charge of the meeting seemed to have the aim of finding out how mad the son was and how mad the entire family was. They felt very different in this meeting in the way everyone was heard and respected, even if they each had different opinions. This was the key difference from the other approach, a comment that they repeated at the end of the OD meetings that we had over a period of one and a half years.

Some simple guidelines for dialogues with people having psychotic experiences

In dialogical practice the main aim of the meeting is to generate dialogue, both between the participants and between their inner voices. This could involve, for example, pointing out that it is natural to have different thoughts about the issues that are being discussed – one does not need to have only one opinion. In this way the capacity to reflect is increased, which in turn makes it possible for those involved to hear more about how other family members have felt about the issues being discussed and to evaluate these different experiences and voices. Often there are surprises for family members – for example, parents may hear that their children experienced issues in their childhood very differently from the way that they did. In such a dialogue, family members may become more willing to share their own experiences and, if they are heard and taken seriously, to listen to other family members as well. This openness to other voices may lead to an increase in one's agency in life, as one comes to understand more about how one's own viewpoints relate to others.

In psychotic crises the task is the same as in other crisis situations, but there are some specific challenges to be aware of. The following four aspects are especially important in psychotic crises:

Having a relational focus throughout

This is the overarching basis of open dialogues. The relational focus is concerned with both horizontal (outer) and vertical (inner) dialogues.

In relation to *horizontal (outer) dialogues*, i.e. the communication between those who are present in the meeting, the main challenge is to cultivate dialogues in which all participants are equally respected and included. Practitioners should support network members to share information and opinions about their lives, whilst at the same time listening and reflecting continually on what they are saying. This does not mean that everyone needs to speak an equal amount, as it is important that everyone is free to participate in the dialogue in their own unique way. In an acute crisis, the meeting is often started by listening carefully to the person experiencing psychosis, whilst at the same time being sensitive to the ways in which other family members react while listening to stories that may every now and then include psychotic utterances. When asking others to respond to such utterances, it is best to emphasise the affective experience of the person who was speaking, instead of getting into a debate as to whether psychotic experiences are 'real' or not. In this way the team can enhance connections between family members and reduce isolation. It is often extremely difficult for family members to accept the reality of the person speaking in a psychotic way. Practitioners can increase network members' acceptance of each other by genuinely respecting the experiences of every family member, including the person having psychotic experiences.

Another domain of the polyphony of voices are the *vertical (inner) dialogues* of every participant, and these should also be encouraged. Those experiencing psychosis do not only have 'psychotic' speech, but also communicate in more everyday ways about their life. Both forms of speech should be respected and listened to. Other family members are in a similar position of having multiple views/feelings. Even if they often feel frustrated and criticise the person experiencing psychosis, they always show care and concern about him/her as well. Furthermore, family members should be encouraged to speak about other aspects of their own life, not only those related to the crisis or the person experiencing psychosis.

Respecting the psychotic experience without conditions

As mentioned above, in optimal dialogues we do not challenge the life view of the other, but rather encourage the person to help us understand more about their way of seeing their life, whilst also listening to the way other participants in the meeting experience the same life issues. This is in marked contrast to the approach often used in psychiatric practice where staff are advised to support people experiencing psychosis to become 'reality orientated', by telling them that what they are saying is part of their psychotic experience (or often 'psychotic illness') and is not real. This kind of statement can be very unhelpful and damaging, especially in that it can lead to a separation and increasing distance between the person experiencing psychosis and professionals (Avdi, 2005). One of the basic elements of dialogical practice is to deepen the speaker's awareness and understanding of what they are saying, by taking this seriously. It is most unlikely that the person experiencing psychosis will be able to start to reflect on their own experiences, and to search for other not yet known aspects for which they do not yet have words, if their points of view are rejected from the very beginning.

Sometimes psychotic experiences and communication can take over a person's life, such that their more constructive voices become silenced, or are difficult to listen to. They may also have diminished agency in their capacity to communicate their experiences (Holma and Aaltonen, 1997, 1998; Lysaker et al., 2003; Roe and Davidson, 2005). In addition, I feel that a good deal of contemporary psychiatric discourse, and the practices associated with it, negatively affect the diagnosed person's agency, by stating that psychosis is a product of a brain disorder which has nothing to do with the life experiences of the subject. Comments such as these can limit the scope of the person's communication with others and thereby constrain possibilities for developing beneficial self-understanding and consequent helpful actions (Avdi, 2005; Harper, 1995; Holma and Aaltonen, 1998; Karatza and Avdi, 2011). When the reality of the person's experience is not accepted by the professionals who are present, this often results in the person feeling even less in control of their thoughts and feelings.

When someone starts to speak in a psychotic way in a network meeting it may mean that, at that very moment, they are beginning to refer to the most difficult/traumatic experiences in their biography, perhaps because these experiences have been 'touched upon' in the dialogue between those who are present. If we start to 'reality orientate' people at such moments, we increase the risk that it will not become possible for them to begin to expand on their ideas as to what has happened in their lives, including painful experiences. Therefore, it is important that team members instead focus on what is happening in the present moment. One can ask, for instance, "what did I say wrong, when you started to speak about that?", or "wait a moment, what were we discussing when M started to speak about how the voices have control over him?" The 'reason' for psychotic manifestations can often become apparent at such crucial points in the conversation.

By fully accepting the utterances of the other, we thereby encourage them to speak more about hallucinations or delusions. In acute crises most people having psychotic experiences think that their hallucinatory voices exist in a reality that is shared with others and it is especially important at this moment to encourage them to share more about their experience/beliefs by asking, e.g. "wait a moment, did I hear correctly when I heard you say that you think your husband is coming to kill you? Can you help us understand more about this? When did you start to think this? Do you think this way all the time or only some of the time?" These questions are examples of how we can include unusual experiences in everyday conversation, instead of defining such experiences as pathological or unacceptable.

It is not always easy to accept the other's psychotic utterances, especially in a time of crisis. It can be particularly difficult if a person, for example, wants to make contact with someone who he thinks is out to 'get him', or hears voices that prescribe the killing of a specific person. One way to proceed in this type of extreme situation is for the practitioner to comment on the emotional part of the experience, by saying, for example, "it sounds like you are in considerable distress and we want to help you", but at the same time staff need to be careful to evaluate what the person could do in practice. In hearing hallucinatory voices that prescribe harm to oneself or to another person it is important to be clear with the person concerned that they must not do what the voice is saying, but instead invite them to start to reflect on their experience.

Later on, in the course of the recovery process, a person may come to think that the hallucinatory voices that they still hear do not exist in external reality, but rather are part of their inner experience, meaning that they are no longer psychotic (Cullberg, 2000). At this point the nature of our dialogue about the voices can be quite different than when the person was in an acute crisis. For example, one woman in psychotherapy started to realise that the voice of her aunt that she had been hearing was not coming from external reality, but actually gave expression to some fears that she had in relation to her aunt.[4] In the course of therapy, we both came to think that the voices she was hearing may be related to the fact that her aunt did not always accept her religious orientation – thus the voices were no longer psychotic, as she could connect them to her life experience. She came to feel that she was no longer willing to carry on the debate with the voices about this issue.

Overall, regardless of whether we are working with someone in an acute crisis or at a later stage in the process, it is essential to have the attitude that our dialogues are with human beings and not with 'schizophrenic/psychotic patients'. If our attitude is that we are talking with a person with an illness, we can too easily become focused on searching for the pathological aspects of their experience, whereas the aim of dialogical practice is to mobilise the positive resources of both the person at the centre of concern and their family members.

Emphasising feelings and the affective aspects of the stories told

A person with psychotic experiences may share extreme stories that could scare both the professional team and family members. These can include auditory hallucinations in which there is a threatening voice commanding the person to do something violent or frightening visual hallucinations. Strong paranoid belief systems may also put professionals in challenging situations. A person having paranoid thoughts may insist on an answer from team members as to whether they share these beliefs. As mentioned above, getting into a debate as to whether experiences/beliefs are real or not is most unlikely to open ways into more dialogical deliberations about the person's life and the role of the belief in it, and one basic dialogical principle is to focus instead on the emotional aspects of the experiences that service users are sharing with us. In dialogues during psychotic crises, it may be especially important to focus on the emotional experience that the person is having when they are telling us, for example, about the persecutors that are after them. This can be done in a simple way, for instance by saying "it sounds like you are in a situation in which you really feel very distressed", or "it really sounds like a scary situation for you. Could you tell me how you feel when you are being threatened?" These responses are only illustrative examples from situations in which I myself have participated. With questions such as these, I have found a way to a more open space in which it is possible to reflect about the person's life, including aspects unrelated to the threatening psychotic experiences.

A preference for being present in the here and now

This is one of the main overall guiding ideas in dialogical practice. Instead of focusing primarily on the content of the conversation, and on what is shared about what happened before the meeting, we concentrate more on what is said in the present moment, and how the responses to what is said affect the experience of the participants in the meeting. Any experiences that have taken place before the meeting can be discussed, but the emphasis is on the key emotions that are felt and expressed during the meeting.

In psychotic crises there are additional elements that emphasise the importance of this way of working. As mentioned above, whilst speaking about something that we as clinicians may think of as psychotic experience, the person concerned may, perhaps for the first time ever, be speaking – although with psychotic utterances – of the most extreme experiences in their life, for which they did not have words prior to this moment. It has been our experience that, in the initial contact with the network in crisis, there is a window of opportunity to discuss delusional thoughts, and the challenge for clinicians is how to be present in a way that supports further deliberation about these delusions. Our ability to do so depends greatly on the way in which we hear the stories that are shared and how we respond to them at these moments. In clinical practice, and from the studies I have conducted (Seikkula, 2002), I have learned to follow a guiding idea of stopping everything else in the dialogue and focusing on what has just been said at the moment that the 'psychotic' communication appears.

In addition to the above, we also need to be present to hear the first reflections that the person starts to have about the experiences they have had, as there could be long-lasting negative consequences for the treatment process if we are not. This became evident in a research study of crises where good and poor outcomes were compared. The research examined the first network meetings and the quality of the dialogue in them (Seikkula, 2002).

In the example below, the person experiencing psychosis (P in the transcription) was speaking about a situation at home which ended with him being violent towards his mother.[5] At the end of his confusing story he started to reflect about his behaviour, but unfortunately the team did not respond to this. Instead they tried to clarify what had happened at home when the violence occurred.

P: Well, it was last weekend; the police came to us. She [his mother] was drunk. When she didn't say anything and started to make coffee in the middle of the night, and I asked... I went out and came into the kitchen, and she turned around and said that it wasn't allowed to speak about it. Then I slapped her. She ran out into the corridor and started screaming. I said that there is no need to scream, why can't she say that... And then I calmed down. At that point, I got the feeling... And the police came and the ambulance. But in some way, I have a feeling, that it is, of course, it is not allowed to hit anyone. But there are, however, situations...

T1: Was that the point when you went into primary care?

P: Yes it happened just before that.

T2: Why did she not say that the police came?

P: What?

T2: Why did she not say that the police had been at your place the previous night?

P: It wasn't the previous night, it was last weekend. I was thinking, all the time I am thinking those strange things, and I knew that they were not true. But when you think about them for a while, after that you have the feeling that things like that can really happen. It is too much... You are only thinking of all kinds of futile things.

T2: And it all started last weekend, this situation?

T1: Yes

In the dialogue above, twice within a short space of time the team chose to focus on the part of P's story that referred to what happened at home when the conflict occurred and did not respond at all to his reflections about his violent act or his "strange thoughts". In both of those situations he was showing interest in his own behaviour in a healthy way and reflecting on this behaviour, but he did not receive any response from the team to help him develop his thoughts about this. In this specific process of care, it didn't become possible subsequently to discuss his psychotic thoughts, and indeed P rejected any offer of help. Not being present at critical moments, neglecting to respond to aspects of crucial topics, can lead to quite dramatic adverse outcomes.

Long-term psychotic experiences

During the period when I was working as a clinical psychologist at Keropudas hospital, I worked primarily on two wards for long-term service users, some of whom had been hospitalised for several decades. In most of these long-term situations we were successful in making contact with their family of origin and arranging meetings with them, together with the service user. This contact, and the process of subsequent meetings, was a very thought-provoking experience for me in at least two respects.

Firstly, we were struck by the number of long-standing 'psychotic' stories that were shared in the meetings. Though initially we could not understand what these stories related to, gradually they started to reveal important meanings, in that they seemed to be related to real experiences in the family. For instance, one man spoke about how he saw blood running out of the eyes of someone and a cannon exploding in his stomach.[6] In the very first meeting with his elderly mother it transpired that, when he was eight years old, he had been a witness to a truck accident in which his father exploded into pieces and died and, on that occasion, blood had really been running out of the eyes of his father. Another person would shoot anyone who came near him with his finger, saying that his fingers were cannons. In the meeting with his sister and cousins it transpired that his father had frequently engaged in shooting, in an attempt to banish children from his yard when they came to swim in a new lake formed by the building of a water-powered mill in the Kemi river. The construction work was a very painful process for the father, who had lost a lot of his farm because of the creation of the lake. It seemed to us that, when he felt threatened, the man repeated the gestures of his father, who had fired shots when he felt threatened in the past.

Secondly, we learnt that hospitalisation had often been a very traumatic experience for the entire family, and it had been even more traumatic because it hadn't been possible for family members to discuss and share their feelings about their relative being hospitalised. The emotional experience of feeling like a failure as parents or siblings, of feeling guilty about the problems of one family member, of feeling anger towards the treatment system that had not managed to cure their son or daughter – all these and other feelings had been stored as if they were unspoken 'deep-frozen' memories. Surprisingly, once we had made contact with the families, these strong emotions appeared very fresh and it was as if things had happened recently instead of, for example, 20 years ago when their son had been taken into hospital. Mothers, for instance, often wanted to have time to speak in detail about the period when their son started to have problems, and how this gradually led to hospitalisation. While speaking about these experiences from a long time ago, they usually became extremely emotional, crying a great deal, and often shared a feeling of having been powerless to do anything that could have helped their son or daughter. It seemed that families could only start to orientate to their present life and plans for the deinstitutionalisation of their son or daughter once they had had the opportunity to recount what had happened around the time of the first hospitalisation. This return to the community was successful on many occasions when we managed to gain good collaboration with family members, including the person who had been hospitalised long term.

Our experience has therefore shown us that, even after long-term hospitalisation, it is possible to engage in/resume dialogical work, work that can have a positive impact on the family and future plans.

Notes

1 This chapter is dedicated to the memory of my close friend John Shotter. Our plan was to write this chapter together and indeed the first outline was prepared together. Sadly, John's illness progressed and he passed away in December 2016.
2 This example was first published in Seikkula et al. (2001).
3 This is a fictitious/composite example based on clinical experience.
4 This is a fictitious/composite example based on clinical experience.
5 This example was first published in Seikkula (2002).
6 This is a fictitious/composite example based on clinical experience.

References

Aas, M., Pizzagalli, D.A., Fjæra Laskemoen, J., Reponen, E.J., Ueland, T., Melle, I., Agartz, I., Steen, N.E. and Andreassen, O.A. (2019) Elevated hair cortisol is associated with childhood maltreatment and cognitive impairment in schizophrenia and in bipolar disorders. *Schizophrenia Research* 213, p. 65–67. doi.org/10.1016/j.schres.2019.01.011

Anderson, H. (1997) *Conversation, language, and possibilities.* New York: Basic Books.

Avdi, E. (2005) Negotiating a pathological identity in the clinical dialogue: Discourse analysis of a family therapy. *Psychology and Psychotherapy: Theory, Research and Practice*, 78(4), p. 493–511. doi.org/10.1348/147608305X52586

Bakhtin, M.M. (1984) *Problems of Dostoevsky's Poetics*, ed. C. Emerson. Minneapolis, MN: University of Minnesota Press. doi.org/10.5749/j.ctt22727z1

Cullberg, J. (2000) *Psychoses: An integrative perspective.* London: Routledge.

Dilks, S. (2013) 'Linking dialogues and emotions in therapy in psychosis' in A. Gumley, A. Gillham, K. Taylor and M. Schwannauer (eds.) *Psychosis and emotions. The role of emotions in understanding psychosis, therapy and recovery.* London: Routledge, p. 40–55.

Goodman, L.A., Rosenberg, S.D., Mueser, K.T. and Drake, R.E. (1997) Physical and sexual assault history in women with serious mental illness: Prevalence, correlates, treatment, and future research directions. *Schizophrenia Bulletin*, 23(4), p. 685–696. doi.org/10.1093/schbul/23.4.685

Harper, D.J. (1995) Discourse analysis and 'mental health'. *Journal of Mental Health*, 4(4), 347–358. doi.org/10.1080/09638239550037406

Holma, J. and Aaltonen, J. (1997) The sense of agency and the search for a narrative in acute psychosis. *Contemporary Family Therapy*, 19(4), p. 463–477. doi.org/10.1023/A:1026174819842

Holma, J. and Aaltonen, J. (1998) The experience of time in acute psychosis and schizophrenia. *Contemporary Family Therapy*, 20(3), p. 265–276. doi.org/10.1023/A:1022408727490

Karatza, H. and Avdi, E. (2011) Shifts in subjectivity during the therapy for psychosis. *Psychology and Psychotherapy: Theory, Research and Practice*, 84(2), p. 214–229.

Karon, B.P. and Vandenbos, G.R. (1981) *Psychotherapy of schizophrenia: The treatment of choice*. New York: Jason Aronson.

Lysaker, P. and Lysaker, J. (2001) Psychosis and the disintegration of dialogical self-structure: Problems posed by schizophrenia for the maintenance of dialogue. *British Journal of Medical Psychology*, 74(1), p. 23–33. doi.org/10.1348/000711201160777

Lysaker, P., Lancaster, L. and Lysaker, J. (2003) Narrative transformation as an outcome in the psychotherapy of schizophrenia. *Psychology and Psychotherapy Theory, Research and Practice*, 76, p. 285–299. doi.org/10.1348/147608303322362505

Roe, D. and Davidson, L. (2005) Self and narrative in schizophrenia: Time to author a new story. *Medical Humanities*, 31(2), p. 89–94. doi.org/10.1136/jmh.2005.000214

Seikkula, J. (2002) Open dialogues with good and poor outcomes for psychotic crises: Examples from families with violence. *Journal of Marital and Family Therapy*, 28, p. 263–274. doi.org/10.1111/j.1752-0606.2002.tb01183.x

Seikkula, J., Alakare, B. and Aaltonen, J. (2001) Open Dialogue in psychosis I: An introduction and case illustration. *Journal of Constructivist Psychology*, 14(4), p. 247–265. doi.org/10.1080/10720530125965

Stern, S., Doolan, M., Staples, E., Szmukler, G. and Eisler, I. (1999) Disruption and reconstruction: Narrative insights into the experience of family members caring for a relative diagnosed with serious mental illness. *Family Process*, 38, p. 353–369. doi.org/10.1111/j.1545-5300.1999.00353.x

Trimble, D. (2000) Emotion and voice in network therapy. *Netletter*, 7(1), p. 11–16.

Van der Kolk, B. and Fisher, R. (1995). Dissociation and the fragmentary nature of traumatic memories: Overview and exploratory study. *Journal of Traumatic Stress*, 8(4), p. 505–525. 10.1007/BF02102887

Section 2

PERSONAL, FAMILY AND PROFESSIONAL EXPERIENCES OF OPEN DIALOGUE

CONTENTS

67

Note

1 This is a fictitious name

EDITORS' INTRODUCTION

We live in an era where the lived experience of service users is being increasingly valued alongside the requirement for evidence-based practice. This new balance is a cause for considerable optimism and is perhaps a climate in which Open Dialogue (OD) can flourish and develop further, with ongoing feedback from both professionals and service users.

In this section of the book we include substantive experienced-based accounts from those who are the initial focus of concern (i.e. those having psychotic experiences), from family members who have participated in network meetings, and from OD practitioners working with networks.[1] The accounts clearly illustrate the OD approach in action, in a variety of different countries, and the personal impact that it had on the lives of those involved. They demonstrate how the approach enables a response to presenting problems such that:

a) these become very meaningful, including a gradual understanding of what led to the crisis and/or how the crisis relates to historical events and experiences;
b) there is usually a partial or more complete resolution of the issues; and
c) the quality of relations between network members improves.

The contributions also highlight how OD offers an important counterweight to the predominant biomedical approach.

Relationships

Whatever has gone before, psychotic experiences nearly always lead to disruptions and disturbances in relationships. Where there is a dominant biomedical focus, professionals can lose sight of the significance of relationships in their meetings with service users. Several of the chapters in this section give a clear illustration of the centrality of relationships in the OD approach, and how these are seen as the key to recovery. Many family members describe how, because of the ways in which network meetings were facilitated, they felt safe enough to start to address issues that they had never been able to speak of before, and thereby to feel more emotionally connected to one another (again). Not only was this beneficial in addressing the specific issues that the family were facing, but it also had a positive impact on communication beyond the meetings and relationships in general. For example, Kirsty (Chapter 5) shares her view that her family's increasing capacity to engage in active listening to one another was often *"enough"*, such that it was possible to experience some of the *"toughest and most revealing conversations we had ever had as a family – some of the darkest"* (p. x).

One of the ideals of OD practice is psychological continuity, i.e. the valuing of the relationships between team members and family/network members, such that the team remain the same throughout the process. Whilst this was the case in most of the accounts in this section, Michels et al. (Chapter 6) describe the difficulty reaching this ideal in their service and the compromise they arrived at, which still rendered OD effective.

Early and late interventions

Chapter 1 emphasised the importance of network meetings being arranged directly following the very first contact with the service. Such early involvement is well illustrated in Chapters 5 and 9, though in neither case did it occur right after the first contact, but a short time afterwards. Kirsty and her family met Yasmin Ishaq and her colleague just after her brother was admitted to hospital and Josh and Debra met Annie Hodgkins and colleague Chris after Josh had already started taking neuroleptics.

Though OD is ideally introduced following the first call for help, it can still be very valuable much later on, when other interventions have not led to good outcomes. From the USA, Mary Olson (Chapter 4) describes how, using the OD approach, she and Jaakko Seikkula were able to flexibly engage with Gabe and his family, after 16 years of hopelessness about his future. They were able to develop this relationship over seven years, with positive results.

Between the ideal of an immediate response and being offered the approach after several years of receiving conventional services, we find the work of Rolf Michels and colleagues from Germany (Chapter 6) and the story of Dan, a Norwegian musician (Chapter 10), which illustrate the use of the OD approach in the community, following a first hospital admission. These powerful accounts contrast hospital experiences with those of network meetings.

Opportunity in a time of crisis

Clinical experience indicates that psychotic experiences can occur when the development of the self has not equipped the individual for coping with life and relationship challenges, but that the outcome, following psychotic experiences, can be a positive transformation in these respects (Sandin, 1992). For instance, it has been proposed that this was the case with the Nobel prize winner John Nash (Jackson, 2015). Veronica (Chapter 7) had, since childhood, been fearful of any expression of negativity, and felt compelled to adapt to the expectations of others. A distressing life event broke this trend, leading to her being flooded by the anticipation of evil being directed towards her. A key point of this chapter is to illustrate the value of flexibly offering psychotherapeutic input (with both family members and individually), well beyond the acute phase, in order to facilitate a more favourable development of someone's sense of self and their interactions with others. The empowerment that Veronica started to experience in this OD process is reflected in many of the other accounts in this section. One common feature of such empowerment is supporting someone to find the words for their experience, as described by Dan in his account of the work with his family (Chapter 10).

There is also a sense of the opportunity in crisis in the striking reflections of Zelda Alpern, Sully, Cathy and Marc on their work together (Chapter 8). Particularly noteworthy in this moving reflection of an OD therapeutic process are:

a) the timing of the intervention, when Sully was suicidal and hallucinating as a 16-year-old;
b) the bringing together of a family who had not previously been able to speak about, let alone address, their collective difficulties, which culminated in divorce, alcoholism, and Sully breaking down with psychotic experiences as he carried much of the emotional burden, protecting his vulnerable parents from his own emotional needs in the aftermath of their divorce;
c) the family's willingness to be vulnerable and to take responsibility in a challenging process; and
d) the therapists' preparedness to be emotionally involved and flexible at crucial points.

It seems clear that Sully was helped positively in his adolescent development by having broken down, with the consequence that his family engaged in a process in which they were able to address their issues together.

Note

1 Editors' note: some of the accounts in this section contain the actual words of family members and have therefore not been edited.

References

Jackson, M. (2015) 'John Nash: Reason's approach to an alternative reality' in J. Magagna (ed.) *Creativity and psychotic states in exceptional people: The work of Murray Jackson*. Hove: Routledge, p. 5–24.

Sandin, B. (1992) 'Schizophrenic strategies for survival' in A. Werbart and J. Cullberg (eds.) *Psychotherapy of schizophrenia: Facilitating and obstructive factors*. Oslo: Scandinavian University Press, p. 50–57.

4

OUR SON IS 'COMING BACK'

A dialogical-network approach to a young adult diagnosed with schizoaffective disorder

Mary Olson
(USA)

> From the power to change a human being into a thing by making him
> die there comes another power, in its way more momentous, that of
> making a still living human being into a thing....
>
> Simone Weil (1939/2006)

I will describe a first meeting with a family that throws into relief the effects of biomedical psychiatry in contrast to a dialogical approach. The effect of the former, with its emphasis on symptom reduction, led to the increased isolation of 32-year-old Gabe, diagnosed with schizoaffective disorder. The introduction of Dialogic Practice, emphasising responsive listening and shared understanding, began to create connection, beginning with the first encounter between Gabe and his parents and the therapists. And then, over time, slowly, this fostered Gabe's greater social participation, e.g. his return to the classroom as a student, and other key developments.

Are you coming back?

It was late October 2011 in the northeast United States. Jaakko Seikkula and I were sitting together with the family of Gabe – his mother, Trudy, and his father, Nate – in their rural home. An unseasonably ferocious snowstorm had arrived the night before, cracking tree branches that still had their leaves and bringing down power lines. The scene outside their New England farmhouse was science fiction-y, slightly apocalyptic, with the blacked-out storefronts and dead traffic lights. My thoughts went to wondering if the early storm was an index of climate change and then to the parallels Gregory Bateson drew between non-ecological thinking and the problems of modern psychiatry, both as failures of the Western systems of thinking.[1]

Trudy, Nate, Jaakko and I sat in chairs together in a circle, while Gabe lay on the sofa. Dark-haired, he appeared occasionally to be in communication with invisible presences. For some reason, I suddenly had a looming image of an intensive care unit requiring split-second dexterity. This image proved significant, as I will go on to explain.

Jaakko was calm. "There is a history behind this meeting?" he asked. The father answered that he and Trudy had been searching on the web for an alternative to the kind of psychiatric treatment that his son had had since the age of 16 and which he had dropped out of some years before. Nate launched into abundant descriptions of these prior experiences and illuminated how they felt the biomedical approach had driven Gabe deeper and deeper into isolation. The father stated that Gabe had learned to stop speaking, because whenever he had said something to a professional, there was an immediate, alarmed reaction: medication was changed, or a hospitalisation recommended. Trudy weighed in, "How would you feel if someone sitting above you only asked you, 'Have you been hearing voices lately?' 'Have you been seeing things?'"

Gabe repeatedly left the room to smoke outside, only to return a few minutes later. Gabe had jumped off a three-story building as a teenager and, though miraculously he had survived, he had been left with a noticeable limp. The earlier image I had of the intensive care unit turned out to be resonant: Gabe had spent many months in intensive care after his suicide attempt.

Early on in the meeting, when Gabe had first got up to exit the room, Jaakko had asked him: "Gabe, when did you know that we were coming to your home?" Gabe stopped and struggled. His parents asked the question again several times in slightly different ways, and he finally answered: "Three days ago", looking directly at us for the first time. "Oh, three days ago", repeated Jaakko.

While the parents continued talking with us, Jaakko, though involved, really tuned into Gabe. After Gabe again briefly left and returned, Jaakko asked another question: "Gabe, when we arrived, I tried to shake hands with you, but you would not. Why not?" Gabe answered, "I do not want to touch you". "Oh, you did not want to touch", Jaakko echoed. "No", replied Gabe.

In this way, instead of starting by assessing Gabe's symptoms (e.g. classifying hallucinations), Jaakko attuned to Gabe's voice, which, at first, consisted of body-based utterances, e.g. not shaking hands, sitting outside the circle, leaving and returning. Jaakko introduced words and encouraged Gabe to use words. Their dialogue had an ancient, musical rhythm. Language itself seemed to be being rediscovered and reinvented.

In response to all the bad stories about prior treatment, I turned to the parents and asked if anything had been helpful. Nate said that some of the short-term residential programmes had. In the context of more hopeful memories, Nate suddenly asserted that Gabe was coming back, not in a literal, but in a symbolic sense. "What tells you that Gabe is coming back?" I continued. Nate thought about it: "his will". "His will", I reflected, now also joining the dance. "Yes", said Nate. I felt a sudden change in the air, as if a new future had appeared. Maybe we were forming a place for Gabe to come back to.

In any event, listening seriously to Gabe's parents' perspectives and sharing their hope for their son's recovery seemed crucial to engaging them. As Nate recounted, it was a counterpoint to what one prior, well-meaning doctor had concluded: there was "nothing there", meaning that Gabe, like a person in a vegetative state, experienced minimal brain activity.

Jaakko and I then turned to each other and began a reflecting talk with the family listening in. Jaakko asked me what I thought. So, I began by describing what had moved me, particularly all the positive stories the parents had told about Gabe as a person, repeating their actual words: "sensitive", "loving", "bright", "protective". I also observed how determined the whole family seemed. Jaakko responded by echoing that he had not heard one negative comment about Gabe and went on to say that he liked how Gabe had participated in the meeting, staying a bit on the outside and listening. Jaakko went back to a question he had put to Nate and Trudy earlier about how much of the time they interacted as a couple versus as active parents. Their answers reassured Jaakko that the couple did protect some private time for themselves and prompted additional exchanges between us. We zigzagged between talking about how everyone, in their way, might be trying to help one another and the practical issues the parents had raised about treatment options.

We then turned and asked the family for their thoughts. Trudy said, "You hit the nail on the head.... You know, about Gabe watching out for us... and I didn't know", catching Gabe's eye, "I was so positive about Gabe". In unison, she and Gabe burst out laughing. "He's laughing", Trudy said. Nate clarified that he did not want to pursue residential care for Gabe but rather wanted to focus on dialogical meetings. Notably, after the reflections, Nate and Trudy shifted to describing their collective isolation as a family, rather than focusing on Gabe's problems as an individual.

After the meeting, we heard from Nate. Gabe had been positive about the meeting. They decided they all would like to meet again with us.

Prefigured by the family's enthusiastic response to our first meeting, the results of our work over the long term have been encouraging. Over the past seven years, the son who had rarely spoken and refused therapy for many years has regularly attended our meetings. In the first year, we averted his commitment to a state hospital, though there were two short-term psychiatric admissions to the local hospital. Over the course of 16 years since he was first diagnosed as a teenager, Gabe had had about a dozen hospitalisations. Since the first year of dialogical meetings, he has not had any hospitalisations. His medication has also been reduced.

Gabe is currently living on a working farm, goes to a hearing-voices group, regularly attends church, and is enrolled in a remedial educational project that prepares adults who have been in the mental health system or living on the streets to enter college or vocational training. He works, on and off, with a peer specialist, and is liked by the farm staff. Everyone agrees that Gabe is ready to live on his own, and plans are underway. Jaakko has remained part of our network by joining our meetings in person on visits and on Skype, periodically, from Finland.

Once, about a year ago, after looking at family photos and remembering happier times, I asked Gabe how we could create more happy memories. He said, "Meeting, talking [silence].... Open Dialogue".

Conclusion

The prior biomedical treatment had made Gabe afraid to talk, because there might be a sudden reaction: a new medication or hospitalisation. It led him to drop out of treatment and retreat further. I felt that biological psychiatry objectified Gabe, which means that it turned him into an object of intervention with the aim of curing a disease. In the dialogical meeting described here, the therapists instead approached Gabe as a subject with an emphasis on generating the engagement that had been eluded before. As the social philosopher John Shotter (2004) has put it, dialogical meetings are based on "withness thinking" as opposed to "aboutness thinking".

Dialogic Practice has arisen from the intersection of Bakhtin's (1975/1981) concept of dialogue with systemic family therapy that draws heavily on the work of Gregory Bateson (1972/2000). Central to both thinkers is the radical division between the living world based on interrelationship and communication and the non-living one based on force and impact. This fundamental difference necessitates different rules for thinking, or epistemologies, and different practical approaches (Olson, 2015). Fixing a chemical imbalance or a broken brain, as Bateson would say, represents an error in thinking, "thingyfication" (Bateson and Bateson, 1987). Instead, Dialogic Practice emphasises connection and attunement and, thus, is aligned with the actual nature of the human sphere.

Note

1 See *Steps to an Ecology of Mind* (Bateson, 1972/2000). Bateson saw resonance between the disturbances created by non-ecological thinking in relation to the natural world and our inability to think contextually about human problems.

References

Bakhtin, M. (1981) *The dialogic imagination*, trans. M. Holquist and C. Emerson, ed. M. Holquist. Austin, TX: University of Texas Press. [Original work published 1975].
Bateson, G. (2000) *Steps to an ecology of mind*. Chicago, IL: The University of Chicago Press. [Original work published 1972].
Bateson, G. and Bateson, M.C. (1987) *Angels fear: Towards an epistemology of the sacred*. New York: Macmillan.

Olson, M. (2015) An auto-ethnographic study of 'Open Dialogue': The illumination of snow. *Family Process*, 54(4), p. 716–729. doi.org/10.1111/famp.12160

Shotter, J. (2004) *On the edge of social constructionism. 'Withness'-thinking versus 'aboutness'-thinking.* London: KCC Foundation Publications.

Weil, S. (2006) *The Iliad or the poem of force. A critical edition*, trans. J.P. Holoka. New York: Peter Lang Publishing. [Original work published 1939].

5

THE EXPERIENCE OF A FAMILY OPEN DIALOGUE APPROACH – A SISTER AND PRACTITIONER REFLECT ONE YEAR AFTER DISCHARGE FROM SERVICES

Kirsty Lee and Yasmin Ishaq
(UK)

Background

The Kent Open Dialogue (OD) Service has been operational since February 2017, but some practitioners have worked with families since 2014. An OD team first met Brett (Kirsty's brother) after he was admitted to an inpatient unit experiencing a first episode of psychosis. Brett had no previous experience of contact with mental health services.

Conversation between Kirsty (sister and network member) and Yasmin (Open Dialogue practitioner)

KIRSTY: I never really understood what crisis meant, never really quite knew the panic that grips you when you see a loved one in crisis, their state of mind spiralling out of control. My mum, dad and I stood on the outside – in an external crisis of helplessness – looking in, no idea where to turn.

YASMIN: I recall that it was about a week after you had tried to manage as a family that Brett was admitted to an inpatient unit. He was frightened that others were out to harm him and his family. I met him about two days into his stay and recall seeing someone in a world of his own, using written words in a crossword process to try to figure out what was happening. During my discussion with him your mum came to visit, and we all agreed that it may be helpful for the team to meet with the whole family on the ward on the following days.

KIRSTY: I recall that when Brett went into hospital, we as a family suddenly all felt distantly removed from him, and therefore also separate from his recovery. The feeling of distance was a prominent feature until we met with you and your team, and our experience changed, with a new destination of long-term hope and the possibility of recovery. The first network meeting with the OD team (with myself, Brett, mum and dad) was in the hospital, in a relatively sterile room, and I recall you asking a simple question like, what is the history to my brother ending up in hospital? With that question I remember the room suddenly filled with an eruption of energy that the practitioners, Paul, Yasmin and Lisa, just absorbed.

YASMIN: I remember asking curious and open-ended questions that created space in a very cramped room for all voices to be heard, from which a rich and full picture of what had happened emerged. There was no need to formulate or label Brett's behaviour. Instead, there was power in just sitting with what had been shared – this enabled words and emotions to be expressed that had not previously been shared.

KIRSTY: It felt so simple – you sat with the energy of our words – and although I am sure that you had some form of structure, not once did we feel there was an agenda or interrogation or pressure to make decisions. There were lingering moments of silence – a pause, a shout, a breath, or just a sigh – and you would sometimes ask clarification questions, to ensure that no-one's voice was lost.

YASMIN: Those first few meetings cemented a relationship with you all that has remained and it felt right that the family meetings continued after Brett was discharged from hospital (after 10 days). As a practitioner it felt liberating to be able to respond to what Brett, you and the family wanted and needed. Also, after the initial period of intensive support, in which we met up to 2–3 times a week, you collectively decided to reduce the frequency of meetings, and trust your own resources as a family.

KIRSTY: I felt that our conversations developed another quality – that of listening – for once we could let listening be enough. We would sit and reflect on what had been said between us as a family and also what you as practitioners shared in your reflections. Having the reflections in our presence ensured that nothing was hidden, nothing was unsaid. We felt that the professional voice was on the same level as ours, and we sat together as mutually authentic human beings. In particular there was no feeling of judgement.

YASMIN: For us, as practitioners, OD has felt like a more authentic way of being with families. New understanding and meaning was generated in each meeting with your family and together we discovered ways forward.

KIRSTY: I gleaned light and positivity from these meetings. However, on occasion, they consisted of the toughest and most revealing conversations we had ever had as a family – some of the darkest – but they stayed in the meeting and we would sit with our feelings rather than trying to reach out for quick solutions.

YASMIN: It was also a lesson for us as practitioners, to sit with the feelings of uncertainty evoked in ourselves and just be curious, rather than problem solving about what we had heard. At times this meant sitting with uncomfortable feelings, both in ourselves and the family. If needed, we were able to explore such feelings in our reflections as practitioners, with the family listening and responding if they wanted to.

KIRSTY: I feel we used the network meetings like tools and my brother was able to find solutions and be the bearer of his own recovery. I feel this way of working enabled us to connect as a network and helped my brother to accept his emotions and that his worry was a normal response to his difficulties. I think my brother felt that his voice was being heard and was able to speak with empowerment. He regained the control that he had lost.

YASMIN: I have worked in mental health services for many years and this way of working has felt like the most authentic and honest way of being with individuals and their families/networks. It enables true 'shared decision making' and prioritises the understanding of distress over hasty treatment decisions.

Concluding remarks

Kirsty and Yasmin: We would like to share that Brett was discharged from secondary care services in September 2017. He had reduced and come off antipsychotic medication by August 2016 and has been able to maintain his work and social interests. The future is hopeful and full of possibilities.

Brett, Kirsty and family were one of the first families to receive this approach in Kent. Since the development of a standalone service in February 2017 over 100 individuals and their networks have had the opportunity to engage in the OD approach. The feedback received so far from service users is overwhelmingly positive, and in addition staff express high levels of work satisfaction. There are still organisational challenges in expanding and growing the model, but these are being positively worked with as there is a will to see this way of working develop.

6

PSYCHOTIC BEHAVIOUR

Symptom of a (brain) disease or an attempt at adjustment?

Rolf Michels, Kerstin Rickert, Birgit Molitor,
Joachim Scheele and Petra Wagner
(Germany)

Maria

Maria, a divorced mother of two grown-up children in her late fifties, was referred to our home treatment team by the public psychiatric community service. They had been contacted by Maria's relatives who were concerned about what they referred to as her "strange behaviour". Some months earlier, Maria had been admitted to the emergency department of our hospital in an acute psychotic state that had developed gradually over five days. As her age seemed advanced for a first psychotic episode, computed tomography (a CT scan) of her brain and a lumbar puncture were performed in order to exclude an organic brain disease. On the ward she had been very agitated, acting in a hostile manner towards staff and other patients, and so some medication had been prescribed (about 4 mg of haloperidol). About a week later she was discharged without any obvious psychotic symptoms, and without any medication or plan for further treatment.

The service

Our team is part of the psychiatric department in a general hospital in Itzehoe, a town in the German state of Schleswig-Holstein. The department has a catchment area of about 130,000 people and has been developing Open Dialogue (OD) since 2008. About 45 staff have been trained in two in-house foundation training courses, with the OD approach mainly being adopted by the team treating people with psychotic disorders. This team provides inpatient care, a day clinic, and outpatient and home treatment services, and can provide the kind of service that seems most appropriate to the needs of those treated.

81

Back to Maria

Seven days after being contacted by the family the first network meeting took place in our outpatient department. The delay was due to the fact that that there was no psychiatrist available at an earlier stage, on this occasion.[1] The meeting included Maria, her partner, and her adult daughter. The professional team for the first meeting consisted of the psychiatrist and a social worker. The beginning of the meeting was very difficult. Maria's partner and her daughter were very upset about her psychotic experiences, which included a feeling that she was being followed by cars (with her recording their registration numbers as though they were personal messages), talking about a shooting that she was convinced had taken place, and a conviction that news items on the TV were about her. Her relatives stated that they could not cope with this any longer. Maria seemed to be in a very psychotic state in the meeting – she was agitated and seemed somewhat confused. She was also hostile and accused her relatives of wanting her to be declared insane. After about 15 minutes she left the meeting. The team members could do nothing other than invite her to rejoin whenever she wanted.

The team was somewhat puzzled and reflected with the relatives about how to deal with the situation. They wondered whether the fact that the meeting was taking place at the hospital could have contributed to Maria becoming upset, because of her previous admission.

About 15 minutes later Maria returned, stating that she wanted to know what had been said about her whilst she was absent. She turned to her daughter with a reproachful attitude: "You know what it is all about. You know what they have done to me!" The daughter was puzzled and said that she had no idea. The team felt that Maria's words might relate to an important issue and tried to clarify what she had said, but their lack of understanding persisted until some minutes later when Maria said that she was sorry that she had spent so little time with her children when they were young. This led the daughter to start to talk about a time 10 years ago when her mother had left the family for more than half a year, adding that, until now, this had never been spoken about. Maria then became very emotional and started to talk about the many hardships she had experienced in her lifetime. She continued to talk for the rest of the session in a calm manner, and in good dialogue with her daughter. All those present at the meeting were very moved by this experience and there were no longer signs of any psychotic experiences. The daughter stated that her mother seemed to be quite normal again and Maria's partner added that she had shared experiences which he had never heard before.

Another meeting was scheduled for the following day at Maria's home. In this meeting she was able to explain how a lot of her psychotic experiences now made sense to her, in that they reminded her of past experiences. She was especially reminded of a time when she was involved in court trials about business affairs with her former husband – the registration numbers of the cars seemed to be identical with the registration numbers of these court trials.

The team continued to see Maria for about half a year. Altogether, there were 13 meetings, comprising a mixture of individual meetings and network meetings. Although there was some suspicion and hostility towards the team in some of the following sessions, Maria did not return to the psychotic state again during the treatment process. Instead, a number of life events could be identified that were related to her psychotic experiences and the focus became more on how she could manage her life going forward, including relational problems.

When Maria herself decided to terminate the treatment, she raised the question about the nature of her psychotic experiences. She stated that they had appeared to her as absolutely real at the time, although she now realised that they were not real. The team therefore offered another session where this was discussed in more depth. During the whole treatment no medication was used. Maria and her relatives were informed that they could contact us should any new problems arise, but this has not happened since our work came to an end and two years later Maria is free of psychotic symptoms.

Comments

The most striking feature of the work with this family was the sudden transition from an acute psychotic state to a normal state during the first meeting. We conclude from this that, at this early stage, the psychotic experience had not become chronic, but was rather a fluctuating state of consciousness that was affected by the way in which the network meeting was conducted. This contrasts with Maria's first treatment episode where the hospital process resulted in an increase in psychotic symptoms and hence the need for neuroleptic medication. In our OD work, it may have been crucial that the team did not classify Maria's behaviour as psychotic, but rather tried to understand what it was connected to for Maria herself. Our desire to clarify the lack of understanding between Maria and her daughter finally made it possible for Maria to talk about an emotional issue that her daughter could relate to. It also seems significant that the team responded to Maria's negative attitude to the hospital environment by letting her decide on the best location for subsequent meetings.

Although this seems to be a good treatment process, with a favourable outcome, there are some shortcomings in comparison to the principles of OD (see Chapter 1). The first contact was not as immediate as it should have been. Fortunately, it seems that, in this instance, it was still early enough. Another aspect that is challenging is how to ensure psychological continuity. Due to staff shift patterns it is impossible to arrange meetings so that the same team members always participate, but we have managed to organise our service so that only a limited number of team members take part in any given treatment process, so that the service users and network can hopefully feel some continuity in relation to the team. This is far from ideal, but it seems to work in many cases, as in this one. In this instance, we were able to arrange it so that at least one team member had participated in the previous meeting. The team consisted of the authors of this contribution (two psychiatric nurses, one social worker and two psychiatrists).

Note

1 The development of OD in our service has changed the role of different professions, especially the nurses, and many network meetings are held without a psychiatrist. However, we still think that it is necessary to have a psychiatrist in our team for an initial meeting.

7

THE STRESS OF TOLERATING UNCERTAINTY

Emails can help!

Giuseppe Tibaldi and Veronica
(Italy)

Introduction

In this chapter Veronica, a service user, and her psychiatrist, who co-facilitated an Open Dialogue (OD) process with Veronica and members of her social network (her parents and boyfriend), describe their experiences. Firstly, Veronica looks back on her crisis and the period before and after it, and shares her understanding of the historical experiences and events which may well have contributed to the crisis. Then Giuseppe Tibaldi outlines what was most significant for him in this work.

Veronica (not my real name)

One year ago, I left the psychiatric ward where I had stayed for a few days. I recall the feeling of freedom I experienced on leaving the hospital building, but also some fear, a lot of insecurity and a need to establish a new order in my mind, as well as in my life.

My main question was: "what had happened to me?" Why did a person who was considered balanced and strong find herself facing a psychiatric admission? Looking back, I can see that several factors contributed to the development of my crisis. The healing process necessarily includes awareness and understanding of these factors.

Surely, a first reason for my emotional fragility was hidden in my childhood: it was not so serene, because family life was deeply influenced by a violent, alcoholic uncle who – for at least 15 years – filled our days with anxiety and fear. He was an intelligent person, sometimes brilliant, but he had misused his talents.

Since childhood, I had been considered to be very gifted and studious, but I started to worry that I would, at some point, act in a negative way. For this reason, I built up, even prior to my adolescence, a strict system of vigilance

85

that prevented me from initiating any unpleasant action towards those close to me. The family atmosphere was full of tension and the ways in which this affected me constituted the first root of my fragility.

A second critical element was the expectations of my parents towards me. I was seen as the daughter who could redeem everyone, who would surely succeed in life. I really loved to study, but these strong expectations weighed on me a great deal. I was not allowed to fail and disappoint my family. So I closed myself off, limiting my relationships with peers, and dedicated myself – body and soul – to study.

When I met my current partner at university I was imprisoned in the character of the perfect daughter and the perfect student. I could even become the perfect girlfriend, since I had at my side a boyfriend whom I considered worthy of great esteem and respect. In this relationship, I continued to adapt myself to my partner's expectations, even if they did not correspond to my wishes, in a continuous effort to seek the benevolence of others ("captatio benevolentiae").

So, when we found ourselves having to decide about an unexpected pregnancy, my position could only be aligned with that of my partner, meaning that I found myself facing an abortion in absolute secrecy, even though I was tormented by feelings of guilt, given my rigid Catholic education which preached absolute respect for life. The suffering I experienced at that time has still not had the chance to surface, to be shared; it remains inside me, unresolved.

I had become what others wanted me to be: kind, helpful, acquiescent; in my private life and at work. My true self, my dreams, my ambitions had dissolved. Deep down, this became intolerable: the load I was carrying was too heavy. First I experienced anxiety, and then an explosive rage emerged, which progressively increased and which I found more and more difficult to contain. On the one hand, there was dissatisfaction and the desire to free myself from every constraint and, on the other hand, there was everyday life: it became a titanic clash, which deprived me of all my strength.

Around the same time, I started to experience a conflict with one of the families in the building in which I live – a family with two children who could seemingly do whatever they wanted. They enjoyed the freedom I had never enjoyed, and their total lack of respect for the rules was unbearable to someone like me, who had chosen rigour as her bulwark.

I had already managed to exclude my parents, after some quarrels, and my partner seemed incapable of perceiving the problems that I was experiencing; I felt alone in an inner and outer world that I did not want to accept anymore.

This was the starting point for my crisis. I began my escape from the real world and invented one of my own. Initially it was harmless and was done by transforming my thoughts into dialogues with neighbours or acquaintances. The empty space was filled with a thousand conversations that satisfied my need for dialogue, but also for support. Gradually, I lost awareness of the fact that they came from me – the conversations took on a life of their own and felt real.

I began to live two lives at the same time: my life in the 'real world' in which I still managed to interact almost normally, and my life in the 'parallel world' that gradually started to predominate and assumed fantastical features: now I could read people's thoughts and talk with otherworldly characters.

My parallel world became populated with evil people, conspirators and demons and started to engulf me, such that I was less able to interact with real people. The tenuous feeling of doubting my perceptions, and thinking that I should ask to be taken to the emergency room, was fading. I pushed my partner to leave and did the same with my beloved cat and my parents; I wandered through the city, chased by evil presences and convinced of having to fight to survive.

I believed that everyone, including medical staff, willed my eternal damnation. My admission to hospital took place in these terrible conditions, in the grip of constant nightmares and hallucinations, auditory as well as visual. I feared that every drug was a poison, that sedatives would make me sleep for years, that this hell would never be over. Crushed by guilt, I knew that I could only be saved by someone who recognised my innocence. I was the executioner of myself, waiting for a forgiveness that could give me hope.

Initially my need to be able to communicate again was opened by low-dose antipsychotic drugs, and then my psychiatrist started a series of meetings. He tried to help me to be more aware of what had happened through dialogue, drawings and diagrams. He tried to build an understanding of my family context with me, in order to prepare me for the involvement of other members of my network. I came to realise that recovery is based on a shared understanding of what has happened, involving all members of one's network, and soon after discharge family meetings began with my parents and partner.

The most difficult phase was the first two months after being discharged. I returned to work immediately, because I felt that contact with real life would have a positive influence. I continued to take medication, at gradually reduced doses, and the family meetings continued, as well as additional meetings with the doctor alone. I started reading books that he suggested, which encouraged continuing introspection, and would send him regular feedback by email.

Involving family members is not always easy. It requires a willingness to put oneself on the line, to share positive and negative experiences, to say what one often does not typically dare to say openly. In small steps, thanks to the mediation of professionals, the initial tensions gradually disappeared and it was possible to face the critical issues, such that, after six months, I felt ready to stop taking the drugs altogether.

Obstacles, however, never end, and when you are fragile, you sometimes see them as insurmountable. After a brief phase of euphoria, I again felt emptied of energy, without a clear goal to reach, without something to drive me.

Furthermore, I felt naked and exposed as the fragilities that I had kept well-hidden were now in front of everyone. My old image was destroyed, and I had to build a new self.

I began to modify some of the behaviours that had led to such deep distress, that threatened to destroy my existence. I started taking care of myself. I clarified and addressed aspects of my relationship with my family and my partner. A number of decisions allowed me to release tension, to resume 'breathing', to imagine a future again. I started to have dialogues with real people, not in hallucinated universes.

Now I feel stronger again, surer of myself. The vivid memories of the crisis have begun to fade. Today I am here to share my recovery journey, to give hope to those still halfway on their journey. The obstacles are many, the path is long, but you can overcome it.

We must help everyone cultivate the belief that both psychic and physical difficulties can be temporary; that medications must not accompany our whole existence; that we can reach a new equilibrium, accepting a need to lean on those close to us, and then find the strength within us – in due time.

Giuseppe Tibaldi

I met 'Veronica' in the psychiatric ward when I was half way through the three-year OD training in London. I initially proposed a meeting on the ward with her parents and boyfriend, but Veronica wanted to postpone such a meeting because her crisis had generated a conflict between her father and boyfriend. I respected this request and offered her some individual meetings instead. She was discharged from the ward earlier than I expected, less than two weeks after admission.

Immediately after discharge, the first meeting took place with Veronica, her parents and her boyfriend. It was a Friday afternoon and the looming weekend seemed full of threatening clouds. Her father feared an immediate return to hospital. Very unusual arrangements had been made to respect Veronica's desire to rest quietly in her bedroom. A kitchen door was brought up from the cellar to limit the nocturnal movements of the cat, and her father (with whom Veronica was not at ease) would come to her house at 10 pm, to sleep in the kitchen with the cat, and would then leave at 7 am the following day. The boyfriend would then arrive around 10 am and leave late afternoon. In this initial meeting I had asked Veronica to keep in touch over the weekend by email, and this proved to be very valuable. Through emails I knew, prior to meeting the following Tuesday, that the most threatening clouds had passed.

In total, 12 network meetings with Veronica, her parents, her boyfriend and her cat took place at Veronica's house, ending a year after her discharge from hospital. My experience of this journey revolves around three OD concepts:

1   **The need-adapted approach** was especially important at the beginning. Veronica's wish to postpone network meetings was respected. Her wish to give meaning to what had happened could not be postponed, however, hence the need for individual meetings. We accepted her desire to resume teaching, even though she, and her relationships, remained unstable. Individual meetings continued in parallel with the family work, without conflict.

2   **Tolerance of uncertainty.** This was very important, but also very stressful during several key periods, as described above.

3   **Trust.** The network meetings were shared with my colleague, Ugo. We developed a good trusting relationship, reflecting well together at different depths of metaphor and language, which paralleled the vital increase in trust between all those attending the network meetings.

A year has passed since the last network meeting. I have since received three emails and am looking forward to the next one.

8

ROOTED IN LOVE – A JOURNEY THROUGH A DARK TIME WITH A TEENAGER AND HIS FAMILY

*Zelda Alpern, Sully Swearingen, Cathy Swearingen
and Marc Werner-Gavrin*
(USA)

Introduction

The Counselling Service of Addison County (CSAC), a community mental health agency in rural Vermont, USA, has a history of utilising reflecting processes that dates back to visits from Tom Andersen and Magnus Hald in the 1990s (please see Chapter 23 for more detail on this). We have worked with over 90 different networks over the past six years. Here we offer selections from the accounts of four persons involved with one of these networks.

The network met 13 times over eight months. The primary network comprised Sully, a high school student, and his divorced parents Cathy and Joel. Marc, a youth and family psychologist, and Zelda, a social worker from the adult crisis team, were the team facilitators. Other professionals and Sully's sister participated in network meetings on occasion. This work was initiated in response to Sully's suicidality and the onset of troubling voices at 16 years of age. He was acting on his suicidal urges at times, and it was unclear whether he would continue with high school. Four years later, Sully is away at college. Although he continues to hear voices, they are now subtle and no longer have the upper hand.

Marc and Zelda asked the family whether they were interested in sharing their experience of our work together. Sully and Cathy responded positively, expressing a preference for Marc and Zelda to first share their reflections to which they could respond. Joel approved of this plan, but chose not to respond himself.

Zelda

These are the pivotal moments and aspects of our collaboration that stayed with me:

- Sully's father, Joel, walking out of a session and Marc running after him and standing in front of his car, urging him to rejoin the conversation. I was struck by Marc's willingness to take this risk – matching the emotional risk that the father was taking.
- Joel's willingness to rejoin and to stay in the process, through difficult emotions. This felt very significant in terms of the eventual positive outcome.
- Sully noting that this was the first time that the family had sat down to talk about the divorce since it occurred many years ago.
- The family's willingness to be vulnerable together, rather than to make this all about Sully and his problems or diagnosis.
- Sully's admiration of his sister's recovery, and the deep painful impression that her earlier years of addiction had had on him.
- The final session when Sully's sister was able to join us and appreciate the family's ability to talk about difficult things, including the repercussions of the divorce.
- The meeting at which Sully's individual therapist, Elizabeth, was present, where the metaphor of him driving his own car, rather than being along for the ride, was coined, and was referred to in sessions thereafter.
- A series of family conversations about the caretaker role that Sully took on as a youngster – protecting his father and mother from the emotional fallout of their divorce and not being emotionally attended to himself. His suicidal urges and self-demeaning voices began to be understood as an opportunity for Sully to fall apart and be attended to. I remember his parents' description of Sully lying in a foetal position and needing to be monitored around the clock by them.
- Meaning-making conversations about Sully's experience of voices and our joint exploration of whether it was in part the opportunity to be taken care of by his parents, and to have conversations with them about the impact of their divorce on him, that made the voices recede significantly. Although he was a child at the time, in the wake of the divorce, Sully became the emotional caretaker of his father. The voices functioned to reverse this and allowed Sully to be the person at the centre of concern. He was able to reformulate his view of himself, with the help of his family, as a person who could have needs – needs which could be met.
- Sully's psychiatrist, Feyza, being truly collaborative in discussions about medication, using low doses and helping him to taper off neuroleptics within seven months of starting them.
- Sully's creativity and resilience: he wrote a memoir about his experiences in one of his high school classes and also wrote a song about the family work. In Sully's memoir he largely attributes his healing process to his connection with one of his closest friends. His friend never came to our meetings, and perhaps this is what Sully preferred, but it does underscore how vital it is to be cognisant of, and to engage, the social network.

Marc

Zelda, your memories correspond with mine. I was flooded with emotions on reading them. My memory is that together we all created, slowly, over time, a sense of safety for each of us to share feelings and thoughts – to offer them, mull them over, respond, and allow differences.

My memory is of love, caring, fear and guilt – all tangled up and stuck. Initially, everybody was so very respectful and careful, and whilst they continued to be respectful, over time the family grew comfortable enough with the process to share their distress, even when they were worried that this might distress others. There was humour too – the family and the clinicians prevented it from becoming intolerably grim by occasionally using humour to lovingly hold and accept each other's quirkiness. At first the focus was on Sully's suicidality, and his parents' struggle to trust in his reassurances that he wouldn't take his life (because of his tendency to try not to worry them). A consensus was soon reached that Sully had spent a good deal of his childhood taking care of his parents emotionally as well as trying to disappear, in order to not be a burden to them during the hard times. This seemed to be especially the case with his dad, who spiralled into depression after the divorce.

I felt most protective of the father, as he could get overwhelmed by the emotions in the room. At times he said that he could barely tolerate being present and he was also afraid that he would say something that would cause pain, something that he would end up regretting. It transpired that all members were fearful of this.

The father was upfront about being a recovering alcoholic. I think that his return to the meeting, after he bolted, was a turning point, albeit one that was built on a foundation that the family had, with much courage, lovingly and patiently created.

Sully's parents stuck it out, gradually showing Sully that they were OK and that they were going to be OK. Yes, there were monsters under the bed, but his parents, in Sully's presence, peered under the bed and, though this was hard for everybody, the monsters gradually became less scary. Sully's parents gave him room to turn towards his own life, to "drive his own car". And slowly, tentatively, with some encouragement and some pushing, he did so.

Sully

I really think that both of your reflections address many of the major emotions and significant points of change that were experienced in our meetings. Zelda, I specifically like and support your paragraph about the caretaker role, because that was one of the biggest struggles for me, and we worked hard on this.

The voices I was hearing in my head at that time were always arguing with each other and with myself. Everyday tasks were extremely challenging because the voices would be constantly critiquing how I should accomplish the task, while shouting insults at me. For example, in the hallways at high school, I couldn't even wave and say hi to my friends in passing without hearing "Don't talk to them. DO NOT LOOK. You are incompetent. No one wants to talk to you". The voices were torturing me, and I had absolutely no control over them, which made me feel completely helpless and vulnerable. I always want to make a situation better by having some degree of control, like when I cared for my parents after the divorce. Being ruled by two foreign voices broke me down and led to panic attacks where I could not hear or comprehend anything besides them shouting uncontrollably. There are still times when I can hear them in my head, but they are much quieter and easier to shake off.

Marc, you and my father formed a pretty interesting relationship and I think you elaborate well on some of the challenges he faced individually in our sessions. In all honesty, I did not see the use in having family sessions at first. Initially I thought they would create more tension between my parents and myself outside of the meetings, but as we became more comfortable and honest, their purpose became irrefutably clear to me. I think about my dark times now and again, and I think you are both heroes, who I associate with that time.

Cathy

I would also agree with most of Marc and Zelda's reflections. I was such a coordinator of care that sometimes it's hard for me to recall the actual time we spent together in sessions. I was constantly organising appointments, school meetings and doctors' appointments. Can you believe that we had Marc and Zelda for family counselling, Feyza for psychiatry and medication management, Elizabeth, Sully's private counsellor, the school team and his paediatrician caring for Sully? Such a massive support team.

One pivotal moment for me was when you, Marc and Zelda, met us in the emergency department after Sully had spent the night in the safe room. I thought that Sully needed inpatient treatment. After breakfast that morning you both met with us and entrusted Joel and I to care for Sully rather than sending him away. Even though it meant 24/7 care and I wasn't sure if I qualified to parent at that point, your calming and trusting demeanour helped us to feel that we could manage. I deeply appreciated your support and encouragement, your really looking out for Sully's best interests, and that, in the family meetings, our parenting and love for our kids took precedence over the resentment between their father and I about the collapse of our marriage.

Writing this sure brings up emotions and jogs some memories but, without this crisis, our relationships would not have reached such a healthy and deep connection.

Zelda

Marc, I am curious about the moment when you told Sully that this work would change the way that *you* will live your life.

Marc

When I'm lost in the forest, with no way out in sight, I try to remember this work, to remember being with and witnessing Sully and his parents taking a chance – trusting that conversations rooted in love can lead to a way out. It's risky business, but it tends to pay off.

9

OPEN DIALOGUE AS A POINT OF ENTRY TO RECONNECT TO THE REAL WORLD OF RELATIONSHIPS

Annie Hodgkins, Josh and Debra[1]
(UK)

Josh

I am Josh, one of Annie's clients, and here is a brief synopsis of my family's experience with Open Dialogue (OD).

At the beginning of my psychosis I felt detached from reality. Even after returning home from university I didn't feel any real connection with anyone. It felt like I was functioning on another wavelength to the people around me and I had no way back. I was distressed by the loss of contact with family and friends, as they were the people I would usually turn to for emotional support and for a different perspective on issues I was experiencing. One of the hardest people to feel disconnected from was my mother, as we had always been particularly close. I felt guilty about being uncomfortable in her presence. I also felt like I was keeping a lot from her because I thought that, if she knew about these things, she wouldn't understand and wouldn't love me.

In the beginning, the OD sessions were very difficult and tense. I remember that I couldn't look any of the other people in the room in the eye. I stared at the ground, playing with a stress ball, and could barely handle being in the room for the hour-long meeting. The emphasis in the first few sessions was on giving us room to speak – a space for my mother and myself to voice our concerns, emotions and grievances. In the sessions I could talk about how I was feeling week to week, and if she had any sudden fears, we all discussed this, giving me a chance to explain myself further. Gradually mum started to understand more about my condition. I was able to talk to her about the issue of suicide, my past drug use and my more extreme delusions. Talking about such issues in the meetings meant that, even if these topics were initially met by a strong emotional reaction, the conversation was sustained long enough for us to work through them, and no meeting ever ended on a bad note. Each issue that we talked about felt like a huge weight off my chest, and as my mum's understanding grew, she was able to give me space when I needed it.

The sense of urgency to return to university went away, giving me peace of mind that I had time to fully recover.

The OD meetings helped us to communicate better – our conversations became less reactive and more understanding. Things that we hadn't been able to talk about directly to each other, because it felt too intense, were defused when we talked with two impartial people in the room. This extended into our everyday life, with our house becoming a more peaceful place, now that we had a better understanding of how each other was feeling, and what we could do to avoid any further escalation.

One issue that turned out to be of particular significance was a dereliction of duty in relation to my responsibility for some younger friends; something that I continued to feel guilty about. Initially I thought that it was a relatively small issue, not especially connected to my psychosis, but as my recovery went on, I realised that it was the underlying theme of my whole condition, and the thing that was stopping me from moving on. This issue made me feel paranoid walking in the street, and when talking to strangers. My work with my care coordinator eventually helped me to reach a place where I felt comfortable sharing the issue in an OD session, a session which turned out to be one of the most eye-opening and positive moments I had had in recent years, and a cornerstone of my recovery. My mum was a little shocked initially, but understood, and by the end I realised that this huge issue, that had plagued me for so long, was not nearly as severe as I had thought.

After the session we hugged, and I had the realisation that there was somebody else in my life, beyond the professionals involved, who knew every notable issue and detail of my condition, who still cared about me, and who didn't see me any differently to before. It felt like I didn't need to hold onto the tension inside of myself, and I was finally able to let go of a huge weight on my mind, and be at peace, with mum and myself. Since that moment I have felt a lot more connected to the world around me. I still get stressed and paranoid, but my support network is so much stronger. I don't think I would have reached a point like this without the OD sessions, to be confident enough to reach out to the person I was closest to.

The improvements in my relationship with my mother had a ripple effect, as I thought that her opinion reflected how my friends and family would feel as well. I realised that my issues weren't mine to bear on my own and didn't make me a horrible person, and this slowly brought me back to reality.

The OD sessions gave me a place to explore my thoughts. Now at peace with my mum, we were able to work through my problems – she provided alternative points of view, based on what she had observed and her knowledge of me. We started to set goals and mini-deadlines together. I would get out of bed each day, wash myself, eat healthily, and she would be understanding if I failed. This was still not an easy time, but each session offered an optimistic viewpoint on the times to come.

Overall the OD sessions were a great experience for me. They helped me to reconnect to my mum, who has been an anchor throughout the rest of my recovery, after I moved away from home. The sessions accelerated my recovery, and even gave my mum a space to voice her anxieties and concerns about her own life. It provided a caring, nurturing environment that helped me to feel safe, and gave me a point of entry to reconnect to the world I live in.

Debra – Josh's mum

Once we got into the swing of OD, I found the sessions really helpful, enabling us to map and explore both the past and future. I know Josh felt that it was a very safe environment to explore feelings and to discuss uncomfortable issues with me. Having both Annie and Chris at those meetings was a real privilege, and I feel we really explored a range of perspectives. I am so grateful.

OD has helped me to understand my son's condition and offer appropriate help and support to aid his recovery. Without these sessions, I would have felt isolated as his carer, with absolutely no idea what he was (and still is) going through; I would have still been angry with him and I could not have responded positively to his changeable moods, behaviours and needs during his recovery (as this is not linear).

I would be very naive if I thought that it was all going to be smooth from now on and I suppose my biggest concern now is that, having had Annie, Chris, Duncan (cognitive behavioural therapist) and me supporting him, Josh is now very much in new and uncharted waters, as he has decided to leave home.

Annie Hodgkins (care coordinator/Open Dialogue practitioner)

I met Josh in the spring, following his first episode of psychosis, which was triggered by the consumption of hallucinogenic substances. Following this episode, he had returned home from university to live with his mum Debra. Josh and I started to develop a good therapeutic relationship through weekly meetings at his home. He was prescribed anxiolytics and neuroleptics, and the very early signs of improvement were promising. Josh's primary goal was to return to university that September, which initially appeared feasible. However, the following month, Josh became increasingly disabled by his distress and socially isolated – he rarely left the house.

Josh's mum Debra had not been involved in his care prior to starting OD. He had consistently dismissed my suggestion that her presence may be helpful, as he didn't "want her to worry". However, my colleague Chris and I had started our OD training at the beginning of the year and so, after our second week of training, we discussed the possibility of him joining Josh, Debra and I for network meetings. Josh and Debra agreed, and we had the first of our 15 network meetings in the summer.

Chris and I arrived at their home with mixed emotions; excitement that we had the opportunity to start to practise OD, along with a degree of anxiety – were we ready? I recall Chris and I attempting to explain the process of OD when we weren't entirely sure ourselves at this early stage of our training. We had no printed information and Josh's discomfort being in a room with the three of us was palpable. Our reflections felt awkward and the silence intolerable.

On meeting Debra, it was apparent that we have much in common – we are professionals, divorced mums of young men, similar in age and background. During the first meeting Debra expressed her anger, disappointment, frustration, love and, above all, fear for Josh's future. It occurred to me that my inner polyphony as a mum had generated an expectation for the trajectory of Josh's progress. I hoped, given his earlier academic successes, that he would go on to fulfil his full potential, a hope I also held for my own son.

I quickly began to value aspects of our OD training that I hadn't fully appreciated the relevance of until we started to practise. A significant feature of the training was team bonding, in order to promote trust. Chris's participation brought a gender balance to the process, and his curiosity invited the perspectives of other males in Josh's network, who were unable to join us. As the sessions progressed, we learnt the value of silence. In the early sessions Josh's verbal communication was minimal, but as his confidence grew, he was able to express himself more, knowing that he would be heard in a space that felt safe.

During the last two sessions Josh made the decision to leave home in order to forward his recovery and ended up moving within a week. Since leaving home Josh has completed a second course of cognitive behavioural therapy and has received help from the early intervention team in the city he has moved to. He lives autonomously, suffers much less anxiety and dissociation, and far fewer psychotic symptoms. He is increasingly able to engage with society and uses exercise to support his recovery. He has withdrawn from his university studies but intends to complete a degree with the Open University to facilitate future travel abroad. He considers himself happy.

Note

1 Josh and Debra decided to publish their story using just their first names.

10

PERMISSION TO SPEAK!

Reiulf Ø. Ruud and Pia Birgitte Jessen
(Norway)

Introduction

This is a story about Dan, a man who, at the age of 18, experienced several psychotic episodes. At the time of the first crisis he was admitted to a psychiatric hospital far away from his local mental health centre, in which there was no Open Dialogue (OD) work being done. On discharge he was referred to the outpatient department in which we worked, which is close to where he was living. We started to work with him using the OD approach, work which lasted for three years. During this time the two of us met with Dan alone and also with Dan and his parents together. John, a psychiatric nurse from the Municipal Psychiatry Service, also participated in some meetings. Recently, we have spoken to both Dan and John[1] about their experience of and thoughts about the work we did together, and what follows is extracts from their accounts of this work.

Dan's story

Dan stated:

> When I was 17, there was a lot going on in my life. I went to study music at high school and wrote lyrics and composed music for a band I played in. We were a well-known and popular band – we made an album, were on the radio, and were very ambitious. I was promised a future as a musician and songwriter. Music became a passion, and the creative urge took me over, such that I didn't sleep for long periods of time. I became immersed in a creative landscape that could both confuse me and drain my energy. I thought that I could achieve everything, without limits. One day I was so tired that I could not go to school – instead I collapsed. After speaking to my mother, I contacted the psychiatric service in the municipality and spoke to John. Soon I was overwhelmed by psychotic experiences, and so I was admitted to a locked ward in a psychiatric hospital for three days where I was treated with antipsychotic medication. During the

admission, the staff seemed to have a very top-down attitude. They thought that they knew best, in an arrogant way. A few days after leaving the hospital, I received a copy of the discharge report from the doctors in the mail. This concluded that I had a diagnosis of schizophrenia, which caused me a lot of stress and anxiety.

Dan says that he experienced his admission to a psychiatric hospital as a threat to his person, worse than the psychotic experience, and also as a threat to his identity, exacerbated by receiving the diagnosis of schizophrenia. However, he felt different once the OD meetings started, as he explains:

Meeting you was good, but it was also scary to talk with a number of people present. It was a good place to get help though, and sometimes it was good that everyone was present in the meetings. The meetings helped me to formulate my thoughts, especially in relation to my father, and I don't think that I would have been able to do this on my own. You recognised what I was talking about and were able to express it in a different way to myself. I was pre-occupied with my father's opinion – he presented things in a way that was not true to my experience. I felt that he twisted issues, and I struggled with this. When my parents were present in meetings, I felt that I had to let the conversation go the way my father wanted it to go. His opinion was that, because of my illness, it was unwise to continue with my music career. This angered me, because music was my life. However, I almost came to believe myself that this is what I needed to do.

In the family meetings we talked about things that we would never talk about at home. We had to put words to things that we would otherwise not speak about, especially my father's alcohol abuse. In one meeting I told my father that he should not point his finger at me. It took a long time before I dared to say this to him, and he was furious with me after this. I knew that it was necessary to address his alcohol abuse, because the only way to deal with the issue was to get him to talk about it. I felt sorry for him because I received help and he didn't. In his view, no-one else could help him with his alcohol abuse – he had to fight it himself. However, I think he realised that his drinking affected my feelings and my stability, and sometime after this he was admitted to a substance abuse clinic. I didn't have a guilty conscience over hurting his pride, because I knew that we had to find a way to discuss difficult topics such as this.

My mother was very submissive in the meetings, afraid to say things the way they really were. She understood the issues in the family relationships but felt that she could not really say anything about these. She was having a very hard time. We understood each other and knew how we felt about the situation – we had a kind of silent alliance.

I used antipsychotic medication during the periods when I had psychotic experiences. You were careful not to prescribe too much medication or for too long, and I really appreciated the way we collaborated on this. I suffered from side effects, especially drowsiness and impaired creativity, and this was hard to live with.

I started to trust you quite quickly. The things my father trivialised, you took seriously. This was good for me. You were good at formulating what I shared. You would say, "so what you think is that...?". You shared your understanding, so that I could hear it back, and be reassured that what I had said was understood. You did not give up until you understood what I meant by what I said. I spoke to you about many things that I had not shared with anyone. In one meeting I spoke about a girl I had been in love with, and you said, "yes, that sounds like a very powerful experience". I felt a sense of relief, because it was an issue that had been downplayed by others for years. You took me seriously and asked questions that helped me to find new words for my experiences. When I spoke these new words, I saw new opportunities.

John, the psychiatric nurse, also thinks that open-ended questions, and the use of OD more generally, created the space needed to reflect on topics that the family hadn't talked about before. The process helped them to understand themselves and their interactions in new ways.

Dan continues:

You asked me questions, rather than supplying the answers yourselves. Generally, I was fearful that someone would change my perception of myself. But I was never afraid when I was with you because you asked me questions. I felt like you were careful in the way you spoke to me, asking questions and not trying to change me. That's what you need when you're in such a situation.

Music evoked powerful forces in me. You took me seriously, and so I felt like I could talk about this. I remember being asked on one occasion whether I experienced music as a vocation. I could relate to this, especially in the absence of a loud voice overriding this idea. It was very important to me that you raised the theme of music, whilst my father listened.

John felt that Dan and his parents had confidence in us. The family knew that they could call either John or us whenever they needed to. It is important that mental health professionals involved with families create an atmosphere of predictability and maintain open lines of communication,

101

so that the families feel taken care of. John felt safe knowing that he could always contact us.

Dan's contact with John has been of great importance, as Dan explains:

> I had one-to-one conversations with John, as well as with you, where I could really say how things were for me. I have been in regular contact with John since I was 17 years old, and this has meant a lot to me. I've been able to talk to him about my plans and get my ambitions in some perspective. I've also been able to contact him when I'm feeling healthy. This means that he knows more about me as a human being than if he had only known me during the periods of illness.

> What I found difficult about being psychotic was that afterwards I had to live with all the things I had said and done whilst psychotic, and all the rumours about me. I have been able to talk about this though, mostly to John, and in recent years have spent very little time concerned with what others think about me. I have become more aware of the responsibility I have, given my level of vulnerability – for example, I'm more careful about having a good routine for sleep.

The authors' reflections

We used the OD approach in our work with Dan, without naming it as such. In our conversation with him about this work he shared what he remembered. In these reflections he highlights certain key aspects of OD as being important in his recovery process. To meet people in this way in any recovery or reorientation process is powerful, as Dan's experience shows. Dan ended by saying:

> I'm well now, thanks to the help I received. I think it's important that those of us who are fortunate enough to recover, contribute by speaking openly about their psychotic experiences.

Dan is today a healthy and well-functioning man, who earns his livelihood from music.

Note

1 Dan and John are both fictitious names.

Section 3

OPEN DIALOGUE TRAINING, INCLUDING REFLECTIONS FROM TRAINERS AND PARTICIPANTS AND ADAPTATIONS IN DIFFERENT SETTINGS

CONTENTS

EDITORS' INTRODUCTION

This section focuses on Open Dialogue (OD) training programmes. Chapter 11 introduces the three/four-year OD training, developed in Western Lapland, and also the most widely used international foundation training, as well as general issues related to OD training. In the chapters that follow trainers and participants share further details and reflect on their experience of these two programmes (Chapters 12 to 15), and then we hear from others who have been involved in similar/related training in different countries (Chapters 16 to 18).

The contributions in this section show something of the extent of OD training that is now being organised in various countries. Whilst in Finland the three/four-year training is considered to be the core training for an OD practitioner, in some of the settings where OD is currently being developed, a one-year foundation training has been the full extent of training on offer. And whilst many teams have been able to start to practise during/after a one-year foundation training, there is a need to determine the extent to which dialogical practice can be developed in services with these shorter training programmes. Hopefully it will prove possible to establish more three/four-year programmes, such that, even when it's not possible for most in a service to engage in longer training, at least a proportion of staff will have the opportunity to do so, in order to enhance the quality of practice across the service.

We have already clarified that OD is essentially a way of organising services as a whole, and in order to achieve this, it is necessary to extend training to as many mental health professionals as possible. This inevitably means that there will be good deal of variation in the skills/experience of those participating in training programmes, and quite possibly differing levels of enthusiasm for the approach and the training (though most participants report very positively on both counts). Some professionals may be used to there being a more practical focus in their day-to-day work, and working therapeutically with families/networks will be very new to them. Therefore, an ongoing challenge is how to make training accessible whilst also structuring/developing programmes such that those participating can develop dialogical practices to a sufficient quality.

If we want to develop OD services, there is of course much more to attend to than the introduction of training programmes. As some of the contributors to this section allude to, there is a risk of training people who have limited opportunity to practise, both during the training and subsequent to it, because of a lack of service development or specific obstacles in the workplace. This is, unfortunately, a not uncommon scenario – see, for instance, Baguley et al. (2000), and see Hopper et al. (2020) for lessons learned from the Parachute Project in this respect. Though it may be possible to find the time, energy and finance necessary to establish a training, unless staff are supported to participate fully in the training and there is also a viable and sustainable plan for service development and ongoing supervision/intervision, limited progress will be made.

References

Baguley, I., Butterworth, A., Fahy, K., Haddock, G., Lancashire, S. and Tarrier, N. (2000) 'Bringing into clinical practice skills shown to be effective in research settings: A follow-up of the 'Thorn training' in psychosocial family interventions for psychosis' in B.V. Martindale, A. Bateman, A. Crowe and F. Margison (eds.) *Psychosis: Psychological approaches and their effectiveness*. London: Gaskell, p. 96–119.

Hopper, K., Tiem, J.V., Cubellis, L. and Pope, L. (2020) Merging intensive peer support and dialogic practice: Implementation lessons from Parachute NYC. *Psychiatric Services*, 71(2), p. 199–201. doi.org/10.1176/appi.ps.201900174

11

INTRODUCING OPEN DIALOGUE TRAINING

Nick Putman
(UK)

Introduction

Towards the end of my first trip to the psychiatric service in Western Lapland in 2012, I asked senior members of staff how they accounted for the very good outcomes evidenced in their research, and the response I invariably received centred on the quality of their training programmes. The fact that, during the period in which the main research on Open Dialogue (OD) in Western Lapland was undertaken (1994–2005), around 90% of those working in the service had completed a three-year programme that meets the national standard for a family therapy training in Finland (later run over four years in association with Jyväskylä University), in addition to their original training (as a nurse, psychologist, psychiatrist, etc.), is testament to their belief in the value of this programme. It is also testament to the strong democratic ethic in their service – the view that any mental health professional can partici- pate in the programme – which helps them to work in a non-hierarchical way together.

The answer I provide in this chapter to the question of what constitutes an OD training is based on my experience participating, coordinating and being a trainer on the full three-year training being run in London,[1] as well as on foundation trainings run in the UK (including in-house in the NHS), Australia and France (which have drawn largely on the training developed by Volkmar Aderhold and Petra Hohn – see Chapter 14), my experience of joining this training in the Parachute Project in New York City for two weeks, two years of participation in the training in dialogical practices developed by Mary Olson in Massachusetts, and my original psychotherapy training with the Philadelphia Association (PA) in London. The PA training shares much of the philosophy and values that underpin the OD approach, rooted as it is in phenomenology and postmodern philosophy (as well as psychoanalysis and other traditions). I would describe my training at the PA as immersion in an ongoing conversation over six years – it was my first introduction to the creative power of truly dialogical activities. Although I cannot neatly articu- late all of the elements that enabled me to practise as a psychotherapist, I am clear that the experience as a whole enabled me to *be* in the room with those I was working with, more fully, more present, and without attachment to theoretical positions. It was extended practice in tolerating uncertainty.

As OD is not specifically an approach to people having psychotic experiences, but rather an approach to any individual/network experiencing a mental health crisis/challenge, training programmes are not specifically focused on working with people having psychotic experiences. However, some attention is naturally given to specific considerations in undertaking such work (see section 'Open Dialogue training and psychosis' below for more details).

Before I outline the nature and content of OD training programmes, I think it is important to consider what we mean by the word 'training'. A glance at an etymological dictionary suggests roots stretching back to the late 14th century, and the meaning "to draw out and manipulate in order to bring to a desired form", and yet my experience of the trainings that have been of greatest value to me are far removed from this, for there has been no attempt on these trainings to bring anyone to a 'desired form', as though there is a singular/pre-defined way of practising the approach in question.

Some have argued that OD training has as much to do with 'unlearning' as it has to do with learning (personal communications), and the argument can then be made that those who have not already had a professional mental health training, those less entrenched in a particular way of working, have less to unlearn and thus may be better suited to the approach and require less training. I think it is important to consider what is meant by 'unlearning' here, and whether this is the best word to use in this instance. For we do not of course forget what we have previously learnt when we train in OD, and indeed, some of our prior knowledge/training may well be useful in our dialogical practice. I think what is meant by 'unlearning' is that in dialogical practice we are asked to let go of prescriptive and habitual forms of responding, as well as practices which tend towards an objectification. Perhaps it is more accurate then to speak of 'releasing' rather than 'unlearning', as it is our relationship to our knowledge/experience which changes – i.e. we are released from formulaic procedures into creative processes, based in human relations.

I would like to propose that, whilst some may have a natural disposition to dialogical practice, and some will indeed have less to 'release' than others, such releasing takes many forms, and our personal development can be just as limiting as our professional learning. As John Shotter writes, "the change we need to make within ourselves...is a very deep one" (2015, p. 8).

If we have been trained to diagnose, to interpret, in a non-collaborative manner, to use technical/prescribed means to treat specific problems, or to view service users from a professional distance, as somehow different from ourselves, then our first forms of releasing in an OD training will most probably centre around these practices/issues. We need to recognise that, in different circumstances, it could be us experiencing such a crisis. In doing so, we move beyond an 'us and them' mentality, and we are more able to *be with* service users.

Another common form of release on OD training programmes is letting go of the tendency to problem solve. We are often taught to problem solve in our training as mental health professionals – that we are the experts who should have the answers and be able to offer something concrete to the people we serve. This is typically one of the greatest challenges for participants on OD training programmes – to slow down, to not need to have the answers, to take time to understand more, to reflect, and to trust in the process – and a good deal of time is dedicated to helping them to do so.

A final form of releasing worth mentioning is related to our tendency to think that we know, that we understand, and that we see what is *actually* in front of us, rather than recognising that we are always viewing the world through lenses, whether these be predominantly professional or personal. We cannot help but see the world through these lenses – so we should never forget that our view is necessarily subjective. A variety of forces can lead us to see sameness where there is difference, such as the need to know or a desire to connect, and we need to guard against this. 'Not knowing' (see Chapter 1), the capacity to tolerate uncertainty, cannot be taught in a class-room format. Rather it is a capacity that develops through conversation and embodied experience, in the training group, in network meetings, in life. As indicated above, trust is a key ingredient in this way of working – trust in your colleague(s) and in the collective dialogue.

One of the most striking aspects of my first visit to the service in Western Lapland was my sense of the quality of the embodied presence of team members in network meetings (see Chapter 1), a sense that has been borne out in recent years, as I have witnessed and participated in meetings facilitated in the English language by experienced practitioners from Finland and else-where, and primarily I think it is this capacity that we hope to cultivate on training programmes.

Whatever the balance of learning and releasing on an OD training programme, there is considerable skill involved in facilitating network meetings: helping the family/network to feel safe enough in a time of crisis; supporting them to open to one another in a way that may not have been possible previously; being open and transparent about our experience of working with families/networks in their presence (rather than behind closed doors); sharing our reflections with colleagues as the family/net-work listen; constructing and maintaining "a dialogic frame in which new meanings can emerge" (Rober, 2005, p. 478–479); sensing what might be an "appropriately unusual" response to the dialogue (Andersen, 1991, p. 34); the capacity to bear intense emotion at a time of crisis, and to respond to the requirements of the moment – to mention just some aspects of the work – are qualities/skills that require a good deal of practice (the practice never ends, of course).

Over the past 30 years a clear plan for organising training programmes has been developed in Western Lapland (though this has undergone some changes in more recent years – as described in Chapter 2). As soon as possible after staff start working in the service, they are enrolled in a foundation programme consisting of 14 days of theory, reflective conversations and supervision. Then, when the next round of the full three- (or four-) year training programme is due to start, as many staff as possible who have not already undertaken this have the opportunity to do so. Having completed this training and gained further clinical experience, staff have the opportunity to apply to participate in a trainers' training programme.

The full training programme at Keropudas Hospital has continued to evolve over the last 25 years or so, and will no doubt continue to do so – for OD training, like the practice, is a reflective process, and thus not a static entity. Different trainers bring different qualities and experience to programmes, though of course organised around shared principles, practices and values. In addition, as more trainings are run in a variety of settings, participants in different countries and from different cultures, with varied backgrounds and professional roles, will affect the processes that unfold in the course of training programmes.

There is a structure to the OD training programmes that have been developed, and some of this will be detailed below. And yet I would argue that it is in the improvisational moments, the qualities of the trainers' responses, that the essence of the approach is most strongly conveyed. For instance, trainers may express different views in relation to a particular issue in the course of facilitating a day of training together, and if this happens, the way in which they leave space for, and attentively listen to, each other's perspectives, such that they may be changed in some way by the experience, is important. Or, if tensions develop between training participants, the way in which the trainers respond is significant, demonstrating how they might respond when tensions emerge in a network meeting. Another example would be the way that trainers sometimes resist answering the questions asked by participants, in the hope/belief that there are answers of value in the participant group (again this reflects how they might respond in a network meeting). Given that the skill of an OD practitioner/trainer is largely embodied, it has been important to involve senior trainers from Western Lapland and elsewhere in Finland when running training programmes internationally, given the limited time that there has been to practise OD elsewhere.

At this point I think it is important to emphasise the difference between structure and manualisation. Manualisation involves a fixed procedure, and is rooted in what Heidegger (1993) referred to as the "technological attitude", the attempt to process people (i.e. trainees/families) through a preconstructed/ordered system in order to replicate outcomes. Such an attitude has no place in the history or development of OD training or practice. Structure, on the other hand, as employed in OD training, is clear but flexible (according to the needs of the group), and is ultimately in the service of the autonomy of training participants to find their *own* way in developing their capacity to respond thoughtfully and flexibly to families/networks. This 'structure in the service of freedom' reflects the process in network meetings, where there is a clear structure, designed to support dialogue, but the content of the dialogue itself is not determined.

Open Dialogue training and psychosis

As mentioned above, OD training is not specifically geared to working with people affected by psychotic experiences. However, some attention is given on training to particular aspects of such work and to the ways in which psychotic experiences have come to be understood within the OD tradition. Most of these aspects have been detailed by Jaakko Seikkula in Chapter 3, and include the following:

1   Psychosis can be understood as a psychological response to very difficult life situations, trauma or unbearable feelings which cannot yet be borne or articulated in coherent narratives.
2   OD practitioners seek to support network members to give expression to their experiences (to get as many different perspectives as possible) and to make sense of psychotic experiences and the ways in which these may be connected to historical events.
3   Practitioners take all communication seriously, however difficult it may be to make sense of. This can be particularly important for people having psychotic experiences, and usually leads to a greater sense of trust in the team.
4   The development of dialogue between inner and outer voices, as well as a focus on emotional experience, can be especially helpful in working with people having psychotic experiences.
5   Related to point 1, an individual may become more psychotic in a network meeting at a point when traumatic/distressing experiences are being spoken of or alluded to, and thus practitioners pay particular attention to what is occurring in the present moment in network meetings.

OD training helps participants to be more flexible and creative in their work, to be both comfortable with and curious about difference, and to take the time needed to understand more, all of which are qualities that are particularly helpful in working with people with psychotic experiences.

Foundation training

As the OD approach has developed internationally there have been variations in the structure of training programmes. Most significantly, foundation training programmes have tended to be longer than in Western Lapland, typically around 16–20 days. One reason for this is that these programmes have been established in services where most (if not all) staff are unfamiliar with the approach. It is a very different experience to be undertaking a foundation training in such circumstances than to be doing so in Western Lapland, where you are already working in your daily practice with experienced teams, as part of a well-developed service. Therefore, there is a need for more time on foundation training programmes run elsewhere to help teams to start to develop their practice.

A foundation-level training is not a substitute for the full three/four-year training, which provides a much more in-depth experience of theory and family of origin and supervision processes (and is considered to be core training in Western Lapland), but it can help participants to start to practise more quickly, with further learning happening through ongoing practice, including intervision/supervision, or through participation in the full training at a later stage. As OD is a way of organising services as a whole, as well as a form of practice, the ability to train larger teams within services is important. However, as things stand in most public mental health services, it is not going to be practical to train everyone fully in the approach (though it is to my mind very important that at least a proportion of the staff are trained to this level). Therefore, the introduction/development of good quality foundation training programmes is important, as long as staff receive the practical support necessary to develop the approach in their service, as emphasised in the introduction to this section and in some of the contributions in Section 4.

On the foundation training that I have been involved in running there is a strong emphasis on *practice*. Having got to know each other through some initial exercises, participants learn about the seven principles of OD (see Chapter 1) and the structure of the service in Western Lapland. We then explore some of the historical developments in family therapy that led to the shift from first- to second-order cybernetics (or in other words from a more structured/objective view/practice towards a more collaborative/subjective/dialogical approach), and in addition the ways in which those developing OD in Western Lapland adapted elements of family therapy practice to suit their dialogical approach. A significant factor in this development was the work of Tom Andersen and his team in Tromsø in the north of Norway, and we explore a good deal of Andersen's philosophy and the thinking behind the development of the reflecting team (see Chapter 2 for more detail on Andersen's work). Participants have the opportunity to practise reflecting in an Andersen-style reflecting team before doing so in the style used in Western Lapland, where those facilitating network meetings also have the responsibility of reflecting during the course of a meeting. Following this we focus on issues relating to the initial contact with a service user/family and decision making around who will be invited to the first network meeting, and then there is extensive practice in the facilitation of network meetings, in which elements of dialogical practice are explored in some depth. Special attention is given to ways of opening meetings, transitioning to reflections and closing meetings. We also explore various forms of responding in network meetings, such as positive/logical connotation, meta-communication, circular questioning, and repeating/responding to the words of network members through a variety of exercises and role plays. As participants become more familiar with the facilitation of meetings, we start to explore more specific scenarios in the work, such as intervening in a crisis, working with people having psychotic experiences, working with families who have experienced violence and/or who have family secrets, working with children, and crisis planning.

Three days of the programme are dedicated to an exploration of participants' own social networks and family of origin, through the use of social network maps and genograms. Students prepare their genograms in their own time between training blocks, having been given specific instructions, including questions to consider in relation to their family background. There are also many opportunities to share personal experiences, relating to either one's professional work or life beyond, in exercises where participants practise facilitation and reflecting, such that the group get to know each other more, and trust can develop. Sharing personal experiences in this way helps participants to have a deeper sense of the approach, and can also support the development of teamwork.

Full training

The three/four-year training programme in Finland is technically a full training to the level of family therapist within the Finnish Quality Assurance programme for Psychotherapy (Pylkkänen, 1989). Though in some respects OD represents a move away from systemic family therapy as historically/generally practised, the training is called a family therapy training in Finland in order to meet with national requirements. There is, however, some resonance with other family therapy trainings, particularly those of a more dialogical persuasion.

The full training programme, as we have organised it in London, takes place over three years, with four blocks of five days per year, and essentially consists of three main elements: 26 theory days, 21 supervision days and 13 family of origin days. On each block there is a blend of theory days and either supervision or family of origin days, meaning that explorations of theory are interwoven with practice and personal work.

On this programme there is a stronger emphasis on each participant taking responsibility for their own process, their own learning and understanding. In the final year participants have to submit a thesis of around 8,000 words, focused on a topic of interest related to dialogic practice and/or the development of OD in their service, including a research component, or an account of their clinical work.

Theory days

The initial focus of the theory days is to introduce the OD service model and its evolution over the last 30 years. Following this the emphasis is on the theoretical (and philosophical) basis of OD, with extensive reading prior to each block, and study groups which meet regularly between the training blocks (either in person or, as is sometimes necessary on international programmes, online). As well as books and papers directly related to the OD approach, participants also read a broad range of material on family therapy, dialogical practice/theory, and related disciplines. On the theory days themselves, as well as discussing and reflecting on required reading, exercises and role plays are introduced to explore particular aspects of the work.

Supervision days

On supervision days the larger group is divided into smaller groups, which remain the same throughout the training, and on each supervision block all participants have the opportunity to present their work once. If they are presenting work done with a colleague who is in the same supervision group, then the primary focus of the supervision session is still on them, on their own experience of and questions about the work. The emphasis in dialogical supervision is not on the network and the issues they are experiencing, or on the supervisor monitoring the work being done, but is rather on the experience of the supervisee. Supervision is another group process within the training, in which there is a lot of potential for group members to learn from each other's work and reflections, as well as the supervisor's facilitation.

The most common format for supervision sessions is for one participant to show video footage of a network meeting they have co-facilitated, and then for the remaining members of the supervision group to share their reflections on what they have seen and heard (typically there will be two rounds of reflections per session). However, the exact format for these sessions varies, according to the preferences of the supervisor (and the group). It can be challenging to expose one's work in these supervision sessions, and yet, as trust develops in the group, it is usually possible to bring more of oneself, such that they can be very rich learning experiences.

Live network meetings can also be arranged on supervision days, i.e. where supervisees invite a family/network that they are currently working with to come to the training venue for a meeting which takes place with the supervision group present. A reflecting team can be set up for such meetings, with further reflections after the meeting has ended. It can of course be challenging for families to come to live supervision sessions, but they may well benefit a good deal from the experience (so far the feedback from families has been positive).

Family of origin days

The family of origin days are a key part of this training programme. Often, when participants reflect on the experience of the training as a whole, it is the family of origin process in particular that seems to stand out. Perhaps this is not surprising, given the very personal nature of the work. Once again participants are divided into small groups (different small groups to the supervision groups), and the intimacy and trust that can develop in these groups, through the sharing of very personal stories in a mutual process, is clearly very significant. The experience is meaningful not only to each of the participants, but also when it comes to working together in teams in the future, where the trust felt between colleagues is important.

It is usually a requirement of counselling and psychotherapy training programmes that trainees undertake their own personal psychotherapeutic work, as we need to understand ourselves and work on our own mental health issues as much as possible when taking on such a role. We need to understand how our experience has shaped our worldview and the ways in which we might be limited by this experience, to disentangle ourselves from unhelpful ways of relating, and to come to terms with difficult/traumatic experiences. Working with families can be particularly affecting, stirring up memories, feelings, associations and dynamics from our own lives and families (of origin). Jaakko Seikkula (2008) describes how our 'inner' voices are activated in the process of doing this work, which he refers to as "vertical polyphony", and the more familiar and reconciled we are with these voices, the more effective our work will be.

Our 'inner voices' are a resource in the work, a springboard for dialogue and understanding, as long as they are used thoughtfully and tentatively (i.e. we can reflect on them and consider what to share). Whether or not we choose to share stories from our own lives (i.e. personal disclosure), as OD practitioners we are personal/subjective in our style – we show our humanity. We allow ourselves to be affected by those we work with, and we share our own thoughts, feelings and associations in the course of facilitating network meetings.

There has been a movement more generally within the family therapy tradition to include a form of personal work within training programmes which reflects a more systemic approach. As a result, rather than requiring students to undertake their own personal individual psychotherapy, they instead participate in a family of origin process, a therapeutic process which has been developed within the OD tradition to be more dialogical, with more reflective processes. The family of origin days work on a number of levels. Primarily, as indicated above, they help participants to understand themselves more fully, within their own contexts, their own family of origin. Through a series of tasks that have to be completed between blocks, and on the family of origin days themselves, participants learn more about significant people in their lives, most commonly their relatives, and the relations between them, as well as family values. They also learn more about significant events/issues in the history of their family/network – how different people have experienced these, the stories that have been told about such experiences (or which perhaps have not previously been told), and the ways in which the family/network have coped. In addressing the (untold) stories in their own family of origin, participants are likely to be more effective in helping the families who they work with to look at their own untold stories.

The tasks given to training participants include work on their own genogram, writing and sending letters to family/network members of their choice and inviting their response, and video recording conversations with them. The genograms, letters and videos are brought to the family of origin days, and are reflected on in various ways. As well as learning more about themselves, the process of engaging family/network members in these tasks may serve to increase understanding and deepen connections within the family/network and may also, in some instances, be a healing experience. Participants choose which family/network members they wish to engage in this family of origin work, which helps to limit the risk involved, but the consequences of engaging in such a process are uncertain, and so it is important that family of origin trainers are available to participants should they need support between training blocks.

One way of thinking about this process is that training participants have an experience of their own family/network being the focus in a transformational/therapeutic process, and I think that such an experience can help them to be more sensitive and humbler in their work with others. Participants also start to have a fuller experience of transformational processes more generally, where subsequent rounds of reflection on the stories being told reveal new elements or aspects, adding to the polyphony, to the variety of perspectives and ways of understanding. This can serve to deepen their appreciation of dialogical processes and their emergent creativity. Although the amount of personal work on an OD training is less than that required on individual psychotherapy trainings, in terms of the number of hours involved, it is interesting to consider the relative benefit of engaging family/network members in this work, and it being a group process on the training, where participants have the opportunity to hear each other's stories, and listen and respond to each other's reflections.

A final aspect of the family of origin days is to help participants to focus on their own values and hopes, so that they can be connected to what is important for themselves in relation to their work, including how they understand their decision to get into this line of work and how they see their identity as a mental health practitioner.

Commonalities in training programmes

Whatever the differences between the training programmes run in different settings (at foundation or full levels), in my experience there are many commonalities. It is important that the training days are conducted in circles, to allow for processes to develop in the space between people, where everyone can see and respond to each other. For this reason, training programmes are typically limited to around 18 to 30 participants (with more advanced/ longer-term trainings tending to be smaller in size due to the greater emphasis on group processes and the depth of work involved). On days where the whole group is together, there is usually a flow between the group sitting in one large circle and in smaller circles in subgroups for exercises and role plays.

It is important to make training relevant to participants, i.e. to link what they are learning to current practices in their workplaces, and so there is usually a good deal of attention given to this, in more structured ways and also in open conversations in the group. If OD is very different to participants' current working practices, then space is given to consider small steps that can be taken to move their work in a more dialogical direction. This includes ways of introducing some of the ideas and practices to colleagues. As Tom Andersen writes, "new ideas will grow unwillingly, if they are imposed from outside the system" (Andersen, 1991, p. 8), and so it is important to include colleagues who are not participating in the training programme in conversations about the approach, once back in the workplace.

The inclusion of peer workers (people with lived experience of mental health challenges difficulties who have been employed in a mental health service to undertake a variety of work with service users) in OD training programmes is now another common feature. In my view, this is a welcome development, for a variety of reasons, but in particular because of the richness of experience that peer workers can bring to such processes and the ways in which this can extend the dialogue (see Chapter 25 for more on the inclusion of peer workers in OD).

In conclusion

Many participants on the training programmes I have been involved in have commented on how different the experience has been from other training that they have done. The family of origin process is often highlighted in this regard, but more generally I think that the collaborative nature of the training is also significant, in which participants are invited to be open and personal and, in the full training in particular, to take responsibility for their own process, within the collective processes. The inclusion of families/networks in mental health services is new to many training participants, raising lots of questions about practice and service development, and yet, probably as a result of their experience working in the field, as well as their learning on an OD training, it makes sense to them that this is a valuable approach to take.

Though the resistance to change within services can be considerable, even when there is good evidence of the effectiveness of a different approach, as more OD training programmes are offered and developed across different services internationally, it seems that there is also now a greater opportunity to develop dialogical practices in our public mental health systems.

Note

1 The full three-year training in London was the first such training to be run outside of Finland. It is currently (2021) running for the second time, and new trainings will be run on a regular basis, for NHS professionals as well as those working in public services internationally and independent practitioners.

References

Andersen, T. (1991) *The reflecting team: Dialogues and dialogues about the dialogues.* New York: W.W. Norton.

Heidegger, M. (1993) *Basic concepts*, trans. G.E. Aylesworth. Bloomington, IN: Indiana University Press. [Original lectures given 1941].

Pylkkänen, K. (1989) A quality assurance programme for psychotherapy – the Finnish experience. *Psychoanalytic Psychotherapy*, 4(1), p. 13–22. doi.org/10.1080/02668738900700021

Rober, P. (2005) The therapist's self in dialogical family therapy: Some ideas about not-knowing and the therapist's inner conversation. *Family Process*, 44(4), p. 477–495. doi.org/10.1111/j.1545-5300.2005.00073.x

Seikkula, J. (2008) Inner and outer voices in the present moment of family and network therapy. *Journal of Family Therapy*, 30(4), p. 478–491. doi.org/10.1111/j.1467-6427.2008.00439.x

Shotter, J. (2015) On being dialogical: An ethics of 'attunement'. *Context*, 137, p. 8–11.

12

REFLECTIONS ON THE DIALOGICAL DESIGN OF THE THREE/FOUR-YEAR OPEN DIALOGUE TRAINING

Jorma Ahonen
(Finland)

The three- (or four-) year training in the Open Dialogue approach (which in Finland is entitled 'Psychotherapy Training for Family and Couple Therapy') is supported by a structured programme which has been developed over the years, based on experiences in different settings (the structure/parallel processes involved in this training are detailed in Chapter 11). Variations on this training have been run in different settings in Finland, as well as the UK and Australia, and I have been involved in most of these. In particular I would like to mention the very significant contributions of Birgitta Alakare, Jaakko Seikkula, Markku Sutela and Pekka Holm to these developments.

Commitment and personal challenges in the process

At a fundamental level, participants need to be committed to attending and observing the schedule of the full training programme. This commitment is developed through jointly discussing structures, roles and responsibilities. In the dialogic approach we 'go slow to go fast'. We take the time to hear every participant's voice, to engage them in the training process from the very beginning, so that they can start to get to know one another, and each other's hopes, fears and aims. As we build a learning community together, participants are invited to challenge themselves openly, to consider how they can be in the learning process in such a way that they get the most out of it. Sharing personal challenges openly in this way helps others to reflect on their own experience and to reinforce communality.

The essential starting point or attitude for dialogical training is that we are all different – we come from different places/backgrounds and inhabit bodies which constrain and enable us in different ways – so there are individual processes alongside the communal process. The aim of the programme is not to try to make everyone look the same. This parallels the work that we do with

119

families, where an appreciation of differences in the communal process is crucial. An explicit sharing of the philosophy behind this attitude is important.

Dialogic aspects within the training and the skill of the trainer

Throughout the training we strive for the active involvement of participants. For example, there are specific topics on theory days, but the conversations about these topics are largely defined by the students themselves, i.e. the questions, issues and experiences that they bring. The trainers' skill is to be present, and to pick up on aspects of these conversations, in order to extend the dialogue and make links to practice and theory, such that the learning is both alive and meaningful to the participants. Theory days have a workshop style, and the learning happens through an internalisation of conversations, self-reflection and practical exercises. As the training proceeds, participants develop their ability to identify moments in their work, in their relationships with the families they work with, which are dialogical, and moments which are not. It is important to learn dialogical skills and explore theory in a dialogical way. This means a continual process of embracing, questioning, discussing and understanding together. This is different from most forms of learning in Western culture, especially in professional training, which are often driven by pre-existing definitions, and the need to master an understanding of these as quickly as possible.

At the beginning of a training process, trainers work to create a positive atmosphere for learning and mutual sharing, and as the training proceeds, to keep this spirit alive. As mentioned in Chapter 11, it is important that trainers embody the dialogical approach in training programmes, i.e. that they are open/transparent and present in the process, as this helps participants to develop their own skills. Having two trainers on theory days is therefore very helpful, as they can be in dialogue and reflect and share their dilemmas openly with each other, in front of the participants.

In many ways the trainers' facilitation of training days mirrors dialogical practice in general – e.g. their appreciation of those participating such that they feel seen and heard, their supporting participants to respect each other's differences, and their capacity to not know what will happen next and to respond to participants' utterances, thereby allowing the process to unfold. In addition, a central question for dialogical trainers (or in other words a feature of their inner dialogue), is when to be dialogical and when not to be, as sometimes we need to be more direct, for instance when sharing information about the history of certain practices/theory. It is important that trainers are able to tolerate their own anxiety, as well as the anxiety of participants, in this uncertain and at times challenging process. It is usually unhelpful to try to rescue participants from challenging situations; instead trainers should help them to stay with the uncertainty/challenge, and support dialogue around this.

When I think about the challenges I have experienced running such programmes, and what I have learnt from these, a couple of things come to mind. Firstly, the importance of ascertaining whether applicants are well placed to fully engage in the training, i.e. whether other commitments in their life could adversely impact on their participation and whether they have the opportunity to develop dialogic practice in their workplace and bring video recordings of their work to the training. Secondly, the importance of being clear about the roles of trainers, i.e. which trainers have responsibility for the different processes in the training and which also have some administrative responsibility.

Working dialogically is not easy, for any aspect of a dialogical training can become emotional and difficult – but if we can face these challenges together, if we can stay dialogical and trust in the process, they can be great opportunities for learning. The best spirit for learning is that we can share our human struggle together, i.e. that we feel safe enough to share our experiences freely. We can learn and develop so much in this way – often nothing else is needed.

13

REFLECTIONS ON PARTICIPATING IN THE THREE-YEAR OPEN DIALOGUE TRAINING

Olga Runciman
(Denmark)

I initially heard about Open Dialogue (OD) through the writings of Robert Whitaker, and many years later I enrolled as a student on the three-year training programme in London, organised by Open Dialogue UK. This was the first time the Finnish trainers had taught the full training programme outside of Finland. The participants came from different cultures, countries and disciplines and included four participants who were users with experience of psychiatric treatment, of whom I was one.

I am a psychologist from Denmark and, before this, I was a psychiatric nurse. I am also a voice hearer who experienced 10 years in the psychiatric system, labelled as a 'chronic schizophrenic' with no hope of recovery. As both a voice hearer and a professional, I am a 'bridge builder' in my daily work, between what is often seen as two polarised worlds. What follows are some of my reflections on participating in the three-year programme.

Supervision

I found the supervision on the training to be a very rich tool for learning, having a very different emphasis from the traditional forms of supervision that I have been a part of. The typical structure of 'case' supervision in the Danish psychiatric system is such that it is very difficult not to talk mostly about the service user (who is not present), as opposed to one's own experience of the relationship. In supervision sessions on the OD training, the focus was very much on me and my work, and this included a consideration of what I bring of myself and my history, which may or may not significantly affect my ability to relate and to be helpful to the service user and their network.

Supervision not only helped us to deepen our understanding of ourselves, but also our working contexts. Many tears were shed in our supervision group, as we watched videos of ourselves holding network meetings over time, with an increasing awareness of the oppressiveness of the system weighing down upon us, as our familiarity with dialogical practice/ethics developed. Yet what also became clear during this process was that, despite the system, meeting people with a genuine desire to truly listen to them, and to understand, opened doors that had not previously been open within these institutions.

Unlearning and healing

Being *present* in this training process (in the dialogue, reflection and deep personal work) precipitated transformations in all of us over time, and I think one aspect of this could be called 'unlearning'. Though I liked to think of myself as having unlearned what I was taught as a psychiatric nurse (a primarily biological approach to distress), after I myself had been subjected to traditional psychiatric treatment, I discovered during this three-year training that there were more layers to my unlearning.

A completely unexpected transformation for me was *the process of healing*. Central to this process was a letting go of/unlearning my *generalised* mistrust, and therefore 'othering' of, in particular, psychiatrists, and instead allowing myself to be curious, to question, to stop making assumptions, and to become close to those who I have for a long time seen as harmful. When bridges are created and the possibility of a shared world of meaning arises, co-created with others in a trusting atmosphere, profound transformations can occur within those relationships, and this is indeed what I, and I think others, experienced. Training people with lived experience alongside clinicians will not automatically ensure that the 'us/them' politics disappear, but it is nevertheless a very welcome development.

Family of origin

When I reflect back on my experience of the training, the part that I find myself returning to again and again is the 'family of origin' work, which I see as pivotal. The process of reflecting on others' stories, and having my own stories reflected upon, created bonds that were new to me, in that I had never before tried sharing deep and personal things within a group setting and experienced the effect that such a process can have. We became a kind of healing family together, and this played a fundamental role in both my aforementioned process of healing and in being more open to and making less assumptions about others in both my professional and personal life.

Had the family of origin work not been an integral part of this training, I believe the process of acknowledging our inner polyphony would have been greatly compromised. In addition, the work done with our own families and networks (as part of the assignments we were given) led to new insights, often through previously untold stories, which I like to think has made me more respectful, and indeed humble, when I meet other families and individuals in distress.

Concluding thoughts

I will never forget the very first day that we were together on this training, sitting in a large circle, and the two trainers present turning to each other to reflect on the death of their friend Markku Sutela, who was to have played a big role in this first training, and openly grieving in the group. I was very moved, and at the same time I was stunned to see such a display of emotion, along with the open sharing of thoughts as to how they were going to approach this training without him. I remember thinking then and there that *this* training is going to be completely different to anything I have undertaken before, and it was. And, as I try to describe the ways in which it was different, I find myself in some difficulty, which is why I often say that it must be lived and not just read about in books!

In a training process such as this, with people from many different professional backgrounds and experiences sharing deeply over a three-year period, there are unique opportunities to connect across the divides and power structures created by different disciplines. This extends possibilities for mutual listening, understanding, equality and respect, and the co-production of meaning and language, such that it becomes extremely difficult to objectify the other. I can only think (and hope) that, as the learning from this training is carried into the workplace, it will have a positive impact not only on the work done with individuals, families and networks, but also on long-term structural changes within systems.

14

THIRTEEN YEARS OF RUNNING OPEN DIALOGUE FOUNDATION TRAINING PROGRAMMES

Volkmar Aderhold and Petra Hohn
(Germany and Sweden)

Since 2007, 90 in-house foundation training programmes have been run in Germany and Switzerland, including within 21 mental health clinics and 40 community psychiatric services, as well as in the Parachute Project in New York and with Open Dialogue UK in London. Most courses have consisted of eight workshops of two days, run over the course of at least one year. The training has been continually adapted and revised, based largely on feedback from participants, and as defined in Chapter 38, the so-called 'key elements of dialogic practice' helped to refine it. Each programme usually consists of around 30 participants and four trainers, with one trainer present (Volkmar Aderhold) throughout all eight workshops.

At the start of each workshop we introduce some new theoretical material and have time to discuss this before moving on to preparatory and self-experience exercises and role plays (and reflections on these in small groups or a plenary session). In preparatory exercises participants learn basic skills of dialogical practice that can readily be used in their workplace with individual service users and later with families, as they are able to include families in the work that they are doing. In self-experience exercises, participants are able to share and reflect on themselves in a variety of ways with other participants of their choosing (developing their experience of how being responded to and reflected on by others affects them – how deep it can be). Typically, we have two 90-minute role plays of a network meeting in each two-day workshop, which are usually based on service users that participants in the training are currently working with (if so, the person working with the service user plays the role of the service user, which helps to make role playing less artificial). During the training everyone has experience of being in different roles.

In actuality, the term 'role playing' is inadequate as participants come to identify very closely with the person they are 'playing'. There seems to be an 'energetic field' of information, i.e. of feelings and embodiment, 'as if' they almost *become* that person, meaning that they get to be in the other's shoes in a very deep way. Usually participants report that they learn a lot about the service user and their networks/families through this experience. Furthermore, if those facilitating the network meeting in the role play ask questions that the person playing the service user feels are quite unhelpful, this person will be much less likely to ask similar questions when they are facilitators, because they have experienced how it feels to be the recipient of such questions. You do not have to preach ethics – you just have to put participants in the role of the service user. Our training is very focused on the practical ability to facilitate network meetings and participants generally say that they learnt the most in the role plays – that changes in their attitude mostly stemmed from these experiences.

In each training two or three live network meetings are conducted with families/networks, with trainers facilitating the meeting whilst the training participants observe. In these meetings we as trainers expose our own abilities to the group, and of course the limits of our abilities, with time for dialogue and reflections on our way of working after the meetings. Before the meeting we ask one or two observers to empathise with a particular network member (i.e. to put themselves 'in this person's shoes') and to give feedback about their experience of the meeting afterwards, including whether they felt heard. Many of these invited networks have made unexpected steps forward after these meetings, and ongoing network meetings can be arranged by the local teams.

We have a curriculum and structure for these training programmes, but we also tune in to the uniqueness of each training situation and so may need to change our plan quickly. It is valuable in these processes to have a variety of trainers (including local trainers who work in the service) in order to make these changes and adaptations.

A Leonardo da Vinci project to develop a European training for peer workers within universities (Utschakowski, 2007) has led to greater inclusion of peer workers in German services since 2008. As a result, we have been able to include peers in our training programmes since 2009, on an equal footing to other participants and with an equal voice. We encourage peer workers to bring their own experience and to find their own style of practising, working in network meetings as part of the team. In our experience peer workers offer a unique contribution, and reflect in a different way, usually with more emotion and intuition. We hope that peer workers can keep their uniqueness, whilst also being equal participants in the process. The more teams can be truly polyphonic, the better they can respond to service users' and families' needs. Sometimes we have also been able to include family members as participants in our training programmes, which has been a positive experience, and we are now trying to expand on this.

We have found that getting management on board is extremely important, and so we invite them to participate in training programmes. When they have been able to do so, typically in the later stages of the programme when participants are more experienced, we have had good results. Without the support of team and organisational leaders to develop services which operate in a dialogical way, with a commitment to new/further training and mentoring opportunities for staff, an ongoing implementation will not be possible.

Reference

Utschakowski, J. (2007) Involvement of Experienced People in Mental Health. Report on a two-year EU-funded project 'EX-IN' (Experienced Involvement), developing training programmes for people with experience of using mental health services to work as trainers and peer supports. *WAPR Bulletin*, 19, p. 14–16. [online] Available at: www. ex-in.info/data/files/188/WAPR_BULL_19_feb2007.pdf [Accessed 5 June 2020].

15

REFLECTIONS FROM PARTICIPANTS ON AN OPEN DIALOGUE FOUNDATION TRAINING

Alan Hendry, Ana Maria Corredor and Mike Roth
(UK)

Editors' introduction

The extracts below are written by participants on the Open Dialogue UK foundation training (described in Chapters 11 and 14) which commenced in London in April 2016. The training was led by Volkmar Aderhold, Petra Hohn, Nick Putman, Mia Kurtti and Iseult Twamley. The participants consisted of members of teams working in the NHS and international public mental health services, including peer workers, and also independent practitioners. Participants were invited to share their reflections on the experience of participating in this training, and a number of themes were drawn out from the responses of the three people who offered to write something.

Practice/role plays

Alan: From early on in the training there was an emphasis on experiential work in groups and practising dialogical skills. This practice led to a dawning understanding that changes in attitude and perspective were called for – a different way of looking at our work was required. Initially this felt uncomfortable and 'clunky'. The ground seemed to shift under my feet as I searched for stability in an unfamiliar process. As the course progressed, however, the experience became smoother. Looking back, the experience of practising on the training seems to have 'soaked in', and has made the wealth of printed material, with which we were provided, richer.

Mike: The role plays, in particular, were totally absorbing – demanding complete concentration and emotional involvement. I gained powerful insights into what it might feel like to be the 'person at the centre of concern', with varying degrees of mistrust into what the people around me were trying to do to me. I also gained insight into what it might feel like to be a distressed family member. As well as this, I had ample experience as an active practitioner, and sometimes as an observer who could reflect on the process.

Ana María: The OD training offered a safe space to use bodily felt experience in a helpful manner. My personal learning was largely embodied and came both from observing the trainers as well as living many 'relational moments' during role plays and exercises. These moments included, as well as words and silences, non-verbal communication and sensations that guided my action towards fellow trainees and the trainers. The structure of the exercises and role plays led to a deep sense of being responded to and heard; an experience fostered by clear guidance from the trainers, such as being present to the speaker and my own experience, working as a team, slowing down, and reflecting within a clear set of guidelines.

Ana María: The OD training helped me to hone and learn useful skills, such as tolerating uncertainty, framing thoughts as personal responses rather than truths, and using people's words to encourage/enable them to tell their stories.

Trainer's presence

Alan: An aspect of the course that made a strong impression on me was the modelling of the approach by the trainers/facilitators. A receptive listening environment was created, within which the whole group gradually became more comfortable. This led to a growing sense of trust that made it safer for everyone to engage, and allowed for differences of view and uncertainty. I believe that this was a new experience for many of us.

Ana María: The trainers modelled a collaborative way of working between them; I valued their calibre and diversity. They brought together a depth of experience from different work settings, genders, countries, professional backgrounds and trainings. Perhaps what I most appreciated was what I saw as their personal commitment to uphold the democratic values of dialogical work. This ethos, combined with technical skill, produced what I experienced as a very personal approach in the way they related to me and other trainees – in the attentive listening, deep respect and carefulness. Trainers' genuine openness to our shared experience, to equality, and to improvised moment-to-moment co-creation was embodied throughout.

Safety, equality and being valued

Ana María: An important aspect of the training was the safety of the space created, despite the size of the trainee group. We came from different backgrounds, including professionals from outside the UK and several peers with lived experience of mental health challenges. When guiding our use of reflections in exercises/role plays, the trainers advised us to begin by finding and verbalising a sense of true appreciation for what had just been shared by those participating. This fostered a sense of kinship and helped generate a safe environment where we could learn by experience. The training was my first experience of peers and other mental health professionals being heard equally.

Ana María: As a trainee practitioner, I was encouraged to use my voice to add something new or different. This invitation to accept, express and almost celebrate my individuality and uniqueness as a person felt positively affirming.

Power/responsibility

Alan: The notion that it's the therapist who holds the responsibility for solving the complexities which unfold in a session gave way to an attitude of 'getting involved', such that the complexities could work themselves out through dialogue in the role plays.

Family of origin

Mike: Each of the small groups on the family of origin days had the full care and attention of one of the trainers, so that in effect we received the same level of care and 'holding' as a network would typically receive in OD treatment. In nearly every case, we found that this led us to an emotional depth and rawness. These sessions also served as a very powerful insight into how vulnerable and exposed family members must feel, when they are expected to open up their personal realities to helping professionals.

Mike: The experience of bringing oneself within one's own family of origin is a necessary part of any OD training. How else would we learn to manage OD sessions sensitively, to create a safe, accepting and empathic milieu for family dynamics to unfold in a dialogical process?

16

BEING 'IN RHYTHM' WITH PARTICIPANTS DURING DIALOGICAL TRAINING

Werner Schütze
(Germany)

As Anderson (2006) and Schön (1983) argue, dialogical training should be a collaborative, reflective process. Thus, any such training should stay as close as possible to the particular needs of participants and their individual development, and consider the experience that is already present in the group, including participants' ability to connect to other people, even in extreme states (as psychotherapy works mainly through the quality of the relation – Norcross, 2010). In this chapter I would like to offer some reflections on dialogical training processes, drawing on my experience of being a trainer on many different kinds of workshops and trainings (held in Poland, Italy, Czech Republic, Germany and the US), which have lasted from a few hours up to 16 days (usually organised in two-day blocks).

In line with Frank (1961), I would like to propose that it is our lived experience, more than the technical skills we acquire, that is most helpful in our work. It is therefore very important that participants in Open Dialogue (OD) trainings become interested in their personal development, i.e. in their own psychological makeup as well as their specific way of embodying the approach. Given this, trainers should do all they can to make training feel like a safe place, in which personal issues can be discussed and participants can develop their relationships with each other. To further this possibility, I offer numerous exercises for small groups – e.g. a group with a speaker, listener and observer, in which the speaker talks about something of significance to them, and the whole group can share something about what was striking for them in the exercise.

I always inform participants that some of the exercises (or roles in the exercises) may not fit their needs. If they do not feel ready to play a particular role, it is acceptable to not do so. It is important for participants to get a feeling for their *own* development, which might differ from that of others, especially if there are very different levels of experience in the group. It is also important for participants to be aware of, and learn more about, their own limits and sense of safety, and to be able to ask for support in relation to this, when needed.

The emphasis on the particular needs of participants and their personal development transforms the idea that there should be a defined goal at the end of each workshop or at the end of a complete training programme, which is something I used to think. I had to learn that a more reflective and collaborative way of teaching means being flexible and changing the schedules established beforehand. Nowadays I offer a headline for each workshop and introduce a few key aspects without using PowerPoint presentations (i.e. I share some of my embodied knowledge), and then ask participants for questions relating to what I have shared and follow the process induced by what emerges. I am convinced that everything we need is in the room. Thus, I see the trainer's role as being a facilitator rather than a teacher.

After new material has been introduced by trainers, on topics such as dialogue, crisis, trauma or reframing, and participants have asked questions about what has been shared, I usually invite them to form small groups to discuss the topic in question. Following these discussions, participants return to the large group and two members of each small group form a circle in the middle of the room and share what was discussed in their groups. The remaining participants listen and can add their reflections afterwards.

Distinct from some of the trainers in previous chapters, I use role plays less and less, and sometimes not at all, as I have found that there is always the possibility for participants to bring their own personal issues, whether from their workplace or their life beyond work, and I usually prefer to work with these, without people taking on roles. For me the most effective way to develop dialogicity is to use it regularly and repeatedly in relation to the thoughts, issues and experiences brought by training participants.

It is inevitable that the motivation of training participants varies from 'some interest' to 'highly motivated' and, as trainers, we need to be aware of the different levels of motivation and the context from which this derives. Almost always some participants are interested, but at the same time sceptical, asking, for example, "does this approach genuinely offer something different to existing practice?" Individuals who feel this way are very important and need special attention, such that their views and assumptions can be explored and worked with. One way of making use of different levels of interest in developing OD is to invite some of the training participants to discuss such differences as a network, whilst others act as facilitators.

I am aware that these explications are very subjective, reflecting a personal interest in being in 'rhythm' with the learning process, and thus that they should not necessarily be generalised. However, I think this style of training may be useful for other trainers as well. As trainers, we should be aware that we also have to develop personally, in order to create more reflective and collaborative ways of training, and that it is helpful to be in dialogue with each other about developments in our approach.

132

References

Anderson, H. (2006) 'Dialogue: People creating meaning "with" each other and finding ways to go on' in H. Anderson and D. Gehart (eds.) *Collaborative therapy: Relationships and conversations that make a difference.* New York: Routledge. p. 21–32.

Frank, J.D. (1961) *Persuasion and healing. A comparative study of psychotherapy.* Baltimore, MD: Johns Hopkins University Press.

Norcross, J.C. (2010) 'The therapeutic relationship' in B.L. Duncan, S.D. Miller, B.E. Wampold and M.A. Hubble (eds.) *The heart and soul of change: Delivering what works in therapy* (2nd ed.). Washington DC: APA Press, p. 113–141.

Schön, D.S. (1983) *The reflective practitioner. How professionals think in action.* Scranton, PA: Basic Books.

17

PERSONAL REFLECTIONS ON THE ITALIAN OPEN DIALOGUE TRAINING[1]

Raffaella Pocobello
(Italy)

The reflections I am sharing here are based on my participatory observation as a researcher of the Italian Open Dialogue (OD) training.[2] I will elaborate on how the training was delivered and how it impacted me and the other mental health professionals involved. Further perspectives on the introduction of OD into the Italian mental health system and the training involved are reported in Chapters 20 and 42.

It was my impression that the Italian OD training was mostly unstructured and, as described in Chapter 11, was instead based on the embodied presence of trainers. For me the improvisational moments of dialogue between trainers and their responsive interaction with trainees were particularly valuable learning experiences.

The training brought about progressively deeper personal and professional changes, and helped us to address our *defensive attitudes*. For example, at the very beginning of the training a critical attitude towards the approach dominated, especially among the more experienced clinicians. They complained about the idea of learning OD, basically saying "we have already been doing this for many years". Others considered OD to be in competition with the Italian mental health reforms and tradition. In response, a mental health service director suggested that we consider OD to be in line with the principles of Basaglia's reforms (Foot, 2014), or even think of OD as a tool to relaunch it, rather than as something better which we need to implement. Thus, a cognitive reframing process has been at the heart of the success of the Italian OD programme.

The primary defensive attitude addressed during the training was however connected to the *service user–professional relationship*. A psychiatrist asked, "how do we maintain distance from the patient using OD?" As was often the case, the trainers did not answer the question. It took us some time to appreciate their lack of answers, but reflecting on it now I think it was key to our being able to work constructively on important issues together. Later, when participating in supervision, I observed that professionals became closer and more engaged with service users when practising OD. As reported else-where (Ziedonis, 2015), professionals become acutely aware of how their own emotions resonate with the emotions of others in the meeting. It was moving to see experienced professionals change, to become more open and respectful and closer to service users – and also more vulnerable.

Trainees provided testimonies of significant *personal and team changes*, such as the rediscovery of a professional purpose. An experienced psychiatrist said:

> I remember why I decided to start this profession. I reflected on the fact that before I always said to my children that I am the director of a mental health service. Now I would say to them that I am someone who helps people with serious mental health issues to recover.

This testimony expresses well how the training brought about a fundamental change in the way professionals experienced their clinical practice, to being more focused on service users rather than their institutional role.

With regards to changes in the team, trainees focused on the relevance of the use of a reflecting team, and how it improved their clinical practice and their relationships with colleagues. It allowed for fuller participation – in training as well as in the OD sessions – for nurses and social workers, valorising their contribution. To me, it was moving to notice professionals developing trust in their team and taking care of each other – for example by showing kindness, being more positive in their feedback, sharing personal stories, and being less competitive on theoretical issues.

However, as reported by others, the training was also characterised by a sort of "transition pain" (Razzaque, 2015). Professionals were enthusiastic about practising OD, but also frustrated because they were not able to do so in their workplaces as often as they wanted to. Due to their workload, it was impossible for most of the professionals to organise teams fully dedicated to OD for all the people they worked with.

Finally, a strong *sense of belonging* to the OD programme emerged, paired with worries about its future. These worries are related to uncertainty about the economical sustainability of OD supervision, training and research once the funding from the Ministry of Health ends. We are currently trying to address these worries by establishing a formal national network dedicated to the development of OD.

Notes

1 This contribution was realised with the support of the Italian Ministry of Health, CCM Programme 2014.
2 The Italian OD training included a preliminary week on family therapy delivered by a team of Italian psychotherapists and a 20-day foundation training delivered by a pool of expert OD trainers. It involved 80 professionals from eight different mental

health departments, and was organised in two classes of 40 trainees. In addition to the training, in-house supervision for each department was provided.

References

Foot, J. (2014) Franco Basaglia and the radical psychiatry movement in Italy, 1961–78. *Critical and Radical Social Work*, 2(2), p. 235–249. doi.org/10.1332/204986014X14002292074708

Razzaque, R. (2015) *Open Dialogue in UK*. Presentation at the international workshop on the introduction of the Open Dialogue approach in the context of mental health services. ISTC-CNR, Rome, 10 July.

Ziedonis, D. (2015) *Open Dialogue & dialogic practice: Research & clinical experience on integrating and adapting into practice in the USA*. Presentation at the international workshop on the introduction of the Open Dialogue approach in the context of mental health services. ISTC-CNR, Rome, 10 July.

18

UK NHS PEER-SUPPORTED OPEN DIALOGUE TRAINING

Russell Razzaque, Mark Hopfenbeck and Val Jackson
(UK and Norway)

A desire to introduce Open Dialogue (OD) into the UK National Health Service, and perhaps to make it standard care one day for all mental health difficulties including psychosis, has driven us to explore, develop and then deliver a training in OD. At the time of writing more than 370 people have undertaken the course which forms the bedrock of a national research trial now launching Peer-supported Open Dialogue (POD) across multiple sites (see Chapter 39 for more on the research for this trial). The key challenge was to design a training that whole teams could attend together. A requirement for each team is that a peer worker (a person with lived experience) learns alongside their co-workers. As a one-year foundation course it is accessible and affordable for busy practitioners. We wanted to make sure that what we were teaching was true to the OD approach, and also that students gained a solid grounding in systemic theory. The systemic part of the training is now accredited as a foundation-level qualification by the Association for Family Therapy and Systemic Practice in the UK and accredited as a graduate or a postgraduate certificate course with London South Bank University.

The course runs over four residential weeks spread throughout the year and it has been developed in collaboration with an international group of OD trainers, with Jaakko Seikkula, Mary Olson, Mia Kurtti and others teaching directly on the course every year since its launch in 2014. The key elements of the course focus on:

- dialogical practice and role plays;
- the contribution of those with lived experience of mental health distress;
- working in teams with service users and their social networks;
- systemic practice, social constructionism and the importance of context including gender, race, age, employment, social inequity, etc.;
- self-work – considering our own family of origin;
- intervision – supporting each other when working dialogically;
- mindfulness or other contemplative practice; and
- understanding mental health difficulties and in particular psychosis as a result of trauma in someone's life.

Our students confirm in their feedback to us that the intense residential nature of the course encourages people to work together, collaborate and engage in experiential and self-work throughout, all of which are crucial to developing a dialogical approach. The time on the training is experienced as a valuable investment in personal development, rather than rote learning. Over the residential weeks strong bonds develop between the trainees, and this has profound effects on the learning experience, as well as the dynamic that develops in the teams. This contributes to creating a sense of trust and safety that is crucial when engaging in crisis work. The training does not begin and end in the residential modules. The real learning takes place when, on a team level, trainees start to organise and engage in network meetings with service users. The trainees are required to write and share reflections around this, which very much cements their learning. The third powerful ingredient is mindfulness, which is taught every day during the residential modules. The purpose is to help the students develop a sense of therapeutic presence and be aware of the sensations, emotions and thoughts they are experiencing, not suppress or push them away, but not necessarily act on them either. Not only does this enable them to be more comfortable with being in the moment during network meetings, it also allows them to recognise their habitual tendencies to intervene with a myriad of more traditional solution-based approaches. Instead, they can simply be aware of them, without letting them dominate the meeting.

An important aspect for us and for the research has been sustainability, thinking about future developments and trying to ensure that POD is not just another passing therapeutic 'tool', but becomes a substantially different way of organising services so that those in need of them feel heard, acknowledged and meaningfully involved in planning their future. As a result, we created further training for mentors, those who have successfully completed the one-year course and want to support and develop the approach within their service. Mentors attend further residential weeks alongside the new cohort, with specific sessions aimed at developing their skills. The sustainability is further enhanced by twice-yearly days of continuing personal development for successful trainees and mentors. A strong focus on the importance of frequent intervision is also emphasised throughout the training. This is a structured space for team members to talk about the personal challenges created by this way of working. It differs from supervision in that there is no hierarchy, no supervisor.

The final key factor is that our training is Peer-supported OD and, as such, the peer element is fundamental to it. Every module contains specific teaching from peer workers around different aspects of peer work, bringing a critical perspective and a richness from their lived experience, while working to establish a more egalitarian and open culture. This is certainly an area of ongoing development, and so our intention is that our growing network of peer workers share and learn from each other as we develop this aspect in a collaborative way.

The challenge for some of our students is the lack of opportunity to practise OD alongside the training as most NHS trusts do not yet offer such inclusive approaches.

Though the course is a stand-alone offer, it is also key to the national trial. As such the course is subject to substantial evaluation and this, as well as the integral system of feedback we have in place, will allow it to continue to grow and develop over time. Our hope is that ultimately, as a result of the trial outcomes, OD training programmes such as ours will become core training for NHS staff in future.

Section 4

INTRODUCING OPEN DIALOGUE IN DIFFERENT CONTEXTS IN VARIOUS COUNTRIES

CONTENTS

EDITORS' INTRODUCTION

As discussed in the opening chapters, Open Dialogue (OD), as it developed in Western Lapland, had two central interlocking features: a particular way of organising the whole psychiatric system, such that mental health issues can be responded to promptly and with a continuity of service and personnel, and the practice of cultivating dialogue within families and social networks. Many psychiatric systems elsewhere cannot be readily restructured, and yet this section describes ways in which aspects of OD have been successfully introduced within existing systems in Europe and the USA. OD is being developed far more extensively than outlined in these chapters, but we hope that they give a flavour of the possibilities for development and the obstacles likely to be met.

Buus et al. (2017) published a full and useful review of the available literature describing the adaptation and implementation of OD in Nordic countries outside of Finland. They summarise organisational constraints, professional benefits and resistances, and a range of outcomes and feedback from family/network members. Overall, the review's findings are similar to those described in this section, and the benefits reported by network members are congruent with those described in Section 2 of this book. Buus et al. highlight the ongoing problem that no service outside of Western Lapland has fully operationalised all seven OD principles (as defined in Chapter 1 of this book), making evaluation of service implementation and outcomes elsewhere problematic. Given the focus of this book, it should be noted that the Buus et al. review does not concentrate on people experiencing psychosis.

This section aims to illustrate the various ways in which OD has been and is being introduced in different countries and contexts, including the possibilities, obstacles and limitations that have emerged. For example, in Germany (Chapter 19) the introduction of OD has been somewhat piecemeal and mostly from the ground up. However, as the dominance of hospital-based care is challenged, systems are changing, and the possibility of insurance company community contracts is making OD implementation more feasible.

In many places in Germany it has only been possible to introduce some elements of the seven principles and outcome research is needed to determine the value of this partial development. In contrast to developments in Germany, a nationally funded Italian project with support from the top-down, in which professionals from eight districts have been trained in OD, is described in Chapter 20. The feasibility of the introduction of the approach is being evaluated, prior to researching outcomes.

UK Early Intervention in Psychosis (EIP) teams share some values and principles with OD. In Chapter 21, Baker and Calzavara, who were supported to do the full training in OD, describe the stepwise introduction of specific OD principles into their EIP service and the challenges they experienced. In another EIP service, this time in Sweden, Sundvall and Wallsten (Chapter 24) describe how and why specific OD principles are appreciated by migrant service users and their families.

In Massachusetts, USA, Gordon and colleagues (Chapter 22) consider OD to be in line with many of the pre-existing service values at their agency, Advocates. A total of 35 Advocates staff were trained in the approach and introduced many aspects of OD to two services: one for young people having psychotic experiences and the other for people suffering from longer-term severe mental health issues. From neighbouring Vermont, Smith (Chapter 23) describes a similar service development, drawing on earlier experience of Tom Andersen's family work. Both chapters clearly convey the enriched experience of service users and families and the work satisfaction of staff. Importantly, Smith highlights the potential for strengthening engagement with existing services.

In Chapter 25, three people who have worked in organisations where peer workers have been included in the development of OD services describe the nature of these developments, the added value of including peer workers in such a service and the challenges that they have encountered. They also offer advice to others who would like to develop the role in their OD service.

The final two chapters focus on the introduction of OD into hospital settings. Schütze (Chapter 26) describes the introduction of OD into German hospitals of different sizes and the many lessons learned. Karlsson and colleagues (Chapter 27) provide evidence of the benefits for service users and families from introducing network meetings into a locked psychiatric ward in Norway, whilst retaining existing structures and hierarchies.

The challenges of introducing Open Dialogue

The challenge of developing the OD approach into existing mental health services is highlighted in many of the chapters. A number of authors argue that OD can stretch limited resources – contributing factors here include the need to network more as a team, the unsustainability of staff working longer hours in order to engage families/networks in the work (for instance, by working into the evenings when more network members are available to participate in meetings) and the amount of investment needed for training and ongoing structures to support practice.

Whilst many professionals are clearly enthusiastic about developing this practice/approach, there are also those who are resistant to and/or feel threatened by such developments, for a variety of reasons, such as an adherence to models or theoretical positions which are incompatible with OD (or perceived to be so), a reluctance to modify existing hierarchical structures and professional roles and a scepticism about the effectiveness of OD or some elements of the practice. Alternatively, some might feel that their service/practice is already similar to OD (which may or may not be accurate) and thus minimise the need for change.

Some authors focus on the qualities that mental health practitioners need in order to engage in dialogic practice, such as the capacity to self-reflect and a willingness/ability to tolerate uncertainty in crisis situations. The view in Western Lapland is that all mental health practitioners in their service have the capacity to engage in dialogical training and practice, but elsewhere some may question the extent to which this is the case in other services. Irrespective of capacity and interest levels, training only a proportion of the professionals within a mental health service may have an adverse effect on team dynamics.

Clearly there is a need to develop a variety of means to address issues such as these. Some express this in terms of a need to adapt the 'ideal' practice from Western Lapland, in order to make local service developments feasible. Others stress the value of trying to develop existing services to be more dialogical, as opposed to trying to create a new 'OD' service. It seems crucial that staff teams are supported to find ways to develop their practice together, and that sceptical voices can be included in this process. It is important to bear in mind that OD is, in one respect, a way of organising a need-adapted service, and therefore many pre-existing practices within existing services may well still have value within an OD service, meaning that the development of OD does not need to be seen as a threat. Finally, it is clear that service development will be more effective where there is both top-down and bottom-up support.

We emphasise again the need for further qualitative and quantitative longer-term research if the enthusiasm and values of OD are to lead to wider service development and the necessary top-down support. If the effectiveness of OD is confirmed, then this could lead to a reinvestment in community services that should address the staffing issues raised by several authors.

For an up-to-date listing of all places known to be developing OD services, please go to the following webpage: www.open-dialogue.net/compendium.

Reference

Buus, N., Bikic, A., Jacobsen, E., Müller-Nielsen, K., Aagaard, J. and Rossen, C. (2017) Adapting and implementing Open Dialogue in the Scandinavian countries: A scoping review. *Issues in Mental Health Nursing*, 38(5), p. 391–401. doi.org/10.1080/01612840.2016.1269377

19

OPEN DIALOGUE IN GERMANY – OPPORTUNITIES AND CHALLENGES

Sebastian von Peter, Anja Lehmann, Nils Greve,
Katrin Herder and Thomas Floeth
(Germany)

When Jaakko Seikkula and colleagues developed the model today known as the Open Dialogue (OD) approach, changes were initiated on two different, but important, levels. Firstly, a culture of dialogical communication between staff, service users and relatives was established. Secondly, community-based, multi-disciplinary teams were implemented that mostly offered outpatient services, leading to a considerable reduction in hospital bed numbers. The Finnish OD model combines both structural and therapeutic elements. In contrast, in Germany, mainly for legal and organisational reasons, most of the structural principles have not been implemented. Instead, practising OD largely means trying to use as many of the therapeutic elements as possible within our conventional, fragmented healthcare system.

The German healthcare system

In Germany there are about 500 institutions, including 117 health insurance companies, sponsoring different parts of mental health services. A psychiatric hospital makes most of its revenue through the occupancy of beds. Outpatient services are highly fragmented, with mental healthcare provision spread among many sectors, characterised by significant regional differences with regard to administration, legal frameworks and financial constraints (Salize et al., 2007).

Why is this important to state? It highlights that it would currently be impossible to fully implement OD with all its therapeutic and structural elements within a catchment area in the current varied German systems. Multi-professional outpatient teams that follow the Western Lapland example are not possible within the legal framework around treatment, rehabilitation and support. The borders between different sectors in the mental healthcare system are rather strict: for instance, once someone has been admitted to hospital, the outpatient psychotherapist or social worker is not paid to maintain contact with that person, and after discharge, hospital staff are similarly not paid for outreach or home treatment procedures.

Despite these challenges, a number of German community-based institutions and hospital departments now offer dialogic network meetings, incorporating most of the therapeutic principles of OD. In Germany, OD is generally perceived as a means of enabling dialogue within social networks, rather than a way of restructuring mental health care systems. However, in some regions, a number of its structural elements have been implemented as well (for instance in Berlin, Bremen, Darmstadt, Hamburg, Itzehoe, Lüneburg, Koblenz, Hamm, Herford, München, Saarbrücken and Solingen).[1]

This chapter describes the implementation of OD in three different mental health settings in Germany, and the associated challenges: a hospital, a community mental health care centre and an 'integrated care' service. The challenges and opportunities differ in these settings.

Open Dialogue within a hospital[2]

At Berlin's St Hedwig Hospital/Charité, during the years 2012–2014, around 30 staff were trained to an OD foundation level, by Volkmar Aderhold and others. We made sure that staff from all wards and professions were represented, resulting in a pool of practitioners with the therapeutic skills to facilitate network meetings (NWMs), and thereby provide a service which is accessible to the entire psychiatric clinic (including all wards and outpatient units).

Three timeslots of 1.5 hours are reserved each week for NWMs, at times when facilitators are available. Slots can be booked in advance by any staff member, who then coordinates plans with service users and their families and participates in NWMs as a member of the professional network. NWMs are facilitated by the same professional team whenever possible. Sometimes NWMs can be arranged outside of the fixed timeslots, to ensure a continuity of facilitators over the course of several meetings.

We focus primarily on so-called 'revolving door' service users and others that staff find difficult to help, especially those who do not fit into the fragmented system, use a lot of resources and repeatedly challenge our convictions about hope and our being helpful professionals. Most suffer from psychotic experiences.

Since starting the OD approach, staff have experienced NWMs as being exceptionally helpful for these service users and their families, and for themselves as facilitators. We have developed a new attitude towards the people we serve, by working in a less goal-orientated and more process-orientated way, being more open to the service user's perspective, and developing our tolerance of uncertainty, amongst other changes. And yet we have also faced difficulties in implementing OD, which we will describe now, hoping that others can learn from our experiences:

- During our training programme, a significant number of trainees dropped out. Many, if not all of us, were struggling to find time for training within our daily routines.
- Some participants were intimidated by the challenge of adapting OD practices to their day-to-day work, of following the high ideals of the Finnish model.
- The implementation of OD in our service has largely been a bottom-up process. Despite formal support, there was never a clear directive from higher management that NWMs should be integrated as an essential component of our treatment plans. As much as we have made efforts to minimise the organisational burden, by providing training and refresher courses, fixed timeslots and rooms that can be booked in advance, NWMs are still perceived as something 'extra' – a luxurious and time-consuming enterprise that is not part of regular care.
- OD places quite a high demand on clinicians, requiring self-awareness and the willingness to question one's own role. Professional hierarchies and knowledge, traditional roles, classification systems and interpretational sovereignty may readily be called into question during NWMs. Presenting oneself as doubtful or uncertain, instead of knowledgeable and superior, may be a challenge for some of us.

Dialogic collaboration in a community mental health centre[3]

The Psychosozialer Trägerverein Solingen (PTV) runs the Mental Health Centre for Solingen (160,000 inhabitants) with a full range of therapy, rehabilitation, nursing and care services[4]. Services are delivered by 150 staff members, organised into 11 teams. Influenced by a group of systemic therapy trainers who are mainly concerned with dialogical approaches (Tom Andersen, Harlene Anderson and Jaakko Seikkula), we began around the mid-nineties to establish dialogical conversations within, as well as between, the teams, including staff members, service users and their families/social networks. Over the years, around 30 staff members from different departments and teams have successfully completed two to three years of training in systemic therapy and counselling, focusing on reflective conversations and OD.

For many years PTV has regularly participated in the annual International Meetings on the Treatment of Psychosis, initiated by Tom Andersen and Jaakko Seikkula in 1996. These conferences have a particularly strong, though not exclusive, focus on OD, and Solingen was the host of the 2015 international meeting. Inspired and encouraged by these meetings, we established a 'conversation workshop' (*Gesprächswerkstatt*) in 2012 that has since offered monthly consultations to anyone working in PTV. Single professionals, teams, case-related systems and families, amongst others, have made use of this opportunity. They come together with members of the 'Gesprächswerkstatt' in dialogical conversations, mostly led by one or two facilitators and including comments by other team members (who form a reflecting team). Also, in 2012, the 'Integrated Treatment' programme (NWpG, cf. section 'Open Dialogue in an integrated care setting' below) was implemented in one of the teams and has contributed to our ideas about dialogical conversation with service users' social networks.

With 20 years of engagement in systemic and dialogical conversation, it is now common practice for us to not target interventions towards a single person (the 'service user'), but rather to collaborate with all persons involved in a particular situation. We have often been able to bridge the gap between professionals and the social networks of service users and between different types of treatment and care. Mutual understanding and respect for differing ideas and concepts has been growing. This all happens much more frequently than previously, but not yet in every situation. Traditional single-person-diagnosis-and-intervention-type concepts are still highly influential, fostered by legal regulations, long-lasting habits and fragmented structures within PTV.

From its very beginnings in 1978, PTV has had a culture of equal footing between service users, families and professionals and we have successfully preserved this culture over the years. OD fits well into this paradigm and has proved useful in influencing our practice; e.g. medication has become a matter of negotiation and agreement, instead of a doctor's order.

Open Dialogue in an integrated care setting[5]

Over the last 10 years, 'Integrated Treatment' services have been developed by various providers of community psychiatry in a number of regions across Germany, based on specific managed care contracts (*Integrierte Versorgung – IV*). The best-known IV contract in psychiatry is named 'Network Mental Health' (*Netzwerk psychische Gesundheit – NWpG*) and is directed towards persons with severe mental illnesses. It was first introduced in 2009, in a handful of regions, but has since spread all over Germany such that it is now in place in about 80 counties, towns or city districts in 12 of the 16 federal states. It includes case management that integrates the service user's personal and professional network, along with a 24/7 crisis service (a hotline, outreach services and residential respite facilities). Integration with hospital care is not included.

Most NWpG providers have adopted the OD approach and have sent their staff members to the OD foundation training developed by Volkmar Aderhold. Although fidelity to the original OD approach has not yet been evaluated, a dialogical attitude has been widely adopted throughout the NWpG teams. Given the usual 'interventionist' attitude in German mental health services, this is a great achievement, and the new services have been very well received by most of the service users who have participated, as well as by their families.

As mentioned above, the OD approach is primarily viewed by German professionals as an attitude and a method of communication and collaboration, rather than a way of re-organising the mental health systems. Yet, due to the recent IV contracts, there are several regions that are now coming close to both aspects of the original OD model, i.e. also including its structural elements: dialogical network meetings, facilitated by mobile multi-professional teams who are available 24/7, and with continuity of the same professionals over a period of at least three years.

One example is the Berlin NWpG programme, which provides a broad range of services for people with mental health problems (supported living, activity centres, therapy, rehabilitation, nursing and care services, delivered by some 600 staff members). Over the last nine years the Integrated Treatment approach referred to above has been offered to around 5,000 service users in Berlin, by 10 multi-disciplinary regional teams, consisting of around 90 staff, including 20 peer workers.

With this structural background and the lived experience of 'trialogue' (the cooperation of professionals, peers and family members on an equal footing, 'auf gleicher Augenhöhe'), all members of the Berlin regional teams went through the aforementioned OD training and we are currently running the 12th course (meaning that more than 300 staff members working in long-term care as well as in the IV programme have now been trained).

A statistical survey was undertaken in 2016 to establish the extent of the service and the resources utilised over the course of a year. The survey found that at that time the IV project was caring for 1,800 service users who accessed our services in Berlin for between one and four years. Each service user had two specific caregivers assigned to them ('Bezugsbegleiter') who offered most of the care together, following the OD principles of psychological continuity and opportunities for reflection. A total of 500 network meetings per annum were being offered. These took place either in a regional office, in the service user's home, in another place of their choice, or – if intensive care was needed – in a crisis respite centre ('Krisenpension').

Discussion

Over the last decade there has been growing support for OD in many mental health institutions in Germany. Meanwhile, a considerable number of community teams, as well as hospital services, have adopted the principles of OD, achieved basic or advanced training, and introduced dialogical elements into their work, to the extent that these are compatible with existing practices. In nationwide meetings and conferences (Netzwerk Offener Dialog), participants

151

usually report a growing acceptance of OD by colleagues who have not been trained, as well as a shift from intervention-based approaches towards dialogue-based concepts, leading to a higher rate of engagement and satisfaction among service users and families.

To date, the scientific evidence for the effectiveness of these developments in Germany is still lacking. Most studies undertaken have not targeted OD in particular. Furthermore, OD in Germany continues to be a rather bottom-up, grassroots intervention, such that its implementation and sustainability depends greatly on the engagement and activities of professional teams or individuals. This may be because the OD approach implies criticism and questioning of well-established hierarchies of power. On a macro-level it questions the biological model and individualistic forms of care, and on a micro-level it may be perceived to be a threat to conventional professional roles.

As a possible consequence, several teams have so far only been able to engage in dialogical practices because of special funding (e.g. NWpG) and the transfer of OD into the regular treatment system hasn't been achieved yet. However, some treatment structures in the German mental health system are shifting towards regularly financed outpatient teams as first-line services, especially for people with severe mental health problems. If these initiatives are successful, new opportunities will arise to combine Western Lapland-like structures with dialogical network meetings. Thus, there is considerable hope of developing regional mental health services along the lines of the original OD model in the long term.

From a legal perspective there is also hope. In 2016, new legislation, allowing for crisis resolution outreach services instead of acute inpatient treatment, opened up new possibilities. It remains to be seen how far dialogical conversations and OD first-line crisis support can be integrated into these services. Further legislation bridging outpatient and inpatient care, integrating the highly specialised treatment services of rehabilitation, community nursing and other forms of support, would help pave the way for the implementation of the structural elements of OD across Germany.

To conclude, despite many developments, OD in Germany is still perceived as something 'special' and 'extra', as something that is not part of regular care. This status is reflected on both a micro-level, as in the three examples above, and a macro-level, given the rather moderate implementation rate of OD across Germany. At the same time, our situation does not seem to differ much from developments in other countries.

Notes

1 For further information see www.offener-dialog.de.
2 Section written by Sebastian von Peter and Anja Lehmann.

3 Section written by Nils Greve and Katrin Herder.
4 www.ptv-solingen.de.
5 Section written by Thomas Floeth.

Reference

Salize, H.J., Rössler, W. and Becker, T. (2007) Mental healthcare in Germany – current state and trends. *European Archives of Psychiatry and Clinical Neuroscience*, 257, p. 92–103. doi.org/10.1007/s00406-006-0696-9

20

OPEN DIALOGUE IN THE ITALIAN NATIONAL HEALTH SERVICE

A view from the borderland[1]

Marcello Macario, Anna Gastaldi and
Luigi Roberto Pezzano
(Italy)

Between 2015 and 2017, eight Mental Health Departments (MHDs) of the Italian NHS participated in a national project funded by the Ministry of Health aimed at transferring and adapting the Finnish Open Dialogue (OD) approach to Italian public mental health services (Pocobello and el Sehity, 2017). Each department covers a population ranging between 300,000 and more than a million. The eight MHDs were (see Figure 20.1):

- 2 MHDs in Turin
- MHD of Savona
- MHD of Modena
- MHD of Trieste
- 2 MHDs in Rome
- MHD of Catania

The project was coordinated by the Department of Prevention within the Local Health Authority of Turin and the pilot study included in the project was carried out by the National Research Council of Rome.

The title of the project translated into English is 'Open Dialogue: an innovative approach to the treatment of first episode crises. Developing and evaluating the transferability of the OD approach into Italian Mental Health Departments'.

The first steps were to:

- provide OD training for all professionals involved in the project;
- assess the potential for developing OD in community mental health centres within the MHDs; and
- evaluate the outcomes of OD-based interventions in a pilot study.

Figure 20.1 The eight mental health departments that participated.

As there was thought to be enough evidence from outside Italy of the effectiveness of OD, the focus of the project was specifically on the impact of the
OD approach on Italian public mental health services.

A point worth making here is that, in our opinion, the field of social psychiatry in Italy is affected by a strong prejudice against anything new from
abroad. Professionals think that we were the first country in the world to close
psychiatric asylums (Mental Health Act 1978 – 'Basaglia Law'), and therefore
conclude that 'the work is done' and there is little to learn from services in
other countries. We wondered about the extent to which this view would affect
this national project.

Our OD foundation training lasted 18 days in total and ran from September
2015 to September 2016. Eight professionals from each of the eight MHDs
were chosen to participate (the usual number of professionals in an MHD is
50 to 100) – see Chapter 42 for more on the Italian training. At the end of the
training we started to use the OD approach as our first option for new psychiatric crises. We established a research project in which, over one calendar
month, all new service users within the catchment area of each OD team had

started OD treatment. A longitudinal observational pilot study with a prospective cohort research design is currently being carried out (Pocobello and el Sehity, 2017). We are following the treatment for a period of 12 months, and are aiming to evaluate the transferability of OD into the context of Italian MHDs as well as the feasibility of a potential future trial focused on the effectiveness of OD.

We feel that our view is from the '*borderland*', because we are practising OD in rural areas and outside academic organisations (one of the authors works in the north and one in the south of Italy), and also because the third author is not a professional, but rather a person with lived experience of psychosis (the mother of a voice hearer). Our interest in developing OD stems from a desire to cross the boundaries between agencies and professions, including the boundaries between professionals and 'lay people'.

Changes to our practice

We would like to highlight three particular aspects of our OD practice in Italian mental health services: a) families being met by a team, as opposed to being met by a single professional, b) the reflective conversations and democratic process in network meetings, and c) peer-worker involvement in the OD team.

Working as a team in an integrated service

We have seen surprise and even disbelief on the faces of the families we have worked with, as we work with them in teams of two or three, listening carefully to their ideas, fears and hopes, in an unhurried manner, without an attempt to provide solutions, but rather with a desire to simply be in dialogue with them. Working in teams was a key element in Italian social psychiatry after the 'Basaglia revolution' (Basaglia, 1968), but it seems that we slowly abandoned this practice, as we began to look more to biomedical approaches, and to creating specific services for specific needs (or sometimes even diagnosis-based services). This 'silo-system' slices holistic life according to its professional division of labour and creates communication gaps and rivalries as to who is 'right' and who has the mandate to steer others. As such our understanding of service users' problems becomes fragmented and they can have a hard time trying to integrate the work of different services and professionals. There are many benefits to the team work and the integration of services in the OD approach.

Reflective conversations and democratic process

Whilst working as a team is a return to our 'Basaglia' roots, reflective conversations during network meetings are something new for us and for the families, bringing greater transparency. Previously, we were used to sharing our thoughts about the work in separate meetings for professionals before and/or after meetings with service users and their families. We thought that we knew what was best for the service user, and therefore we saw the only issue as being how to make them comply with our plans. OD has taken us back down to the same level as everyone else involved, in a democratic process; now each of us is involved in the dialogue with our embodied self, in such a way that we can show our emotions and express our uncertainties, without any strategic aim to change the other.

Peer involvement

The involvement of a peer worker in the Savona OD team is having a strong impact, helping to improve the relationship between service users and professionals and promote trust and dialogue in the meetings. Embodied experience is probably central to this impact, because a peer worker can listen to what a service user is saying whilst also referring to their personal experiences in psychiatry, and this helps people to feel accepted and under-stood. In addition, a relationship between professionals and peers that is based on respect, support and affection seems to have a good effect on service users; they feel more comfortable in meetings and are more likely to speak. Also, it is more likely that a peer worker will stay in touch with service users between meetings, such that the service user does not feel alone or abandoned. We'd prefer not to have 'classic' OD on one side and 'peer-supported' OD on the other; we think that having peer workers involved in OD teams along-side professionals could be the best choice for standard practice, because the presence of peers can have a positive and unique impact on professionals and the service user and their family.

The seven principles as viewed by trained and untrained professionals

A self-administered questionnaire was given to eight OD-trained professionals from the health and social services of Savona and 23 colleagues from the same services not involved in the training – the 'untrained' group (Macario, 2017). Table 20.1 shows that some responses confirmed impressions that we already had, whilst others surprised us. Respondents rated each of the seven OD principles (see Chapter 1) as close, distant or neutral (neither close nor dis-tant) in relation to their working style.

The OD-trained participants differed significantly from the untrained participants in their evaluation of the following principles:

Psychological Continuity (Chi2 (31; 1) = 6.126; p = 0.047)
Dialogue and Polyphony (Chi2 (31; 1) = 6.149; p = 0.046)

Table 20.1 OD principles. The two groups' responses to the questionnaire (all figures are percentages)

	OD-trained group (n=8)			Untrained group (n=23)		
	Distant	*Neutral*	*Close*	*Distant*	*Neutral*	*Close*
Immediate Help	50	12.5	37.5	21.7	30.4	47.8
Social Network Perspective	50	37.5	12.5	17.4	26.1	56.5
Flexibility and Mobility	12.5	50	37.5	39.1	26.1	34.8
Responsibility	0	37.5	62.5	13	39.1	47.8
Psychological Continuity	0	50	50	47.8	39.1	13
Tolerance of Uncertainty	25	50	25	26.2	56.5	17.4
Dialogue and Polyphony	12.5	12.5	75	8.7	60.9	30.4

Half of the OD-trained participants rated Psychological Continuity as *close* to their daily practice (following training) as opposed to only 13% of the untrained participants, 47.8% of whom rated this principle as *distant*. 75% of the OD-trained participants rated Dialogue and Polyphony as *close* to their daily practice compared to only 30.4% of the untrained participants, 60.9% of whom rated this principle as neutral. We understand these results in the following way: treatment as usual in our services tends to be monological, involving a good deal of top-down communication – it is work that can be undertaken by and passed on to equivalent professionals. Therefore, it is not surprising that OD training, and the resulting changes that professionals made in their practice, would have a particularly strong impact on the principles of dialogue/polyphony and psychological continuity.

An unexpected outcome, although not reaching statistical significance, was that 50% of OD-trained participants rated Immediate Help and Social Network Perspective as distant to their current practice (after OD training), whilst these percentages in the untrained professionals group were only 21.7% and 17.4% respectively. If this were confirmed statistically it would indicate that current service structures do not permit OD-trained clinicians to offer sufficiently early help or to adequately involve members of the social network. Furthermore, we think that the low percentages for untrained professionals reflect a different understanding of these aspects of service provision. For the non-OD-trained professional, urgent help means meeting a service user within 7–10 days, whereas for OD practitioners this means within 24 hours. A social network perspective for the average professional means having a *separate* meeting with relatives who are invited by the professional and not, as in OD, involving the family/social network directly in meetings with the service user, who decide together who to invite.

Two open-ended questions about the involvement of the social network and reflective conversations were included:

What do you think about the involvement of family members and the social network from the very beginning of treatment?

What do you think about the practice of having all discussions between professionals in the presence of the service user and their relatives?

In the OD-trained group seven professionals out of eight (87.5%) affirmed that the involvement of family members and the social network is important and effective. Only one OD-trained professional expressed some worries about the involvement of the family members ("it could be stressful for them"). More than 50% of OD-trained professionals highlighted the deep emotional impact that the reflective dialogue during the meeting could have on those participating (both family members and professionals).

In the untrained group, 43.5% of the combined responses to the two questions contained either a negative (n=2) or a doubtful (n=8) statement, with the criticism focused especially on the reflective conversation. Some wrote that a decision should be taken in each meeting as to whether or not to include a reflective conversation. Some wrote that a space should be kept for professionals to talk about service users and their family without them being present. There was strong criticism about the idea that we should say everything in the presence of the service user and their family, with some feeling that they may need to be protected from some 'inconvenient truths'.

Looking at the different professional roles (across both the trained and untrained groups), psychiatrists were the most worried about the involvement of the social network and the openness of communication (66.7%) and social workers were the least worried (only 9%), with nurses (50%) and psychologists (33.3%) falling in between.

In *Zen and the Art of Motorcycle Maintenance* (Pirsig, 1974), the almost autobiographical story of a motorcycle trip across America, the author recounts how, when he came to a crossroad, he would always take secondary roads so that he could meet "people who are not going anywhere and who are not too busy to be courteous. The 'hereness and nowness' of things is something they know all about" (p. 15). We think of OD as, in some respects, similar to an unknown road, where we can drive slowly and have time to pay attention to the people we meet. And it feels significant to us that this invocation for dialogue is coming from a person with lived experience of psychosis; in fact, Pirsig was diagnosed with schizophrenia and was treated with electroconvulsive therapy, spending time in and out of psychiatric hospitals between 1961 and 1963. We hope that the introduction of OD in the Italian public mental health system will reflect something of the exploration of the secondary roads that Pirsig describes: "Roads where when you stop to ask for directions or information the answer tends to be longer than you want, rather than shorter, where people ask where you're from and how long you've been riding" (p. 15).

Note

1 This chapter is dedicated to our colleague and friend Cristina Balestra, who shared the Open Dialogue training experience and the initial steps in practice with us, and who is no longer with us. We infinitely miss her gentle smile, her humble curiosity and her points of view. "Even her absence is something that's with me" (Pessoa, 2007, p. 77).

References

Basaglia, F. (1968) *L'istituzione negata [The institution denied]*. Torino: Einaudi.

Macario, M. (2017) Crossing some boundaries. The building of a local network between different health and social services as a possibility to deal with 'multi-problem' clients and families using the OD approach. *Thesis*, Three Year OD Training Programme: London.

Mental Health Act (1978) Legge 13 maggio 1978, n. 180, Accertamenti e trattamenti sanitari volontari e obbligatori [Law 13 May 1978, n. 180, Voluntary and compulsory health checks and treatments], *Gazzetta Ufficiale* 16 maggio 1978, n. 133.

Pessoa, F. (2007) *The collected poems of Alberto Caeiro*, trans. C. Daniels. Bristol: Shearsman Books.

Pirsig, R.M. (1974) *Zen and the art of motorcycle maintenance*. New York: William Morrow & Company.

Pocobello, R. and el Sehity, T. (2017) Evaluation of Open Dialogue in the context of the Italian mental health services. Technical Report for the Italian Ministry of Health, ISTC-CNR, Rome.

21

THE CHALLENGES OF INTRODUCING OPEN DIALOGUE INTO A UK EARLY INTERVENTION IN PSYCHOSIS SERVICE

Darren Baker and Simona Calzavara
(UK)

Context

We learned about Open Dialogue (OD) at different times but shared similar initial responses to the approach. The principles and values of OD seemed to fit closely with ours and reflected the way in which we wanted to work. However, the culture of dialogic practice felt so different from that in which we worked, and the organisational changes required to move towards an OD system seemed so great, that it felt virtually impossible to achieve. Yet, inspired by developments such as the US Parachute Project and the initiation of the UK clinical trial of Peer-supported OD, we have tried over the last five years to introduce aspects of OD into the NHS Early Intervention in Psychosis (EIP) service where we work. It is located in a busy, diverse part of London and is for people aged between 18 and 65 experiencing a first episode of psychosis. It offers a period of up to three years in a multi-disciplinary team that works as flexibly as possible and tries to involve service users' families and support networks, where appropriate. Our service has a strong emphasis on hope and recovery.

Rationale for introducing Open Dialogue

EIP services have been shown to provide clinically important benefits over standard care (Bird et al., 2010) and to be cost-effective (McCrone et al., 2010), and often receive positive feedback from both service users and their families, who value them for their ethos and approach (The Schizophrenia Commission, 2012). Given this, why would we want to try to introduce a new approach into such a service?

Firstly, the positive outcomes for people with a first episode of psychosis published by the OD team in Western Lapland (see Chapter 37) significantly exceed anything produced by EIP services. The outcomes are also maintained at long-term follow-up (Seikkula et al., 2006). This contrasts with EIP services where research has shown that benefits may not be maintained in the long term, particularly after the service has been withdrawn (Marshall and Rathbone, 2011).

Feedback within our own service supports the view that service users and carers are satisfied with EIP services. For example, in response to a survey, 90% of service users and 100% of carers said they would recommend our team to friends and family. However, within this overall level of satisfaction, there were significant variations. For example, only 36% of carers felt able to question the treatment options offered by the team.

OD and EIP appeared to us to be a good fit, because they share some important values and principles, such as the central involvement (where appropriate) of family members, carers and other important members of the social network. In the UK, the National Institute for Clinical Excellence (NICE) guidelines for EIP services recommend that they should work in partnership with service users and their carers and "take time to build supportive and empathic relationships as an essential part of care" (NICE, 2014, p. 11).

How we went about introducing Open Dialogue

As Seikkula and Arnkil (2006, p. 9) argue: "Good practices simply cannot be duplicated. The difference of contexts and actors should always be taken into account". We began by instigating and facilitating numerous dialogues both within our team and in the wider organisation. Through these dialogues, a growing interest in and commitment to the approach began to evolve, and as part of this, we (the authors) were funded to participate in the first full three-year OD training outside of Finland, which commenced in London in 2015. We were drawn to this particular training because it most closely replicates the training in Western Lapland.

Once the training was underway, we worked together with service users who requested the involvement of their families, using the concept of 'network meetings'. As a team, we tried to find ways to introduce small service developments that would help move the team as a whole towards the OD approach. For example, by encouraging people newly referred to our service to bring members of their social network with them to their first appointment (if they wished), we hoped to begin to shift our service culture away from a focus on the individual towards a social network perspective. In tandem, we tried to disseminate the skills and knowledge we were acquiring through the training to other team members, through a combination of training, supervision and experiential learning.

Challenges of introducing Open Dialogue

Introducing any new approach into a busy team that has multiple demands on its time and resources is never easy. Recent years have been particularly demanding for UK EIP services; many have expanded their remit to work with people up to the age of 65 (previously services worked with 'young adults') and some have also begun working with people deemed to be at risk of developing psychosis. In addition, demanding targets around waiting times have been introduced at a national level, which has led to a significant increase in workload, despite increased investment in staffing. Consequently, staff sometimes struggle to find time to attend in-house workshops and supervision or to consider some of the necessary and challenging changes to their clinical practice.

Initially we used the term 'Open Dialogue' liberally. However, we were a long way from a comprehensive OD system. As one of our carers stated: "We did a lot of reading of articles, and looking at the people involved in OD... We found out that what we were getting wasn't the same... We wanted other things to happen that were more in line with this approach". As a result, we have started to talk more in terms of introducing specific aspects of dialogical practice, such as network meetings.

It has been challenging to introduce aspects of a new approach to others, whilst at the same time learning and developing our own skills and knowledge. We are positioned locally as the 'experts' in OD, when in reality we feel far from expert, and in fact the expert position is discouraged in dialogical approaches. We have tried to encourage our colleagues to work together to introduce the approach, rather than looking to us to 'tell' them how best to go about it.

One of the most challenging issues we have faced is a lack of continuity, partly due to the turnover of staff, but also because of the fragmented organisation of services. Our EIP, Crisis/Home Treatment and inpatient services are all provided by different teams. Continuity of care is one of the key principles of OD (Seikkula and Arnkil, 2006) and breaks in continuity have been highlighted as challenging by service users and family members. The fragmentation of our services is very different to the OD system in Western Lapland. We have, however, now reached the point where we are beginning to introduce OD to these other services too and to think how best to provide a more unified approach across services.

To finish on a positive note

When thinking about introducing a more dialogic culture into our workplace, it is easy to become preoccupied and pessimistic about the number of significant challenges involved. However, our initial forays into the approach have resulted in some very positive outcomes, with many service users and family members having talked about how helpful network meetings are and how they have led to significant improvements in their situations.

We asked service users and family members who attended network meetings to rate their level of satisfaction with a range of aspects of the service delivered and compared this to previous data. We found that both service users and family members attending network meetings were significantly more likely to state that they felt involved in the planning of treatment and care and able to question the treatment options offered. Carers were more likely to report that they were given time to discuss their own needs. Collecting this data has been instrumental to ensuring that we have retained the backing of our organisation to continue with this work.

On a personal note, developing a more dialogical practice has been both inspiring and transformative and has renewed our enthusiasm for and commitment to our work. We find the approach profoundly human and humane. This is illustrated by the following quote from one of our service users: "The biggest thing for my recovery was being able to bring someone I loved into the room, bringing in their point of view and feelings".

References

Bird, V., Premkumar, P., Kendall, T., Whittington, C., Mitchell, J. and Kuipers, K. (2010) Early intervention services, cognitive–behavioural therapy and family intervention in early psychosis: Systematic review. *British Journal of Psychiatry*, 197, p. 350–356. doi.org/10.1192/bjp.bp.109.074526

Marshall, M. and Rathbone, J. (2011) Early intervention for psychosis. *Schizophrenia Bulletin*, 37, p. 1111–1114. doi.org/10.1093/schbul/sbr110

McCrone, P., Craig, T.K.J., Power, P. and Garety, P.A. (2010) Cost-effectiveness of an early intervention service for people with psychosis. *British Journal of Psychiatry*, 196, p. 377–382. doi.org/10.1192/bjp.bp.109.065896

NICE (2014, February 14) *Psychosis and schizophrenia in adults: Prevention and management*. [online] Available at: www.nice.org.uk/guidance/cg178/resources/psychosis-and-schizophrenia-in-adults-prevention-and-management-pdf-35109758952133 [Accessed 11 April 2020].

Seikkula, J. and Arnkil, T.E. (2006) *Dialogical meetings in social networks*. London: Karnac Books.

Seikkula, J., Aaltonen, J., Alakare, B., Haarakangas, K., Keränen, J. and Lehtinen, K. (2006) Five-year experience of first-episode nonaffective psychosis in open-dialogue approach: Treatment principles, follow-up outcomes, and two case studies. *Psychotherapy Research*, 16, p. 214–228. doi.org/10.1080/10503300500268490

The Schizophrenia Commission (2012) *The abandoned illness: A report from the Schizophrenia Commission*. London: Rethink Mental Illness.

22

TWO OPEN DIALOGUE PROGRAMMES AT ADVOCATES, FRAMINGHAM, MASSACHUSETTS, USA

*Christopher Gordon, Brenda Miele Soares
and Amy Morgan*
(USA)

We first became aware of the practice of Open Dialogue (OD) through the journalism of Robert Whitaker, in 2009. We recognised similarities between the system of care in Western Lapland, and the services we offered in our non-profit mental health agency. These included the values underpinning our work: a strength-based, person-centred and person-directed approach to care; a wariness of psychiatric diagnoses as unduly pathologising and demoralising; and a belief that care in the community is generally better than in institutions. We also had in place a mobile crisis team, available 24/7, 365 days a year, and outpatient and community residential services with experienced clinicians and therapists for people experiencing extreme emotional/psychiatric states. It seemed that we could use our existing structures and resources to adapt OD principles to our environment.

We were immensely lucky; through Robert Whitaker we met Jaakko Seikkula, a founder of OD, who was lecturing in the US at the time, and Mary Olson, his principal US collaborator. About an hour from us, Mary Olson was preparing to open her Institute for Dialogic Practice with a faculty from Finland. With a grant from the Foundation for Excellence in Mental Health Care, and financial support for training from the Massachusetts Department of Mental Health, we trained 35 members of our team for two years at Mary Olson's institute.

The Collaborative Pathway

About six months into our training we created two programmes using OD principles. The first, the Collaborative Pathway, offered network meetings in the home, along with related psychiatric services, for young persons aged 14–35, experiencing current or recent psychosis, regardless of their particular

165

diagnosis. The Collaborative Pathway attempted to replicate the Western Lapland services as closely as possible, using the seven fundamental principles of OD (see Chapter 1).

We created the Collaborative Pathway as a formal research project in partnership with the Center for Psychiatric Rehabilitation at Boston University (Gordon et al., 2016). We recruited participants primarily from people who contacted our crisis team. We were unable to fully provide one OD principle, psychological continuity, since our team was unable to follow participants if they were admitted to a psychiatric hospital. However, we provided a clinical team of at least two OD-trained clinicians to offer home network meetings for up to one year. Network meetings which needed to include a psychiatrist were held in the clinic to save the cost of travel time for the psychiatrist. The service was expensive, with third-party reimbursement covering less than a quarter of the total cost of care, since costs included a second clinician, travel time and supervision, none of which was reimbursable through insurance. We covered these costs with grant supports.

Our feasibility study of the Collaborative Pathway (Gordon et al., 2016) reviewed our experience with the first 14 families we served. This is summarised in Chapter 43. The average age of persons at the centre of concern was 22.7 years and the average duration without treatment of the new episode of psychosis at initial contact with us was 41.1 weeks. As suggested by the long duration of difficulty prior to contact with us, practically all participants had already had substantial – and often negative – experiences with the mental health system. Usually, the contact with our team was precipitated by a new crisis. Clinical outcomes were generally positive, with a significant improvement in symptoms, functioning and need for care (Brief Psychiatric Rating Scale, $p < 0.001$; BASIS-R, $p=0.002$; and Strauss Carpenter Level of Functioning Scale, $p<0.001$). Generally, the service was safe with no substantial adverse outcomes. Participants used network meetings to make decisions about medications: some reduced or eliminated antipsychotics, others adjusted their dosages or choice of medications, and some began antipsychotics. Staff satisfaction was very high.

Both service users and family members in the Collaborative Pathway rated the service very highly, expressing appreciation for:

- the opportunity to receive services in their home;
- extended time with the clinical team and psychiatrist, compared to standard care;
- the transparency and openness of professionals in the reflective process;
- feeling empowered from shared decision making, particularly around the use of medications; and
- the general tone of friendliness and warmth pervading the programme.

Since the study, a couple of individuals have been excluded from the programme due to threats of violence toward family members and/or staff; this is consistent with recently published long-term outcomes in Finland in which aggression seemed to be a harbinger of greater need for services and poorer long-term outcomes (Bergström et al., 2017).

Open Dialogue in Community Based Flexible Supports

The second programme we initiated was OD in Community Based Flexible Supports (OD in CBFS), offering network meetings using dialogic principles to people we were already serving with long-term, complex and serious psychiatric conditions, and for whom we provided residential, outreach and other psychiatric supports. The experience of providing OD services in this programme has been very rich. It was not constructed as a formal research programme. Instead, we applied dialogical principles to our clinical work in the community, including the use of two facilitators in network meetings, practising transparency, and other elements of dialogic practice (see Chapter 38).

Network meetings in OD in CBFS have involved family members and other participants in the person's natural support network, just like the Collaborative Pathway, but some people were estranged from their families. In these instances, some of our professional staff have functioned as network members, while others served as facilitators. For example, a service user we worked with in the community with a history of severe suicide attempts wanted to have greater control over her medications, and the professional staff were divided about how to balance the person's rights with concern for her safety. This person was estranged from her family and staff cared about her considerably. These staff participated in network meetings with her as concerned members of her network, along with two facilitators trained in OD. The service user felt heard and also appreciated the opportunity to understand the deep concerns and fears of the staff members who cared for her.

Many family members and service users have reported positive experiences of OD in CBFS. One service user even convened wider network meetings involving other parents and siblings and fellow religious congregants, and reports that these have been a source of great support and comfort, and have helped to mobilise resources. Another family reported that, after 25 years in the mental health system, this was the first time they had ever known what clinicians were thinking. These network meetings seemed to be of great benefit, as the service user has been able to avoid hospitalisations – which had previously been frequent and prolonged – for a substantial period of time.

Not all families were happy with the network meetings in OD in CBFS, and in the Collaborative Pathway. Some families seemed to be so committed to a primarily bio-medical paradigm for understanding their loved one's experience, and so concerned about their loved one's suffering and safety, and then so convinced that adherence to antipsychotic medication protocols was the primary solution to their difficulties, that they experienced the team's attempts to honour and amplify their loved one's voice as 'anti-medication' or even 'anti-psychiatry'. This occurred in spite of the fact that our team prescribed medications and recommended their use when appropriate, and tried to reflect appreciation for the family's love and concern, and to validate their fears. In one instance, a family requested that their relative, who struggled both with psychosis and suicidal impulses, be transferred away from our agency in order to, from their point of view, rescue her from a process that they considered harmful.

Other families, however, even when their relative's clinical course has been extremely turbulent, requiring multiple hospitalisations, have valued the network meetings as a place to come together to process what has happened and how to move forward.

Challenges and lessons learned

In both programmes, we have been challenged to provide network meetings in the homes of persons in crisis at times convenient for them and their families. Since many people work, families often request evening and weekend meetings. Staff managing demanding clinical responsibilities and productivity targets have found it difficult to respond promptly and at the requested times, especially in a crisis, when frequent meetings are often needed. This comes down to funding. Our agency, like most non-profit mental health providers, runs on the slimmest of margins, and providing services which are not reimbursed is very challenging. With adequate funding we would be able to provide services at hours and places people want. As it is, we have to stretch resources, and often clinicians are providing services on top of their regular duties, because they love this model. This is not a way to build scalable services. So, our main obstacle is money. In this we are fortunate – some people have to overcome serious barriers of values, language and philosophy – we didn't.

Another significant barrier in the Collaborative Pathway programme has been identifying people early on in their crisis before they encounter substantial – and often negative – experiences in the mental health system. Most had already taken antipsychotic medications, sometimes not willingly. Only once did we have an opportunity to serve a young person and their family from the very beginning of their distressing psychosis, and in this instance she and her family opted (successfully) to try to manage her difficulties without medications.

168

The main lessons we have learned from our two programmes are:

1   Meeting people and their support networks in a dialogical manner is generally experienced by all as more authentic, caring, inclusive, respectful and empowering than standard care.
2   Staff engaging in this work have generally found their experience to be professionally and personally rewarding.
3   Meeting dialogically has seamlessly integrated with other practices, including our Certified Peer Specialist Team and our medical psychiatric practitioners – with little or no conflict between dialogic principles and practising in a psychiatric environment, due to using medications and diagnostic language in a careful and caring way.
4   This model is expensive due to the amount of training, supervision and travel time involved, as well as the use of multiple therapists; we have only been able to manage because of grant income and support from our parent company.

A painful lesson has been that, for a few young people experiencing extreme states and psychosis, in which the psychosis was so extreme and/or the behaviour so dangerous, network meetings seemed unhelpful or even counterproductive. Examples include an instance in which a young person seemed offended or otherwise put off by the process of reflection and by the inclusion of family members; in another situation, a young person engaged in repeated behaviours that seemed dangerous and unmanageable. In some instances, involuntary hospitalisations involving substantial coercion therefore occurred, such as the forced administration of antipsychotics, including long-acting, injectable ones. Confronted by outcomes such as these, we have at times questioned our own level of skill in practising OD, and wondered whether it would have made a substantial difference if we could have engaged the network much earlier in the course of their difficulties.

All in all, we conclude that the process of OD, as we have practised it, does not generally dissolve psychosis entirely, but family/network support and the experience of being heard and empowered can certainly improve psychosis. While OD is not helpful for all families, it does create conditions of connection, safety, collaboration and meaning-making that can be profoundly helpful to many young people and families dealing with psychosis. It can create conditions for improved shared decision making and informed consent concerning medications, compared with standard care. It attenuates the stigmatising and demoralising language and process of much standard psychiatric treatment and can help people to avoid getting stuck in the mental health system. It promotes recovery and self-fulfilment and strengthens and protects family connections. All of us strongly believe that, if a loved one of ours were struggling with an extreme state involving psychosis, OD is the model we'd want for our family.

References

Bergström, T., Alakare, B., Aaltonen, J., Mäki, P., Köngäs-Saviaro, P., Taskila, J.J. and Seikkula, J. (2017) The long-term use of psychiatric services within the Open Dialogue treatment system after first-episode psychosis. *Psychosis*, 9(4), p. 310–321. doi.org/10.1080/17522439.2017.1344295

Gordon, C., Gidugu, V., Rogers, E.S., DeRonck, J. and Ziedonis, D. (2016) Adapting open dialogue for early-onset psychosis into the US health care environment: A feasibility study. *Psychiatric Services*, 67(11), p. 1166–1168. doi.org/10.1176/appi. ps.201600271

23

IMPLEMENTING OPEN DIALOGUE-INFORMED PRACTICES AT THE COUNSELLING SERVICE OF ADDISON COUNTY IN VERMONT, USA

Alexander Smith
(USA)

Implementing Open Dialogue (OD) within an existing publicly funded service system is likely to be a complex undertaking, even in the best of circumstances. The system-wide crisis and closure of our state psychiatric hospital, following flooding from tropical storm Irene in 2011, allowed for a meaningful exploration of the possibility of implementing OD in three of our 10 regional community mental health centres, including our agency: Counselling Service of Addison County (CSAC), Vermont, USA. Legislation redirected funds to reduce the need for psychiatric hospitalisations by encouraging more creative responses to psychiatric crises, further encouraged by state leadership. The funding structure allowed for more flexibility than traditional billing procedures.

Antecedents

In the late 1980s and early 1990s our agency hosted Tom Andersen and his Norwegian colleagues, who led training and consultation sessions for staff, focusing on applications of their work with 'reflecting processes'. Several of those staff were still working with us as we began to consider OD, some 20 years later, including two family therapists who had continued to use reflecting processes. The rest of us, although still influenced by that training and Andersen's ideas (about dialogue, language, and conversations conducive to new understandings that lead to change), had not felt the continued use of reflecting processes to be viable, given the pressures of our funding frameworks.

Our readiness to move towards these practices was bolstered by relatively low staff turnover for a community mental health centre, including within our leadership, which helped enable a collaborative culture based on relationship and the pursuit of innovative practices that might yield better results.

How we got started

After the 2011 flood, hearing that the Howard Centre (a nearby programme under Dr Sandy Steingard's leadership) was looking to apply aspects of OD in their new crisis outreach services, we realised that we too were in a very good position to develop these practices. We therefore formed a multi-disciplinary planning team including staff from across the agency and also consulted with Advocates Inc. of Massachusetts and the Parachute Project in New York City.

Our in-house expertise with family work and reflecting processes readily allowed for pairings with facilitators newer to this way of working, such that we could start offering OD-informed family/network meetings. Referrals came from our crisis response team in situations where there was receptivity to a family/network approach, prioritising first episode and early episode psychosis presentations. Some of this work mirrored the principles of OD as a service system model, as outlined in Seikkula and Arnkil (2006). We developed a range of other dialogic network applications in existing services, including one-time or short-term consultative sessions in which we utilised reflective processes with service users receiving long-term team-based services.

At the time of writing, we have conducted dialogic network meetings with about 100 different service users and families. We estimate that about 25 of these would meet 'fidelity' criteria (see Chapter 38), in terms of how we organised our service and conducted meetings in a dialogical manner – see Chapter 8 by Alpern et al. for an example of this work.

Our current assessment of this project

Qualitative research of our project is under way. Early results and interviews with family members correspond with staff observations that:

- network meetings have been highly engaging with rich and often intense conversations;
- families valued practitioners taking time to carefully hear all perspectives on matters of concern; and
- conversations were had that would not have been possible otherwise, and these helped all reach new levels of understanding.

However, while most responses were very positive, negative comments from family members spoke of their hopes being too high for a 'fix', and uncertainty as to whether there could be further progress, other than a better understanding of their loved one's experience. Given that these were anonymous comments from a survey of families and service users in a wide range of circumstances, we don't have much context to inform our interpretations of the findings. Hopefully further project evaluation will tell us more. We recognise that when a new practice is introduced for conditions that often result in long-term severe life disruption, family members may come with high hopes.

In working with people experiencing psychosis, we think that dialogical practice helps us to better listen, understand and respond to language, meanings, emotions and actions, both in network meetings and other treatment contexts, leading to better service user engagement and more effective treatment. We are able to help families and individuals to understand psychotic experiences in their life context and no longer dismiss such experiences as 'just symptoms'.

The impact on staff

The impact on staff has been notable:

- Staff consistently describe a quality of dialogue in network meetings conducive to movement in a positive direction, often marked by surprising variations from the predicted patterns of conversation.
- Dialogical teamwork helps staff to hold a space of mutuality, collaboration and transparency, with a greater ability to keep 'fix it' pressures at bay, whether these be from external providers, family members or staff's own internalised pressures. This frees up their shared attention to the conversations at hand, supporting calmer and slower dialogues, a greater tolerance of uncertainty, and the cultivation of shared meaning and understanding.
- There is a striking contrast between the dialogical approach and standard crisis services, where explanations and responses can be very narrow and limited. The positive outcomes we have seen are often surprising for our experienced practitioners, who might otherwise anticipate poor outcomes based on their prior experience.
- Staff report a stronger emotional connection with colleagues and feeling re-energised by working in this way.

It has become evident to both our front-line OD practitioners and programme developers that it is critical to be closely allied with others doing this work at different levels:

- Network meetings need to be co-facilitated by at least two staff members.
- Staff members need to be supported by a larger work group, through training processes and joint planning of further practice developments.

- Members of our team have benefitted greatly from regional collaborations and sharing with a broader practice community (including the northern European network).

We see a striking parallel between the need for a social/professional network in a time of crisis and our own need for a network to support our practice, especially because it is outside of the norms, assumptions and structures of existing service paradigms.

Some challenges

The following are some of the challenges we have experienced in our development of this practice:

- Longer-serving staff, with well-developed professional roles and knowledge bases, can find it particularly challenging to 'unlearn' and be more selective in their use of professional knowledge.
- Staff members less directly involved in the new practice have voiced a sense of an 'outsider dynamic', have felt put off by some of the language used, and express concern that there may be too much emphasis on this practice, given other needs at hand.
- It is a struggle to create enough time in a pressured and underfunded service system to train and practise this way, and there is a tendency to slip back into previous ways of working, with the constant pressures from existing paradigms in the surrounding system.
- There is a concern about the project's reliance on staff working overtime, as we move from the initial enthusiasm to a sustainable programme.
- The most fundamental challenge, in publicly funded service systems in the US, is the lack of service reimbursement frameworks to support two or more practitioners being in one meeting. However, if health care funding reforms lead to outcome-focused reimbursement structures and private insurers seek alternatives to costly hospitalisations, there may well be opportunities in the future.

The programme leaders are clear that this work supports values long espoused. OD has led to new ways of being more truly collaborative, person-centred and empowering of our service users, with a strengths-based focus and an emphasis on connectedness and relationship. Considering staff dynamics, we have always believed that we have a collaborative organisational culture, but we now see more diverse perspectives expressed within staff discussions. Furthermore, in using this approach, the adverse impact of external system pressures and requirements often become more transparent to all involved, such as pathologising diagnoses and definitions as well as unhelpful defensive processes related to professional liability.

Considerations regarding implementation

Engaged and motivated practitioners are essential if dialogical practices are to be implemented effectively. In contrast to the ways that highly manualised evidence-based practices are often mandated by programme and regional administrators, we recommend collaborative practice development, with latitude to make adaptations to the specific practice context.

Dialogical approaches can clearly energise practitioners, reconnecting them with, and more fully developing, values that originally brought them to this work, creating a virtuous circle, reinforcing and being reinforced by the values of the organisation in which they work. We find that these approaches align very well with other emerging practices and paradigm shifts in the field, such as the hearing voices movement, Intentional Peer Support, and other approaches that emphasise personal meaning making, relational connectedness, and normalising language for describing the range of human experience.

At times, OD and related practices are associated with wholesale criticism of existing service frameworks. However, our experience has been that the OD related practices we are developing in our setting offer a collaborative meta-framework for planning that is more likely to help strengthen engagement with those services than to conflict with existing treatment approaches, so long as the service system itself is flexible and open to change.

Reference

Seikkula, J. and Arnkil, T. (2006) *Dialogical meetings in social networks.* London: Karnac.

24

MIGRANT FAMILIES

Experiences using the Open Dialogue approach

Maria Sundvall and Margit Wallsten
(Sweden)

As clinicians who used to work in an outpatient, first episode psychosis team in a multicultural town in Sweden, we experienced the need to move flexibly between different domains of understanding, such as the domains of the psychiatrist, the social worker, the parents and the manager of the workplace. Introducing the Open Dialogue (OD) approach into a traditional psychiatric culture was challenging, but often proved to be very helpful. Working with migrant families meant further challenges, as we attempted to facilitate a process in which they could start to voice previously unexpressed perspectives on their experiences of migration and aspects of their culture.

When the first episode team in our mental health service was introduced in 1997, its practice was inspired by both the Swedish Parachute project for first episode psychosis (Cullberg et al., 2002) and by the OD approach. In evaluating the first few years of our work, the positive reactions of the families involved, irrespective of background, were striking. They appreciated the fact that their relative received help early, and that the staff gave time, offered continuity, and were caring of the family members (Götmark et al., 2003).

We later followed this evaluation up with a series of informal interviews with migrant families. To explore their experience of the way we engaged with them, we used part of a Swedish cultural formulation interview (Bäärnhielm et al., 2009). The cultural formulation approach was later developed into a cultural formulation interview in the fifth edition of the Diagnostic and Statistical Manual (DSM-5), and is recommended as a way of exploring a service user's subjective position as well as cultural variations in perceptions of illness, help-seeking behaviour and expectations of care. The interview's purpose is to enhance service user–clinician communication in order to inform diagnosis and treatment planning (American Psychiatric Association, 2013). We found the questions relevant and useful in an OD context, reflecting our desire to explore the migrants' perspectives, and they helped to stimulate dialogue within the family.

All the service users had a diagnosis of psychosis and the families had backgrounds in South America, Africa or the Middle East. Initially, the families told us that they had been bewildered by the experience of psychosis; several had never heard of this kind of problem prior to their contact with services and were without words in their own language to describe their experience.

At first the families had been sceptical about seeking help from psychiatry and, in some cases, there was conflict within the family about this. Some had previously sought help from traditional healers in their country of origin and some feared that letting persons outside the family know about their difficulties might have stigmatising social consequences. Families often chose not to use an interpreter, not trusting the interpreter's capacity to maintain confidentiality. Some people even preferred talking in Swedish. Family members shared experiences of discrimination in health care, for instance not receiving the same care as Swedish-born persons, or a fear of this happening.

Home visits seemed to be crucial to building up trust, to creating a safe context for dialogue. Often family members were able to share symptoms and traumas with each other for the first time, such that it gradually became possible to understand more about the psychiatric problems that they were experiencing, and to see how these had emerged from traumatic life experiences, often related to extreme vulnerability and stress at different stages in the migration process.

The families expressed their appreciation of the contact with our team and saw us as a bridge to the sometimes incomprehensible society outside. Our own experience was that, in keeping with OD principles, having a 'not knowing' and reflecting position helped us to be respectful and to let all voices be heard. In situations where the patriarchal structure of the family was strong, there was often an expectation for a more authoritarian intervention, and it was especially helpful in these circumstances to be very attentive to every person's needs. This was particularly evident in instances of generational conflict around following one's own path in life as opposed to family traditions. Together with the family, we negotiated a way of allowing all voices to be heard, hoping to facilitate a dialogue in the long run. In some instances this involved meeting family members separately for a period of time.

Given issues related to stigma with these families, and the lack of words in everyday language to describe their experiences, the OD approach became a way of creating new, joint language. By investing time, being flexible and taking an active interest in their everyday realities, the families started to trust us, such that we could be in dialogue.

References

American Psychiatric Association (2013) *Diagnostic and statistical manual of mental disorders: DSM-5* (5th ed.). Arlington, VA: American Psychiatric Association.

Bäärnhielm, S., Scarpinato Rosso, M. and Pattyi, L. (2009) *Kultur, kontext och psykiatrisk diagnostik. Manual för intervju enligt kulturformuleringen i DSM-IV [Culture, context and psychiatric diagnostics. Manual for interviewing according to the cultural formulation in the DSM-IV]*. Stockholm: Transcultural Centre, Stockholm county council. doi.org/10.1521/psyc.2014.77.2.130

Cullberg, J., Levander, S., Holmqvist, R., Mattsson, M. and Wieselgren, I.M. (2002) One-year outcome in first episode psychosis patients in the Swedish Parachute project. *Acta Psychiatrica Scandinavica*, 106(4), p. 276–285. doi.org/10.1034/j.1600-0447.2002.02376.x

Götmark, H., Olsson, M., Öhlund, L., Askerstam, M. and Henriksson, M. (2003) *Utvärdering av ett behandlingsprogram för nyinsjuknade psykospatienter 'NIP-projektet' i Södertälje psykiatriska sektor*. FoU-rapport *[Evaluation of a treatment program for first episode psychotic patients – the 'NIP project' in the Södertälje mental health services. Report for the section of Research and Development]*. Stockholm: Stockholm County Council.

25

PEER WORKERS IN OPEN DIALOGUE

Leslie Nelson, Helene Brändli and Edward Altwies
(USA and Switzerland)

Editors' introduction

One of the developments in Open Dialogue (OD) practice, as it has spread internationally, has been the inclusion of peer workers in network meetings, perhaps beginning in Germany, as a result of the foundation trainings organised by Volkmar Aderhold and others. Peer workers also featured strongly in the Parachute Project in New York City, where trainings in OD were offered to both peers and clinicians, alongside Intentional Peer Support (IPS) trainings. The peer worker role has now been developed/extended in various ways in several other locations, including Western Lapland (as the work there is influenced by developments overseas). In some settings, peer workers are involved in co-facilitating network meetings. In others they take a different role in such meetings. In Advocates in the USA, for instance (see Chapter 22), peer specialists decided that they didn't want to be part of the facilitating team in network meetings, but rather wanted to participate in meetings purely in their role as a peer specialist (if the person at the centre of concern would like this), in order to preserve the integrity of the peer specialist role and not conflate this with a clinical role.

The inclusion of peer workers in OD services can raise questions such as:

- In which ways can peer workers be involved in network meetings and can services develop different options for this?
- What might the advantages and disadvantages be, in any given situation, of a peer worker sharing the responsibility for co-facilitation of a network meeting as opposed to taking up a different position/role in the meeting?
- One of the contributions that peer workers can make in network meetings is to share aspects of their lived experience and their journey of recovery. But when and in what ways is self-disclosure helpful, and how, through training programmes and other means, can peer workers develop their capacity to use their experience skilfully? This is also a question for OD

practitioners generally, who may have different views about the value of self-disclosure in facilitating network meetings.

• An OD service is need-adapted and therefore needs to provide a range of therapeutic options. In such a service, what are the ways in which peer workers could engage in work with network members outside of network meetings, in addition to attending network meetings as either a member of the professional team or a co-facilitator?

The contributions that follow indicate that there is a lot of potential in including peer workers in an OD service, though there are likely to be challenges in the attempt to do so. In order to include different voices in this chapter, we asked three people who have worked in peer-inclusive OD services to respond to four questions about the peer work in these services. Leslie Nelson worked as a peer worker in the Parachute Project and now works in an OD-informed service in Vermont. Helene Brändli has worked as a peer worker in various psychiatric services in Switzerland. Edward Altwies worked in the Parachute Project as a psychologist.

In what way(s) have you been able to include peer workers in your Open Dialogue service?

Edward Altwies

In the Parachute Project the trainers set the expectation for peer workers, organising training such that they could co-facilitate network meetings. On the ground, however, the peer workers' role varied significantly across the mobile crisis teams in the three boroughs developing the approach – from not participating in network meetings (doing individual peer work only) to fully co-facilitating meetings with a clinician and in some instances, later in the project, to peer workers jointly co-facilitating meetings. A primary reason for this variance was team managers and clinicians having differing levels of comfort, especially at the beginning of the project, about a more egalitarian practice. Overall, however, the trend as the project developed was towards more peer workers co-facilitating network meetings.

Leslie Nelson

At the Howard Centre where I currently work, peer workers co-facilitate network meetings, and in doing so share equal responsibility with other mental health professionals. However, some aspects of the work are fulfilled by specific professionals. Psychiatrists, for example, are called upon to fulfil certain functions that require them to be able to exert power over persons who are either gravely disabled or who pose serious risks to self or others. In my experience, it is helpful to talk about roles and responsibilities before beginning work together.

Helene Brändli

In our services peer workers can co-facilitate network meetings with clinicians, though it's also the case that sometimes two clinicians co-facilitate due to the limited availability of peer workers. At other times two peer workers may co-facilitate meetings, as all peer workers in our service have several years of work experience and have participated in an OD foundation training. Most clinicians are supportive of peer workers co-facilitating meetings, but some are still reluctant for them to do so.

What do you think peer workers add to your Open Dialogue service?

Leslie Nelson

Initially when we meet a network for the first time, I am another mental health professional sitting in the room. But something happens when the network hears me share that I too have had such experiences. After a pause, I offer my qualifications as a 'peer'. Maybe this is the first time they have met someone who has had similar experiences and who is now working as a provider. I demonstrate that there is life after psychiatric crisis, including after psychosis. This sense of hope and possibility can be powerful. As peer workers we actively change the narrative on mental illness, and perhaps especially psychosis, when we talk about strength, determination and resiliency, with expert authority. In addition, having peer workers directly involved in the work emphasises to our service users and their networks that we value and respect individuals with psychiatric histories.

As a peer worker my way of being is not limited by the boundaries that exist for licensed clinical professionals. Greater limitations and expectations are put on clinicians, both by the (legal) systems in place and by families – as peers we have more freedom to be ourselves. The family/network does not expect us to have the answer or be the expert, and with the weight of expectation lifted, I have more freedom to be bold, authentic and rough around the edges.

Helene Brändli

Because of their lived experience, peer workers can trust that the solutions are in the network – I know from my journey that it was the work I did for myself that was most significant, so I am sceptical that solutions that come from outside the network will be helpful. My experience helps me not to fall into the trap of trying to help from the outside. Instead, I try to stay open, with a searching/questioning attitude – for I know that this is life-long work.

I wonder whether it may be easier for peer workers than clinicians to embody the open and searching attitude of OD, even after both groups have participated in an OD training, as they have been less socialised in classical psychiatry. It seems to me that this applies to service users as well – the longer they have been socialised in the system, the harder it is for them to engage in an OD process. Peer workers may also find it easier to build bridges, to understand what a person in crisis or a family member is talking about.

Sometimes I let the network know in a meeting that I am a peer worker with lived experience. But even when I haven't shared this information (but instead have just mentioned my role without any explanation), network members have told me after meetings that they felt my presence was different from what they are used to. Sometimes I may also share something particular about my lived experience – my suffering and difficulties dealing with crises – in the flow of the dialogue. In one network meeting a father said that it was helpful to hear about my experience – because he was not emotionally related to me, it was easier for him to listen.

Edward Altwies

When peer workers and clinicians collaborate well together in front of the service user and their network, this can significantly increase the degree of trust between all involved, heightening a sense of the possibility of the service user recovering.

In the Parachute Project, clinicians came to value peer workers sharing their own experiences of altered states and of conventional treatment – the ways in which this helped to forge connections with and validate/clarify the experiences of service users and network members, especially in meetings when the peer worker spoke openly about their experience of psychosis. For example, I recall a meeting in which a mother, when her son mentioned hearing voices, sternly stated, "You don't hear voices…you are never to speak like this again". In a subsequent meeting, when the son's sister mentioned, in passing, that the family gave her brother a limited amount of money because he had previously "given it away in the streets", the peer worker spontaneously and light-heartedly shared her own experience of giving away her phone and cash to people in the streets, having been instructed by voices to do so, in order "to save the world". Later in the meeting, the mother listened intently, without interrupting, when her son spoke in detail about the voices he heard the night he gave away the money. The peer worker's intervention appeared to be a turning point for this particular network. The mother later shared that she had been too scared to acknowledge her son's voices, before learning that the voice-hearing peer worker was doing "OK".

One welcome development in Parachute was clinicians beginning to acknowledge and share their own personal mental health issues and history with one another. In my opinion, this was due to the emphasis on equality in dialogic practice as well as the peer worker practice of sharing one's story. Another change was a gradual reduction in the use of pathologising language and an increase in the use of the words of network members, as a result of specific training exercises and a general emphasis on language in the trainings/approach, which I think contributed to peer workers vocalising issues related to this.

What challenges/obstacles have you encountered as the peer worker role has been developed in your service?

Leslie Nelson

Peer workers may not be supported to become integrated into a team and may be supervised by clinicians who have little understanding, knowledge or experience of working in the role they are supervising. Peer workers are hired to be experts by experience but may receive the message that their experience isn't expert or professional: a frustrating situation at best. Alternatively, services may not be well informed about the peer worker role and may inadvertently encourage peer workers to become more like clinicians. It is freeing not to share the clinical responsibility, but it can be tough when there are differences of opinion and peer workers have to follow the clinician's decision, because of their clinical responsibility.

Edward Altwies

We experienced a reluctance on the part of some leaders and team members to embrace the OD approach generally, but more specifically the inclusion of peer workers. From my observations, the latter was in part due to scepticism about the competence of peer workers and partly because many clinicians maintained their crisis assessment-oriented perspective, fearing scrutiny from a traditional risk-management perspective if an incident occurred. All this was especially difficult in mobile crisis teams developing the OD approach, as peer worker roles were not yet established in these services, meaning that most clinicians were unfamiliar with peer workers. The multiple simultaneous changes overwhelmed some team members.

Helene Brändli

Occasionally I feel somewhat confused in my role. As a facilitator of network meetings, I need to be omnipartial (i.e. partial to everyone) but, as an advocate for the service user (a role I am often asked to fulfil), I can find it difficult to ensure that every voice is heard equally and openly in network meetings. The voice of service users has been overlooked too often, and the quest for meaning can be taken over by professionals, which increases the risk of my dropping the role of facilitator in order to take the side of the service user.

What advice would you give to people who would like to develop the peer worker role in their Open Dialogue service?

Leslie Nelson

There is a literature about what agencies should do before considering introducing peer work and this should be utilised in any new development (e.g. Legere, n.d.). It's not enough to have slots for peer workers on trainings – you need to also plan a service carefully, such that the peer worker role is clearly defined and peer workers have enough support. After training, peer workers need ongoing support in their role. Many are coming into a work environment for the first time in a long while, and a psychotic crisis can really shake your confidence in your abilities. Also, if we believe that peer workers are of value in services, we must provide them with opportunities to continue to define/refine their role. In future projects it will be important to develop positions of leadership for peer workers, so that they can share responsibility with clinicians for decisions about service provision and development.

Edward Altwies

Having consulted with Chris Hansen, lead Intentional Peer Support (IPS) trainer at the Parachute Project, we would like to make several recommendations:

- For long-term success, the values of the host organisation should align with both OD and IPS values.
- Job descriptions for peer workers should make explicit key aspects of these two approaches and selection should be based on suitability for the approaches.
- Part-time employment options should be offered to enable more qualified peer workers to work in services.
- OD trainings should, like IPS trainings, foster more awareness of the traumatising and marginalising aspects of using/surviving conventional psychiatric services.
- Peer workers should carry the emotional load and responsibility equally with clinicians, in order to meet OD/IPS standards of care, and should therefore receive equal pay to their social worker colleagues. Such a policy is likely to have a positive impact on the recruitment of qualified peer workers, long-term team collaboration, and the quality of care.

Helene Brändli

It is very important that clinicians familiarise themselves with the concepts of recovery and empowerment, and with the peer worker role. It should not be the case that peer workers alone have to adapt in order to enable co-working. I think it is necessary for peer workers to follow an educational programme in peer support, such as EX-IN (Experienced Involvement), as well as an OD training programme, and it's also important for them to gain sufficient work experience with some form of supervision. In this way peer workers are no different from other OD practitioners who have to follow their original professional training and then an OD training with supervision. They should therefore be seen as equal members of an OD team, with the same rights, tasks and obligations.

Reference

Legere, L. (n.d.) *The provider's handbook – on developing & implementing peer roles.* [online] Available at: www.psresources.info/images/stories/A_Providers_Handbook_ on_Developing__Implementing_Peer_Roles.pdf [Accessed 10 March 2020].

26

THE CHALLENGE OF DEVELOPING OPEN DIALOGUE IN HOSPITAL SETTINGS

Werner Schütze
(Germany)

In writing something about the possibilities of developing the Open Dialogue (OD) approach in hospital settings, I did not find anything substantial or helpful in the existing English literature. However, a Norwegian group have since published a study on the subject of 'Open Dialogue behind locked doors' (Jacobsen et al., 2018) and give an account of their work in Chapter 27. Nevertheless, hospital settings still seem to be 'unexplored territory' within the development of OD, perhaps because OD was developed to reduce the need for hospital treatment. As far as I know, whilst there have been attempts to develop OD in a few hospitals, similar to the work described by Jacobsen et al., only Keropudas Hospital in Western Lapland makes comprehensive use of dialogical and reflective practice.

The development of OD in the context of a psychiatric hospital sometimes feels like a clash of cultures to me. How can a traditionally very hierarchical organisation, supported by legal demands and following its own rules of dealing with psychosis, meet a culture of not knowing, open-endedness, dialogue and shared expertise? How could these ever go together? Well, it will be of no surprise to the reader to learn that it is difficult, and maybe even very difficult.

Nevertheless, in recent years more inpatient staff have become interested in OD, resulting in some training being introduced in Germany and Poland. I will refer to developments in three different hospitals. In two of them I was active in implementing OD structures as the head of a psychiatric department (in the second I was also an OD trainer), and in the third I was an observer for many years. I will describe the developments in these three places and summarise my reflections on the processes involved.

Hospital 1

This was a small department of psychiatry located in a general hospital, with 60 beds, two day-care units, and an outpatient unit. The process of change started in 2007 in a top-down manner, as it was led by myself, as head of the psychiatric department. Initially a series of conversations took place with people who I thought would have to be involved in the change process – both staff inside the hospital, including the CEO, and psychiatric workers outside in the community. Fortunately, a budget was available to engage a trainer to run a three-year in-house training for a third of the staff, including colleagues from other local services who were working in cooperation with the hospital. The training consisted of five two-day workshops per year, and staff members in leading positions were consistently included. This relatively small department already had a tradition of shared decision making and rather flattened hierarchies, enabling the development of a dialogical educational process in staff meetings.

After the first year of training, participants who had been actively involved in the implementation of the approach asked me whether they could introduce further aspects of what they had learnt into their work routines. This was an important step, as now a bottom-up movement began, as staff started to articulate their own wishes. The staff wanted to initiate the use of reflecting teams and did so on one of the wards. Soon the practice spread to the other units, in spite of the sceptics and critics of this new approach.

One year later another step was taken, when some staff wanted to start offering home treatment. As a result of this growing interest in practice, with backing from myself, some of the most experienced staff members involved in the training organised teams in order to gain initial experiences of facilitating network meetings with service users and families in crisis, including home treatment. They started with people suffering from first episode psychosis. They collected data, had regular supervision, and published two papers about their experiences (Schütze, 2015; Schütze et al., 2010).

Another important step was the introduction of 'treatment conferences', which developed out of the use of reflecting teams, in which the service user could participate along with staff members who held significant relationships with them in the treatment process. These staff members worked more dialogically, using reflective processes in such meetings. Later these conferences developed into in-house network meetings, to which members of the service user's social network were also invited.

Parallel to this, organisational negotiations took place with insurance companies to implement a new model of funding, called a regional budget. This further supported OD developments, as hospitals had more control over how they spent the money allocated to them. However, in 2012, even though the model seemed to be successful, some insurance companies suddenly favoured another model of financing and so OD development had to be stopped.

What did I learn from these developments?

- When implementing an approach like OD it is important to be aware of the size of the department as a lot of time is needed for communicating/ networking to find new ways of working together.

- A 'top-down' movement has to be supported by a 'bottom-up' movement, as the new approach has to be established/supported by those working on the ground.
- The implementation of OD can only proceed step-by-step.
- Home treatment in acute crises is a domain for experienced staff.
- There can be major obstacles that inhibit further development, e.g. financing structures.

Hospital 2

The second example comes from a somewhat bigger department, with 80 inpatient beds, two day-care units and one outpatient unit, where a regional budget had been in use since 2006. In 2008 staff participated in an OD foundation training and, due to the engagement of one of the senior psychiatrists in this training, they were able to establish treatment conferences in the hospital, as described above for Hospital 1.

Nothing else specific was added or developed in the staff team's practice, until they met again for 'refresher' training days in 2015, with the intention of establishing a home treatment team. In the following years they organised another training course, in order to get more staff involved in this way of working, and invited members of organisations who were cooperating with the hospital to participate as well. The home treatment team was founded and consisted of three to four members (a nurse, social worker and two psychiatrists), who were sometimes also able to work in the hospital. This team continues to work together, benefitting from the regional budget and a change in the financial system in Germany, which enables home treatment as a substitute for inpatient treatment.

What did I learn from these developments?

- Leaders should be actively involved in the process of change, otherwise it takes much longer to develop OD structures.
- It takes engaged leaders/representatives/deputies/senior psychiatrists to keep the flame burning through the years, when other organisational needs have to be addressed.
- OD practices have to be adapted to institutional needs and routines (i.e. some compromises are necessary).
- It can be difficult for inpatient staff to work in a home treatment team, having been socialised into a very different way of working on hospital wards.
- New or rotating staff members have to be included in trainings and practice on a regular basis.

Hospital 3

This is one of the biggest psychiatric departments within a general hospital in Germany, with more than 170 inpatient beds, three day-care units and a large outpatient unit. A senior psychiatrist, responsible for an acute ward, the crisis intervention unit and the outpatient unit, wanted a change – from mainly inpatient treatment, which was largely custodial in nature, to a more dialogical approach. In 2011 it was agreed to start an initial training course for about 40 staff members, lasting 18 months. This first training included the head of the department and other leading or senior psychiatrists, as well as members of all professions. In two of the six wards they soon started to introduce treatment conferences and, as a second step, network meetings. However, some OD principles had to be compromised in order to fit with the rules and organisational principles of the institution – tolerance of uncertainty was difficult with the need for a knowing position, embracing polyphony was challenging in the hierarchical structure, and shift work meant that psychological continuity was not always possible. All three day-care units also managed to integrate treatment conferences and network meetings into their weekly routines. Benefitting from a special contract with an insurance company, some staff founded a home treatment team, whose members are mainly OD trained.

What did I learn from this observation?

- The larger an organisation, the greater the forces preventing change, and this needs to be acknowledged and addressed in the course of development.
- The regular turnover of staff members makes it necessary to create structures in which new members can learn on the job, in addition to more in-depth trainings.
- You cannot convince every staff member, and so specific solutions have to be found for those who remain sceptical.
- Even if it is only possible to introduce some aspects of OD, it is still worth it.

Summary

Implementing OD in a hospital setting, outside of Western Lapland, is still a new endeavour. You learn to be patient and humble as you encounter the complexity and conflicts within each institution. Small changes, such as the introduction of reflecting processes, can be a big step. Development can be like a patchwork in the institution, that hopefully becomes tied together over the course of many years. The more restrictive the practice is on a ward, e.g.

the use of forced treatment modalities, the more difficult it will be to bring in changes.

One aim of introducing OD into a hospital should be the reduction of inpatient treatment and bed numbers. In working toward this goal, staff face new challenges, but these can be personally rewarding, e.g. the opportunity to meet service users on a more equal level. Trainers need to be aware that work in a psychiatric hospital is hard and sometimes frustrating. We should be careful that, in adapting our teaching to this situation, we do not make it even harder for staff members by pointing at all the differences from treatment as usual, but rather support them to reflect on their existing practices and develop these in a more dialogical direction.

References

Jacobsen, R.K., Sørgård, J., Karlsson, B.E., Seikkula, J. and Kim, H.S. (2018) 'Open Dialogue behind locked doors' – exploring patients', family members', and professionals' experiences with network meetings in a locked psychiatric hospital unit: A qualitative study. *Scandinavian Psychologist*, 5, e5. doi.org/10.15714/scandpsychol.5.e5

Schütze, W., Karwinkel, U. and Aderhold, V. (2010) Am Beispiel Nauen. Bedürfnisangepasste Behandlung nach finnischem Modell [Using the example of Nauen. Need-adapted treatment according to the Finnish model]. *Kerbe*, 3, p. 11–15.

Schütze, W. (2015) Open Dialogue as a contribution to a healthy society: Possibilities and limitations. *Postępy Psychiatrii i Neurologii*, 24(2), p. 86–90. doi.org/10.1016/j.pin.2015.05.002

27

OPEN DIALOGUE BEHIND 'CLOSED DOORS' (A LOCKED WARD)

Bengt Karlsson, Ritva Jacobsen and Jorunn Sørgård
(Norway)

Both national and international political guidelines emphasise the need to develop mental health strategies that consider service users' perspectives (Puras, 2017). Dialogical practices are one way of addressing this, not only because of the procedures involved, such as network meetings and the use of reflecting teams and processes, but also due to the attitudes towards service users in dialogical approaches, which emphasise recovery, user involvement, shared decision making and the acknowledgement of the person's own lived experiences. Over the last 20 years in Norway, there has been an increase in the development and implementation of practices related to and inspired by Open Dialogue (OD). However, so far it hasn't been possible to initiate a comprehensive reorganisation of the Norwegian mental health care system along the lines of the service in Western Lapland.

Our project 'Open Dialogue behind closed doors' is nevertheless based on, and inspired by, the OD approach – especially the way network meetings are organised, in which a dialogical attitude develops within and among the participants. The project was established in our inpatient unit in 2010 and is ongoing. It was initiated by the director of the unit together with a group of senior staff members who had been trained as facilitators of network meetings. From the beginning other senior and junior staff members have participated in the same training programme. The aim is to organise network meetings and further the possibilities for dialogue, but not to change the overall psychiatric system.

Our context is a locked psychiatric hospital ward where people are often brought against their will. They are diagnosed as having a severe mental illness, some with a combination of substance misuse and risk of violent behaviour. Therefore, the unit has a considerable focus on structure and security. There is a clear hierarchical structure in the organisation of the professional team, in the following order: psychiatrists, psychologists, nurses and social workers.

Within this context, service users invite their family members and other important persons to network meetings that mostly take place in the unit. The project aims to develop dialogical practices, such as reflecting teams and processes, alongside conventional psychiatric discourses, both in the ward generally and in the network meetings especially. A tension remains, however, between coercion and service user involvement in these dialogical practices.

In 2017, we evaluated the project by interviewing the professionals on the ward who participated in network meetings. We also used focus group interviews and written narrative evaluations from the service users and family members. Data were analysed using systematic text condensation (Braun and Clarke, 2006). The findings show that the use of OD in a locked psychiatric ward can be of significance for professionals, service users and their social network, and can be summarised as follows:

- Our study indicates that it is possible to practise OD in network meetings behind closed doors.
- Our approach helped to develop service users', relatives' and professionals' confidence in the power of dialogues, as well as their courage to be open in collaborative therapeutic activities and conversations.
- Professionals, service users and family members participating in network meetings highlighted various positive developments, including the experience of sharing, having sufficient time to address a number of topics in enough depth, a focus on hope and new opportunities, and possibilities for continuing the dialogue.
- Service users and family members felt seen and heard, and welcomed the collaborative nature of the work. They described having a more active role in the process and decision making, including decisions about who would participate in meetings, where the meetings would take place after discharge from hospital, and what the focus of meetings would be.

We have published an article in English that elaborates further on our dialogical work (Jacobsen et al., 2018). Our hope is that others can be inspired by this work and create spaces and possibilities for OD in network meetings, regardless of the context.

References

Braun, V. and Clarke, V. (2006) Using thematic analysis in psychology. *Qualitative Research in Psychology*, 3(2), p. 77–101. doi.org/10.1191/1478088706qp063a

Jacobsen, R.K., Sørgård, J., Karlsson, B.E., Seikkula, J. and Kim, H.S. (2018) 'Open Dialogue behind locked doors' – exploring patients', family members', and professionals' experiences with network meetings in a locked psychiatric hospital unit: A qualitative study. *Scandinavian Psychologist*, 5, e5. doi:10.15714/scandpsychol.5.e5

Puras, D. (2017) *Report of the Special Rapporteur on the right of everyone to the enjoyment of the highest attainable standard of physical and mental health.* [online] Available at: https://digitallibrary.un.org/record/1637420?ln=en

Section 5

OPENING THE DIALOGUE
WITH OTHER APPROACHES

CONTENTS

EDITORS' INTRODUCTION

In this section authors explore the similarities and differences between Open Dialogue (OD) and other therapeutic approaches to people having psychotic experiences and highlight possibilities for integrating some aspects of these approaches into an OD service or introducing network meetings into existing services.

Steingard (Chapter 38) contrasts the OD service in Western Lapland with psychiatric services which are based largely on a biomedical model of psychosis. In the latter there is a less selective use of neuroleptics and greater emphasis on diagnosis. She argues that elements of the OD approach could be consistent with a more biomedical model and points out that increasing numbers of psychiatrists are questioning at least some aspects of current diagnostic systems. She identifies a number of reasons why psychiatrists could benefit from working in an OD service.

In Chapter 31 Granö and colleagues further develop this theme in their description of the use of network meetings and OD principles in their psychiatric service in Helsinki (the Early Psychosis Centre of the Department of Psychiatry within Helsinki University). There appears to be a stronger focus on diagnosis and symptoms in this service, as well as on cognitive functioning, and yet there are also parallels to the service in Western Lapland.

Other contributions to this section focus on a specific therapeutic modality. In considering systemic therapy, Burbach (Chapter 29) argues that OD network meetings can be seen to be a form of systemic therapy. He sees parallels between contemporary systemic therapy and OD, with both having a focus on resources rather than pathology and with shared aspects to their practice, such as a team reflecting in the presence of the family. In his second contribution Burbach (Chapter 30) outlines Cognitive Behaviour Therapy (CBT), focusing on psychosis. He argues that CBT has evolved from its more technique-based origins to a more relational approach which includes acceptance and mindfulness, and that individual CBT for psychosis could be a useful option within an OD service. Similarly, Martindale (Chapter 33) advocates that psychoanalytic psychotherapy may also be a useful option, subsequent to the initial crisis in which network meetings may well be the most useful approach. Martindale reminds us of the significance of psychoanalytic theory in Need-Adapted Treatment and in some of the OD developments in Western Lapland. He likens some aspects of psychoanalysis to OD practice, such as the concept of free association, and argues that a fuller understanding of unconscious defences would add to the skill of an OD practitioner in furthering the understanding of the meaningfulness of psychotic phenomena.

In Chapter 32 Sempere and Fuenzalida introduce Interfamily Therapy (IFT), which has drawn on the OD approach. By working with multiple families together, they claim that IFT can be seen as a fuller embodiment of social constructionist practice, extending the polyphony further, in a 'mini-society'. The concept of polyphony is also central in Chapter 35, in which Eugster highlights its significance (along with dialogue) in both music therapy and OD. He draws a parallel between the collapse in musical dialogue, often found in music therapy with people having psychotic experiences and Jaakko Seikkula's description of the stuckness of networks at a time of a psychotic crisis, and explores the potential for working with families, drawing on both OD and music therapy practices. In Chapter 34, Putman contrasts OD with Therapeutic Communities (TCs), drawing in particular on Rapoport's four core principles of democratisation, permissiveness, reality confrontation and communalism. An intriguing prospect is the provision of TCs within an OD service, as an alternative to hospital.

OD is by nature an inclusive approach, and in a need-adapted service there is value in having available a range of approaches to people experiencing psychosis and their families/networks. The extent to which approaches which have a (very) different theoretical basis can exist within an OD service remains to be seen. However, one crucial factor must surely be the willingness of practitioners in such a service to be in dialogue, to explore and develop a fuller understanding of the similarities and differences between their therapeutic approaches, and to further their understanding of when a specific form may be well suited to a particular service user and their family. We hope that this section is a valuable contribution to the dialogue between those practising in different ways.

28

WORKING WITH OPEN DIALOGUE WITHIN THE NEUROBIOLOGICAL MODEL – CHALLENGES AND OPPORTUNITIES

Sandra Steingard
(USA)

Introduction

Since the concept of dementia praecox, subsequently called schizophrenia, was introduced to psychiatry, many have assumed that an underlying pathophysiology would be identified. While this remains an unrealised goal, many psychiatrists consider schizophrenia to be a neurodevelopmental disorder for which antipsychotic drugs are essential to effective treatment, with a host of psychosocial interventions deemed important adjuncts to good care as recommended by the National Institute for Mental Health (NIMH, 2019). This chapter is written especially, but not exclusively, from a USA perspective, where a neurobiological model is dominant, and aims to address the challenges and opportunities when working with the Open Dialogue (OD) paradigm in such a setting.

Conceptualisation of schizophrenia

The contemporary neurodevelopmental view of schizophrenia is often traced back to Kraepelin's era. General paralysis of the insane was found to be caused by syphilitic infection and Alzheimer's dementia was found to be associated with specific pathologic brain changes. Kraepelin thought that what he called 'dementia praecox' would also be found to be due to brain pathology, and even though subsequent researchers failed to identify specific tissue pathologies, his notion that schizophrenia is a chronic condition became codified with modern diagnostic conceptualisations, particularly since the publication by the American Psychiatric Association of Edition III of the Diagnostic and Statistical Manual (APA, 1980). However, alternative hypotheses regarding mental states characterised as psychotic existed both before and contemporaneously with Kraepelin. This includes the ideas of Charcot and Janet,

197

who posited that these altered mental states are dissociative in nature, related to traumatic experience, and could be relieved with psychotherapeutic approaches (Moskowitz et al., 2019). Furthermore, the Kraepelinian model of schizophrenia as having an inevitably bleak course has been challenged for decades (Harding, 1988).

The neurodevelopmental model

Within the biological frame, a neurodevelopmental model of schizophrenia developed and has come to dominate in many countries in recent decades (Owen et al., 2011). This posits that a genetic vulnerability interacts with some sort of environmental trauma, resulting in impaired brain development (Rapoport et al., 2012). The trauma typically referenced is intra-uterine, although nutritional deficiencies and traumatic birth have also been proposed. The areas of the brain thought to be affected by this genetic/environmental interaction are frontal lobe circuits (Weinberger, 1988), which are important in many areas of complex cognition and abstract thought. The so-called negative symptoms of schizophrenia, such as apathy and impaired social functioning, are also observed in individuals who have experienced damage to their frontal lobes. These brain regions do not fully mature until late adolescence, which might explain why psychosis often manifests for the first time around this age. The so-called positive symptoms of schizophrenia – hallucinations and delusions – are thought to emanate from impaired connectivity between the frontal lobe and other brain regions (Boksa, 2009).

A complimentary hypothesis is the stress-diathesis model, which acknowledges that social experiences can contribute to the onset of psychosis. This concept is accepted by some who adopt the more neurobiological model of psychosis, but it is more complementary to OD, because it allows for a broader consideration of the triggers that may contribute to the development of psychosis, including traumatic life events (Jones and Fernyhough, 2007).

Role of antipsychotic drugs

Antipsychotic drugs (APDs) were first introduced to mental hospitals in the 1950s and 1960s and have become first-line treatments for most psychotic disorders. In the early 1990s, largely due to the influence of the neurodevelopmental model, the hypothesis that antipsychotic drugs forestall further clinical deterioration gained wide acceptance (Wyatt, 1991). Withdrawal of APDs led to a higher psychosis relapse rate compared to those who continued taking them, leading to consensus recommendations that APDs should be initiated as soon as possible and continued indefinitely (Goff et al., 2017). This – along with financial pressures to reduce expensive hospital care – resulted in a system, certainly in the USA, where shorter-term hospitalisation was encouraged. Here, if a person wants to try an alternative approach, there is usually little support from anyone; professionals, insurers, even ethicists typically argue that any delay in the initiation of APDs slows down the treatment process and prolongs hospitalisation.

Conflicts between Open Dialogue and the biomedical model

There are two main conflicts between OD and standard treatment guidelines. The first concerns diagnosis: in the biomedical model, formulation of a diagnosis is considered essential to treatment, whereas in OD diagnosis is not essential to care. Second, OD suggests a slower and more cautious approach to APDs; they are not started immediately and if they are used, they are not considered essential for optimal long-term recovery. Even though the OD approach may, in this respect, seem to conflict with standard guidelines, current medical knowledge is entirely consistent with a more cautious use of APDs and recently psychiatrists have raised questions about the early use of drug treatment, and even the validity of psychiatric diagnosis (Frances, 2012; Insel, 2013). Thomas Insel, then director of the US National Institute of Mental Health, wrote that the "DSM diagnoses are based on a consensus about clusters of clinical symptoms, not any objective laboratory measure" (Insel, 2013). In addition, some academic psychiatrists openly question the validity of the 'schizophrenia' diagnosis (Van Os, 2016). Thus, a model of care that does not privilege the diagnostic system is consistent with the perspective of at least some respected psychiatric researchers.

The use of antipsychotic drugs in OD is quite different from current American Psychiatric Association (APA, 2010) and British National Institute of Clinical Excellence (NICE, 2014) standard treatment guidelines, which support APDs as first-line treatment. In a Finnish study of need-adapted treatment services for people diagnosed with first-episode non-affective psychosis, six regions were studied. In three regions (of which Western Lapland was one), APD use was intentionally minimised, and 42.9% of subjects did not take neuroleptics at any point in the two-year study period. This compared with 5.9% not taking neuroleptics at any point in the other three regions where neuroleptics were used routinely as standard practice. Outcomes were generally good in both groups and slightly better in the group who had less exposure to drugs (Lehtinen et al., 2000). In subsequent studies of OD in Western Lapland most individuals were never prescribed APDs and only a small minority were taking them at five-year follow-up. And yet the reported outcomes, in particular the low level of hospitalisation and disability status and high level of study and employment, are superior to those reported in other settings where APDs were integral to care (Seikkula et al., 2006).

The suggestion to begin drugs as soon as possible arose from an influential paper (Wyatt, 1991) and was supported in a recent expert consensus review (Goff, 2017). However, the papers cited in this review did not definitely confirm that drugs were protective. One paper reported that *both* biological and psychosocial early interventions were correlated with improved outcomes (Pentilla et al., 2014). In another paper, researchers evaluated an early detection model used to identify individuals experiencing psychosis (Melle et al., 2008), which found a reduction in 'negative' symptoms in the early detection group, sustained at two-year follow-up. Those identified were offered *both* drugs and psychosocial support. However, since not everyone in the experimental group was given drugs, this study does not support the notion that early use of drugs, in and of itself, improves outcomes – it does though support the OD approach, where there is a rapid response to those experiencing psychosis.

It is usually recommended in the USA that drugs are continued indefinitely because studies have shown a higher rate of relapse among those who stop compared with those who continue to take them (Goff et al., 2017; Thompson et al., 2018). However, this recommendation can be challenged by a review of the scientific literature. For instance, Harrow et al. (2012) followed individuals for 20 years and found that those who stopped taking medications had better outcomes than those who continued, even when controlling for pre-morbid characteristics that might predict better outcomes. Furthermore, Wunderink and colleagues (2007) tracked those randomly assigned to either remain on drugs continuously or to stop using them and only resume if symptoms recurred. Reporting *two-year* outcomes, those who continued on drugs had a lower relapse rate. However, over *seven years* (Wunderink et al., 2013), those who continued on drugs had a worse functional outcome than those treated with drugs only when symptoms re-emerged. The authors also found that the relapse rate between the groups at seven years was similar; drugs appeared to delay but not prevent relapse.

Psychosis can result in an individual behaving in extreme ways which put the person affected in harm's way or cause significant disruption for the family and community. This can overwhelm a network's ability to respond and drugs can be helpful in such situations. Some individuals may find them so beneficial, or the psychosis so fearful, that they choose to continue to take them. However, the data suggest that it is at least reasonable, in many situations, to offer people a chance to address their psychotic experiences without using drugs. It also does not definitively refute an approach where drugs are used intermittently and tapered off once a person is more stable. OD provides a way to both tolerate the uncertainty that our current knowledge base would suggest is warranted and to have the difficult conversations that the topic warrants, with an exchange of ideas among everyone concerned.

Psychiatrists who retain some or even all of the medical model might nevertheless welcome aspects of OD. Those who work in services where rapid assessments lead to brief interactions with as many service users as possible within a given time frame, as often occurs in the USA, might welcome an approach where a) time is given to understand the complexity of the person they are asked to help, b) sleep problems and severe anxiety are attended to by psychological approaches and sometimes non-neuroleptic medications, and c) neuroleptics are used as needed to support or complement other interventions rather than considered essential to good care.

Acknowledgement: The author thanks Christopher Gordon MD for his assistance in reviewing an earlier version of this chapter.

References

American Psychiatric Association (1980) *Diagnostic and statistical manual of mental disorders III.* Washington, DC: American Psychiatric Association.

American Psychiatric Association (2010) *Practice guideline for the treatment of patients with schizophrenia (Second Edition).* [online] Available at: https://psychiatryonline. org/pb/assets/raw/sitewide/practice_guidelines/guidelines/schizophrenia.pdf [Accessed 10 April 2020].

Boksa, P. (2009) On the neurobiology of hallucinations. *Journal of Psychiatry and Neuroscience*, 34(4), p. 260–263.

Frances, A. (2012) Predicting psychosis risk is pretty risky. *Huffington Post.* [online] Available at: www.huffingtonpost.com/allen-frances/psychosis-risk_b_1289022. html [Accessed 10 April 2020].

Goff, D.G., Falkai, P., Fleischhacker, W.W., Girgis, R.R., Kahn, R.M., Uchida H., Zhao, J. and Lieberman, J.A. (2017) The long-term effects of antipsychotic medication on clinical course in schizophrenia. *American Journal of Psychiatry*, 174(9), p. 840–849. doi.org/10.1176/appi.ajp.2017.16091016

Harding, C.M. (1988) Course types in schizophrenia: An analysis of European and American studies. *Schizophrenia Bulletin*, 14(4), p. 633–642. doi.org/10.1093/ schbul/14.4.633

Harrow, M., Jobe, T.H. and Faull, R.N. (2012) Do all schizophrenia patients need antipsychotic treatment continuously throughout their lifetime? A 20-year longitudinal study. *Psychological Medicine*, 42(10), p. 2145–2155. doi.org/10.1017/ S0033291712000220

Insel, T. (2013) *Post by former NIMH director Thomas Insel: Transforming diagnosis.* National Institute of Mental Health. [online] Available at: www.nimh.nih.gov/ about/directors/thomas-insel/blog/2013/transforming-diagnosis.shtml [Accessed 10 April 2020].

Jones, S.R. and Fernyhough, C. (2007) A new look at the neural diathesis-stress model of schizophrenia: The primacy of social-evaluative and uncontrollable situations. *Schizophrenia Bulletin*, 33(5), p. 1171–1177. doi.org/10.1093/schbul/sbl058

Lehtinen, V., Aaltonen, J., Koffert, T., Räkköläinen, V. and Syvälahti, E. (2000) Two-year outcome in first-episode psychosis treated according to an integrated model. Is immediate neuroleptisation always needed? *European Psychiatry*, 15(5), p. 312–320. doi.org/10.1016/s0924-9338(00)00400-4

Melle, I., Larsen, T.K., Haahr, U., Friis, S., Johannesen, J.O., Opjordsmoen, S., Rund, B.R., Simonsen, E., Vaglum, P. and McGlashan, T. (2008) Prevention of negative symptom psychopathologies in first-episode schizophrenia: Two-year effects of reducing the duration of untreated psychosis. *Archives of General Psychiatry*, 65(6), p. 634–640. doi.org/10.1001/archpsyc.65.6.634

Moskowitz, A., Dorahy, M. and Schäfer, I. (eds.) (2019) *Psychosis, trauma and dissociation: Evolving perspectives on severe psychopathology* (2nd ed.). Chichester: Wiley.

National Institute for Clinical Excellence (2014) *Psychosis and schizophrenia in adults: Prevention and management.* [online] Available at: www.nice.org.uk/guidance/cg178/chapter/1-Recommendations#first-episode-psychosis-2 [Accessed 10 April 2020].

National Institute of Mental Health (2019) *Schizophrenia.* [online] Available at: www.nimh.nih.gov/health/topics/schizophrenia/index.shtml [Accessed 10 April 2020].

Owen, M.J., O'Donovan, M.C., Thapar, A. and Craddock, N. (2011) Neurodevelopmental hypothesis of schizophrenia. *British Journal of Psychiatry*, 198(3), p. 173–175. doi.org/10.1192/bjp.bp.110.084384

Pentilla, M., Jääskeläïnen, E., Hirvonen, N., Isohanni, M. and Miettunen, J. (2014) Duration of untreated psychosis as predictor of long-term outcome in schizophrenia: A systematic review and meta-analysis. *British Journal of Psychiatry*, 205(2), p. 88–94. doi.org/10.1192/bjp.bp.113.127753

Rapoport, J.L., Giedd, J.N. and Gogtay, N. (2012) Neurodevelopmental model of schizophrenia: Update 2012. *Molecular Psychiatry*, 17, p. 1228–1238. doi.org/10.1038/mp.2012.23

Seikkula, J., Aaltonen, J., Alakare, B., Haarakangas, K., Keränen, J. and Lehtinen, K. (2006) Five-year experience of first-episode nonaffective psychosis in open-dialogue approach: Treatment principles, follow-up outcomes, and two case studies. *Psychotherapy Research*, 16(2), p. 214–228. doi.org/10.1080/10503300500268490

Thompson, A., Winsper, C., Marwaha, S., Haynes, J., Alvarez-Jimenez, M., Hetrick, S., Realpe, A., Vail, L., Dawson, S. and Sullivan, S.A. (2018) Maintenance antipsychotic treatment versus discontinuation strategies following remission from first episode psychosis: Systematic review. *BJPsych Open*, 4(4), p. 215–225. doi.org/10.1192/bjo.2018.17

Van Os, J. (2016) 'Schizophrenia' does not exist. *British Medical Journal*, i375, p. 1–2. doi.org/10.1136/bmj.i375

Weinberger, D.R. (1988) Schizophrenia and the frontal lobe. *Trends in Neurosciences*, 11(8), p. 367–370. doi.org/10.1016/0166-2236(88)90060-4

Wunderink, L., Nieboer, R.M., Wiersma, D., Sytema, S. and Nienhuis, F.J. (2013) Recovery in remitted first-episode psychosis at 7 years of follow-up of an early dose reduction/discontinuation or maintenance treatment strategy: Long-term follow-up of a 2-year randomized clinical. *JAMA Psychiatry*, 70(9), p. 913–920. doi.org/10.1001/jamapsychiatry.2013.19

Wunderink, L., Nienhuis, F.J., Sytema, S., Slooff, C.J., Knegtering, R. and Wiersma, D. (2007) Guided discontinuation versus maintenance treatment in remitted first-episode psychosis: Relapse rates and functional outcome. *Journal of Clinical Psychiatry*, 68(5), p. 654–661. doi.org/10.4088/jcp.v68n0502

Wyatt, R.J. (1991) Neuroleptics and the natural course of schizophrenia. *Schizophrenia Bulletin*, 17(2), p. 325–351. doi.org/10.1093/schbul/17.2.325

29

SYSTEMIC THERAPY AND OPEN DIALOGUE

Frank Burbach
(UK)

Introduction

Chapter 2 acknowledged that systemic family therapy ideas and skills have informed the practice of Open Dialogue (OD) and, although OD is a radically different service delivery approach, one could argue that as a therapeutic approach OD is, in essence, a form of systemic therapy. Many systemic and OD practitioners have a great deal in common due to the sharing of experiences, ideas and practices, but one could also view OD and systemic therapy as having evolved in parallel in reaction to the earliest forms of systemic family therapy.

Systemic therapy is a broad church

What is sometimes confusing is that systemic therapy is a broad church (between 15 and 20 models are described in the *Handbook of Family Therapy*; Sexton and Lebow, 2015) and has gone through numerous phases of development (see e.g. Dallos and Draper, 2010). An initial concern with pattern and process (cybernetics) developed into a focus on beliefs and meanings (constructivism), followed by a focus on social and cultural contexts (social constructionism). The latter phases developed out of a critique of earlier practices such as strategic interventions and the use of a one-way screen for observation. Contemporary systemic therapy, like OD, is 'postmodern', with the therapist valuing a multiplicity of stories and avoiding taking an 'expert' position. Problems are seen as being 'created' by language and to 'dissolve' during collaborative therapeutic conversations, through the development of mutual empathy and positive affect, and from people recognising their stuck patterns.

Contemporary systemic therapy

Contemporary systemic therapy, like OD, no longer focuses on family 'pathology' but views the family and significant others in the wider system as a (potential) resource. It considers competence and solutions and aims to challenge the prevailing 'problem-saturated' discourses of 'illness', 'pathology' and 'dysfunction'. Both systemic family therapy and OD can be categorised as one of the 'resource-oriented' (strengths-based) therapeutic approaches (Priebe et al., 2014).

Are there differences between systemic therapy and Open Dialogue?

So, is there any difference between collaborative, social constructionist (post-modern) systemic therapy and OD? Though most contemporary systemic therapists do not have a service context in which to practise all of the principles of OD (because OD is both a service delivery approach and a therapeutic approach), they would in my opinion endorse all seven principles of OD, all 12 elements of dialogical practice and the three additional principles of OD as described in Chapter 1.

When it comes to practice, many contemporary postmodern systemic therapists may be largely indistinguishable from OD therapists. OD therapists and collaborative systemic therapists, such as Andersen (1995) and Anderson and Goolishian (1998), will hold similar therapeutic conversations, closely tracking the utterances of family/network members. Both will reflect with each other in front of the family/network, and use therapeutic forms of responding such as 'positive connotation' and 'systemic reframing'. For example, an OD therapist could reflect on a negatively framed account of a 'lazy son' by wondering if the son might also be staying at home out of concern for his parents.

However, many contemporary systemic therapists integrate aspects of earlier phases of systemic therapy into their practice. Compared to an OD therapist, in my experience, their style tends to be more active. They are more likely to hypothesise or to try to create new stories and use a greater range of questions with the aim of provoking change, in contrast to OD therapists and collaborative family therapists, who focus more on meaning construction in the dialogical encounter than the uncovering of dominant social narratives, intergenerational beliefs, or interactional patterns that may be maintaining problems.

A dialogical conversation tends to have a slower pace, allowing for multiple inner and outer dialogues to develop; the therapist relies on this process, rather than actively directing or intervening. These differences are only a matter of degrees, however, as a dialogical therapist will also (tentatively) offer particular thoughts or observations if they have not yet been raised. Systemic therapists who have 'retrained' as OD therapists do report having to make a conscious decision to be less active in the session, to listen more and ask fewer questions, and to focus on being 'fully present' or attuned (Val Jackson, 2015, personal communication). However, the 'clever' systemic questions often highlighted in textbooks actually make up a small proportion of any session and most systemic therapists would agree that listening is more important than the manner of interviewing (Anderson, 1997). An interesting paper by Monk and Gehart (2003) concluded that there were more similarities than differences in the theories and practices of collaborative and narrative therapists, but that the former's positioning as 'conversational partner' (Anderson, 1997) and the latter's positioning as 'sociopolitical activist' ("liberating subjugated knowledges and life stories" – White and Epston, 1990, p. 102) lead to differences in the style and pacing of the therapeutic conversation.

References

Anderson, H. (1997) *Conversation, language, and possibilities: A postmodern approach to therapy*. New York: Basic Books.

Andersen, T. (1995) 'Reflecting processes; Acts of informing and forming. You can borrow my eyes, but you must not take them away from me' in S. Friedman (ed.) *The reflecting team in action: Collaborative practice in family therapy*. New York: Guilford, p. 11–37.

Anderson, H. and Goolishian, H. (1988) Human systems as linguistic systems: Evolving ideas about the implications for theory and practice. *Family Process*, 27, p. 371–393. doi.org/10.1111/j.1545-5300.1988.00371.x

Dallos, R. and Draper, R. (2010) *An introduction to family therapy: Systemic theory and practice*. Maidenhead: McGraw-Hill Education.

Monk, G. and Gehart, D.R. (2003) Sociopolitical activist or conversational partner? Distinguishing the position of the therapist in narrative and collaborative therapies. *Family Process*, 42(1), p. 19–30. doi.org/10.1111/j.1545-5300.2003.00019.x

Priebe, S., Omer, S., Giacco, D. and Slade, M. (2014) Resource-oriented therapeutic models in psychiatry: Conceptual review. *British Journal of Psychiatry*, 204, p. 256–261. doi.org/10.1192/bjp.bp.113.135038

Sexton, T.L. and Lebow, J. (eds.) (2015) *Handbook of family therapy*. New York: Routledge.

White, M. and Epston, D. (1990) *Narrative means to therapeutic ends*. New York: W. W. Norton and Company.

30

OPEN DIALOGUE AND COGNITIVE BEHAVIOURAL THERAPY (CBT)

Frank Burbach
(UK)

General principles of CBT

The general principle underlying CBT is that the way we make sense of events or experiences (our thoughts) affects how we feel (our mood) and what we do (our behaviour), and this in turn affects the responses of others in our environment. For example, if we stop going out, we may lose contact with friends, leading to fewer people being around to provide validation and emotional and practical support. CBT often involves identifying 'safety behaviours' (things that we do to make us feel better in the short term) or patterns that reinforce beliefs which may cause distress in the long term. CBT involves a process of exploration ('assessment'), understanding how a person's current difficulties may have arisen and are being maintained ('formulation'), considering alternative perspectives ('developing alternative thoughts/beliefs') and trying out new behaviours ('behavioural experiments'). In CBT the consideration of new perspectives is largely, but not solely, related to present events. It can involve reconsideration of the past (e.g. modification of guilt or shame) and the future (e.g. consideration of different options). However, it is argued that ideas and conversational practices from solution-focused and narrative therapies offer more in enabling people to go forward in their lives than CBT, and this has led to the development of integrated approaches (e.g. see Burbach and Stanbridge, 1998; Rhodes and Jakes, 2009).

CBT is a broad church

CBT is a broad church; most contemporary models have moved on from the original, more technique-based approaches for anxiety and depression, which focused on developing alternative beliefs and coping strategies, to a more relational approach which focuses on acceptance and mindfulness. This theoretical and clinical development can arguably be traced back to the approaches developed for working with psychosis (CBTp).

CBT for psychosis

The core CBT approach, which involves the exploration and gentle challenging of unhelpful thoughts and schemas, was substantially modified for people with psychosis. CBTp is not a "quasi-neuroleptic" (Birchwood and Trower, 2006) as it does not usually focus on symptoms and the challenging of unhelpful beliefs, but rather aims to reduce distress and improve quality of life through the mindful acceptance of experiences, which can in and of itself be beneficial, but which can also lead to new insights and support the development of new coping strategies through a gentle exploration of the links between events, thoughts, feelings and behaviour within a safe therapeutic relationship (Tai and Turkington, 2009). Although CBT is most often practised as an individual therapy, it pays a great deal of attention to context and relationships and is a very useful framework for couple and family therapy (Baucom et al., 2012).

CBTp is based on collaboration and recovery-oriented practice (Brabban et al., 2017; Cupitt, 2018; Hagen et al., 2013) and shares many of the same values as Open Dialogue (OD). It also views "experiences and beliefs commonly regarded as symptoms of psychosis (as) highly understandable reactions to adverse life events" (Psychosis Research Unit, n.d.).

Outcomes and CBTp

CBTp has been included in National Institute for Clinical Excellence guidelines (NICE, 2009) following research trials indicating its effectiveness. There is little clarity regarding the effective therapeutic components of CBTp and randomised controlled studies indicate that it is not significantly better than befriending or support. This is evidenced in the review of 20 research trials for Cochrane by Jones et al. (2012). Perhaps all therapeutic approaches achieve good outcomes through active, embodied listening, collaborative meaning making and, in particular, the emotional exchange (the therapeutic relationship).

Extending the dialogue through CBTp and other approaches

The importance of the therapeutic relationship is increasingly acknowledged in all forms of psychotherapy; in OD the key to a successful therapeutic encounter is considered to be the service user receiving a response and entering into dialogue. Seikkula and Trimble (2005) consider the emotional resonance with the facilitators and the emotional exchange between network members to be the core driving force of the encounter and the facilitation of recovery.

There may be additional forms of response that extend the dialogue/polyphony in network meetings. For example, the exploration of links between events, thoughts, feelings and behaviour, to help someone develop new, more helpful perspectives (CBTp); noticing exceptions to problems and further developing these solutions (solution-focused therapy); exploring how our lives and identities are multi-storied and developing possibilities for the future (narrative therapy); and exploring understandable ambivalence about change (motivational interviewing) might all be useful. However, for these conversations to have a therapeutic effect they will need to be experienced as collaborative, affirming, and part of an emotionally attuned relationship (see Burbach, 2016).

References

Baucom, D.H., Whisman, M.A. and Paprocki, C. (2012) Couple-based interventions for psychopathology. *Journal of Family Therapy*, 34(3), p. 250–270.

Birchwood, M. and Trower, P. (2006) The future of cognitive-behavioural therapy for psychosis: Not a quasi-neuroleptic. *The British Journal of Psychiatry*, 188(2), p. 107–108. doi.org/10.1192/bjp.bp.105.014985

Brabban, A., Byrne, R., Longden, E. and Morrison, A.P. (2017) The importance of human relationships, ethics and recovery-orientated values in the delivery of CBT for people with psychosis. *Psychosis*, 9(2), p. 157–166.

Burbach, F.R. (2016) 'Brief family interventions in psychosis – a collaborative, resource-oriented approach to working with families and wider support networks' in B. Pradhan, N. Pinninti and S. Rathod (eds.) *Brief interventions for psychosis: A clinical compendium*. Cham: Springer, p. 119–137.

Burbach, F.R. and Stanbridge, R.I. (1998) A family intervention in psychosis service integrating the systemic and family management approaches. *Journal of Family Therapy*, 20(3), p. 311–325.

Cupitt, C. (ed.) (2018) *CBT for psychosis: Process-orientated therapies and the third wave*. London: Routledge.

Hagen, R., Turkington, D., Berge, T. and Gråwe, R.W. (2013) *CBT for psychosis: A symptom-based approach*. London and New York: Routledge.

Jones, C., Hacker, D., Cormac, I., Meaden, A. and Irving, C.B. (2012) Cognitive behavioural therapy versus other psychosocial treatments for schizophrenia. *Cochrane Database of Systematic Reviews*, Issue 4. Art. No.: CD008712. doi.org/10.1002/14651858.CD008712.pub2

National Institute for Health and Clinical Excellence (NICE) (2009) NICE clinical guideline 82. Schizophrenia: Core interventions in the treatment and management of schizophrenia in adults in primary and secondary care. *Update of NICE clinical guideline*, 1.

Psychosis Research Unit (n.d.) *About the Psychosis Research Unit*. [online] Available at: www.psychosisresearch.com/about-psychosis-research-unit/ [Accessed 20 May 2020].

Rhodes, J. and Jakes, S. (2009) *Narrative CBT for psychosis*. Hove: Routledge.

Seikkula, J. and Trimble, D. (2005) Healing elements of therapeutic conversation: Dialogue as an embodiment of love. *Family Process*, 44(4), p. 461–475.

Tai, S. and Turkington, D. (2009) The evolution of cognitive behavior therapy for schizophrenia: Current practice and recent developments. *Schizophrenia Bulletin*, 35(5), p. 865–873.

31

EXTENDING NEED-ADAPTED INTERVENTIONS IN A CONTEMPORARY OPEN DIALOGUE SERVICE IN HELSINKI

*Niklas Granö, Olli Niemi, Laura Salmijärvi, Marja Pirinen,
Jukka Anto, Jorma Oksanen, Tuula Kieseppä, Päivi Soininen
and Jukka Aaltonen*
(Finland)

Introduction

Traditionally, Open Dialogue (OD) has been used in the treatment of psychosis as a need-adapted therapeutic platform for family/network-orientated therapies. A recent focus on developing interventions for psychosis has been in the early course of psychosis – in first episode psychosis (FEP) and in the clinical high risk (CHR) of developing FEP. A deterioration in social and occupational functioning and deficits in neuro-cognitive performance are often already present in the early stages of psychosis. However, these alterations are often poorly recognised and treated. Hence, it is important, when developing an OD service, to offer individually tailored and need-adapted treatment choices, targeted at a wide variety of problems.

The Early Psychosis Centre

The Early Psychosis Centre (EPC), of the Department of Psychiatry within Helsinki University Hospital, provides an example of a modern variation of need-adapted care, where OD is a platform for a variety of treatment choices, according to current needs. The EPC focuses on FEP, or possible FEP, and on the CHR stage of developing psychosis among an adult population. In addition to providing family/network meetings, facilitated similarly to those in Western Lapland, the treatment options cover both need-specific medication and intensive psychological treatment. A multidisciplinary case-specific team (of three people) evaluates the person's functioning and neurocognitive, negative and other clinical symptoms. This case-specific team then works with the person in network meetings throughout the treatment process. Depending on the nature of the problems/symptoms, the team may also organise a joint meeting with a particular EPC team member possessing the knowledge and skills to introduce additional treatment option(s) that might be suitable. If the person is motivated, this work will start alongside the network meetings. The EPC consists of physicians, nurses, occupational therapists, psychologists and social workers.

Range of therapeutic approaches offered alongside network meetings

Individual and group-based cognitive remediation (CRT) is offered for cognitive rehabilitation (Medalia et al., 2009). When CRT is offered as group therapy it is called a 'Skilled Thinking Group' and is practised in a classroom with computerised training software. Following a personalised computer training session, participants discuss together their neurocognitive difficulties in a 'bridging' session, where experiences and ideas are shared in the group. Some sessions are action based, e.g. playing board games together. Individual CRT is based on the metacognitive model of CRT (Reeder et al., 2017), which focuses on the recognition of dysfunctional cognitive strategies (e.g. in working memory, attention, planning), using metacognition to train more functional strategies in handling everyday tasks. Social Cognition and Interaction Training (SCIT) is a group therapy for remediating deficits in social cognition. It is based on Roberts' and Penn's model (Roberts et al., 2015). Here, therapy is focused on biased social cognition, which is often a particular difficulty in psychosis, affecting social functioning.

Multifamily Groups (MFG) in EPC is based on the idea of "Families helping Families" (Bloch Thorsen et al., 2006) and involves several families who have a family member experiencing psychosis. Each session begins with a lecture on a relevant theme, given by both a professional worker and an "expert by experience". Following this, people who have experienced psychosis and parents form separate groups, with two facilitators in each group, to discuss the topic and share ideas from their own experience. The aim of MFG is to normalise psychotic experiences, give psychoeducation, provide peer support through the sharing of narratives, and support independence.

Cognitive Behavioural Therapy (CBT) is mainly based on the French and Morrison model (2004), adapted for both CHR and FEP. It focuses actively on psychotic beliefs and their alternative, normalised beliefs, which are tested by behavioural experiments in natural surroundings.

Interventions for people with CHR are organised with vocational schools and colleges through mobile and consultative work. If health care personnel or teachers detect psychotic-like symptoms in their students, personnel can consult the EPC. Network meetings at school clarify and address worrisome symptoms using case-specific EPC teams with the service user, their parents and school staff. No formal referral is needed; a phone call is enough. If the person meets CHR criteria, CBT techniques are used as an intervention method, with OD as the overall platform.

Summary

Early psychosis interventions should be targeted to the large variety of differences between people experiencing psychosis, including negative symptoms, defects in social functioning, and cognitive problems, besides overt positive psychotic symptoms. Our EPC uses OD as a platform for a need-adapted way to work within the field of early psychosis, and over time we have added additional evidence-based interventions to the approach.

References

Bloch Thorsen, G., Grönnestad, T. and Öxnevad, A. (2006). *Family and multi-family work with psychosis.* London and New York: Routledge.

French, P. and Morrison A.P. (2004) *Early detection and cognitive therapy for people at high risk of developing psychosis – a treatment approach.* West Sussex: John Wiley & Sons Ltd.

Medalia, A., Revheim, N. and Herlands, T. (2009) *Cognitive remediation for psychological disorders. Therapist guide.* New York: Oxford University Press.

Reeder, C., Huddy, V., Cella, M., Taylor, R., Greenwood, K., Landau, S. and Wykes T. (2017) A new generation computerised metacognitive cognitive remediation programme for schizophrenia (CIRCuiTS): A randomised controlled trial. *Psychological Medicine*, 47(15), p. 2720–2730. doi.org/10.1017/S0033291717001234

Roberts, D.L., Penn, D.L. and Combs, D.R. (2015) *Social cognition and interaction training (SCIT): Group psychotherapy for schizophrenia and other psychotic disorders, clinician guide.* Oxford: Oxford University Press.

32

INTERFAMILY THERAPY

Application of dialogical practices in the multifamily group

Javier Sempere and Claudio Fuenzalida
(Spain)

*Why might **dialogues in social networks** be of interest to professionals?*

For the surprising and unexpected resources that can be found if we think together.

(Jaakko Seikkula and Tom Erik Arnkil, 2006, p. xvii)

Following on from this we, the authors, ask:

Why might interfamily dialogues be of interest to professionals?

Because of the astonishing resources that can be found if families think together.

Introduction

The Interfamily Therapy Centre (CTI), located in Elche (Spain), makes psychotherapeutic activities readily accessible to service users and their families, whilst also promoting research and professional training. Professionals from health, education and social disciplines in the CTI team have been deeply influenced by the Open Dialogue (OD) approach during the last 15 years and are especially focused on utilising OD approaches with people experiencing psychosis in multifamily settings.

Interfamily therapy

Interfamily therapy (IFT) is a model of multifamily group work[1] (MFG) based on/inspired by dialogical and collaborative practices. The forum in which the therapeutic process develops is the multifamily group, which goes beyond the boundaries of the family and the professional team into a wider community setting involving several families. Depending on the institution, the families in the group might suffer similar problems (e.g. having a member with a psychotic disorder) or different problems. The facilitators of multifamily groups promote dialogue within the whole group, with each family contributing according to their own experiences, communicational dynamics and sociocultural characteristics.

The main characteristics of IFT are:

1   It has an open and spontaneous group setting, enabling a greater number of people to access therapy and benefit through the power of group therapy.
2   It is a clear, straightforward methodology based on dialogical practices that can easily be learned by professionals from different backgrounds, thereby facilitating integration of their diverse therapeutic contributions.
3   It is complementary to other therapeutic, social and educational interventions that can be carried out concurrently.
4   It is cost-effective, since more service users and families are treated simultaneously.
5   Some have stated that families are resistant to attending MFGs, but this has not been our experience. This may be a consequence of the individualistic focus of many professionals/institutions who underestimate the significance of a social/group approach to therapy. We encourage families to hold joint responsibility in all treatment steps, from the first contact with the person experiencing psychosis.
6   Recent research has demonstrated the efficacy of IFT. Sempere and Fuenzalida (2017) studied 181 participants in IFT, finding a clinically statistically significant symptomatic improvement in most of the items measured by the SCL-90 R test (Derogatis and Savitz, 1999), including 'hostility', 'paranoid ideation' and 'psychoticism' symptom dimensions. Similar improvements on the 'hostility' dimension were found in relatives of those experiencing psychosis, leading to a reduction in critical emotional expression in these families. IFT was the preferred treatment of service users, when compared with their experience of individual and single-family therapies.

Theoretical and methodological background of IFT

IFT brings together the power of family therapy with the power of group interventions. As with OD network meetings for a single family, multifamily meetings do not have a predetermined agenda. The main purpose is to generate a conversation where experiences can be shared, and emotions can be expressed within a space of solidarity and commitment. The role of the facilitators is to help families connect to each other, as if the professionals were 'architects of dialogue' (Asen et al., 2001), i.e. they promote a collaborative and polyphonic dialogue within the group, following the main principles of dialogical practices. This takes place simultaneously on three levels: an inner dialogue in each participant (intra-psychic), a dialogue among members of the same family (intra-family) and a dialogue among members of different families (inter-family).

Participants come to recognise how they interact with members of their own family and their social environment through mirroring effects (Pines, 1997), i.e. they identify their own communication patterns, as reflected in other individual/family dynamics within the multifamily group. The main goals are to increase the capacity for exchanging experiences, to be able to reflect together, and to create new meanings and new relationships through shared dialogue.

Contribution of IFT to dialogical practices

IFT does not necessarily replace individual or single-family interventions, which can be held concurrently and coordinated by the same professional team. Both individual and group processes can be complementary and enrich one another, through the sharing of new narratives created in both contexts. This can result in a greater capacity to create yet further narratives and to resolve conflict. IFT integrates all participants in a *reflective team*, first described by Andersen (1991), that includes not only the professionals but also the non-professional members of the multifamily group in a meta-dialogue that aims to generate new narratives.

Conclusion

IFT represents the fullest implementation of a social constructionist approach in therapy. The greater the number of voices included in a poly-phonic, multicultural and cross-generational dialogue, the greater the opportunities for understanding. We get sick in society and now we can find therapeutic places to recover in society. Badaracco (2000) stated: "The presence of users, relatives and therapists constitutes a mini-society, a heterogeneous setting where 'madness' can show/unfold its true nature" (translated from Spanish).

The first implementation of IFT in Elche (Spain) and the surrounding areas began about 15 years ago and since then it has spread exponentially, being implemented in treatment programmes for both early psychosis and more chronic psychosis in many Spanish institutions, especially in the provinces of Alicante, Madrid and Barcelona. IFT breaks the isolation of people with psychosis by enabling their voices to be heard in an open social space. Furthermore, in IFT people with psychosis actively contribute to the process with their responses to and reflections on the experiences of other members of the group.

Note

1 Multifamily group therapy is a model of therapeutic intervention carried out in a setting where several identified service users and their families gather together. Peter Laqueur (1976), an American psychiatrist, developed this approach with service users and their families in New York in the 1950s. Some years later, the Argentinian psychiatrist García Badaracco (2000) applied psychoanalytic theory in the multifamily context, establishing Multifamily Psychoanalysis.

References

Andersen, T. (1991) *The reflective team. Dialogues and dialogues about dialogues.* London and New York: W. W. Norton.

Asen, E., Dawson, N. and McHugh, B. (2001) *Multiple family therapy. The Marlborough model and its wider applications.* London and New York: Karnac.

Badaracco, J. (2000) *Psicoanálisis multifamiliar [Multi-family psychoanalysis].* Buenos Aires: Tecnipublicaciones.

Derogatis, L.R. and Savitz, K.L. (1999) 'The SCL-90-R, Brief Symptom Inventory, and Matching Clinical Rating Scales' in M.E. Maruish (ed.) *The use of psychological testing for treatment planning and outcomes assessment.* New Jersey: Lawrence Erlbaum Associates Publishers (p. 679–724).

Laqueur, H.P. (1976) 'Multiple family therapy' in P.J. Guerin (ed.) *Family therapy, theory, and practice.* New York: Gardner (p. 405–416).

Pines, M. (1997) *Circular reflections. Selected papers on group analysis and psycho-analysis.* London: Jessica Kingsley Publishers.

Seikkula, J. and Arnkil, T.E. (2006) *Dialogical meetings in social networks.* London: Karnac Books.

Sempere, J. and Fuenzalida, C. (2017) *Terapias multifamiliares. El modelo interfamiliar: la terapia hecha entre todos [Multi-family therapies. The interfamily model: The therapy made between all of us].* Madrid: Psimática.

33

PSYCHOANALYSIS AND OPEN DIALOGUE

Brian Martindale
(UK)

My interest in psychoanalytic contributions to psychosis has many rich sources, but practical applications stem especially from Need-Adapted Treatment (NAT), an important precursor to Open Dialogue (OD) (Alanen, 1997). It is curious that references to NAT in the OD literature often do not stress the centrality of its psychoanalytic psychotherapeutic underpinnings, in terms of theory and psychotherapeutic attitude, considering that Alanen's published results are comparable to the excellent results of OD. A range of approaches were available within NAT, as individually needed, not only from within psychoanalytic frameworks, and it continually developed according to outcome research, as summarised in Chapter 36.

The development of OD in Western Lapland represents a success story, extending further the shift taking place in Finland away from the previously dominant paradigm, which emphasised medication and hospitalisation. This shift was mainly facilitated by the Finnish National Schizophrenia Project, again led by Alanen, utilising the goals or principles developed from NAT (see Chapter 36 and Alanen, 1997, p. 159–166).

This chapter raises questions about whether psychoanalytic ideas continue to influence OD, even if not named as such. In considering these psychoanalytic ideas for psychosis, readers should not have in mind the traditional psychoanalytic method of using a couch, fixed time frames, and focusing more or less exclusively on interpretation of the unconscious. A key aspect of NAT as the approach developed was the increasing flexibility of the frame when responding to those with psychosis. A good example is the inclusion of family members in meetings, which was, in my view, one of the most important developments.

Working with families

Today, it is unusual to hear of psychoanalytically based family work, even though psychoanalysts were prominent in drawing attention to significant family issues decades ago (Martindale, 2017). A factor that possibly detracts from the offer of family psychotherapies in psychosis (despite long-standing evidence of effectiveness) is concern about blame – that families will judge that they are being blamed if offered therapeutic work; perhaps, as a consequence, therapists avoid working with families (Martindale, 2017). With the OD approach this crucial obstacle has been successfully overcome, as evidenced by numerous favourable reports from family members, including those in this book.

In general, the contemporary problem seems to be that mental health trainings, and most psychotherapy and psychoanalytic trainings, do not result in professionals confident in working with more than one individual, let alone working in the setting that the family and network prefer, most often the home.

Free association, interpretations, tolerance of uncertainty and authority

The invitation to free associate, and for consequent multiple cadencies and hesitancies to be carefully listened to and reflected on, is at the heart of psychoanalysis (Laplanche and Pontalis, 1973). The psychoanalyst Donald Winnicott (1969) argued that the (psychoanalytic) specialist does not need to be clever, but rather needs to be able to provide a natural and dynamic human relationship in a professional setting while the person gradually surprises themselves by the production of ideas and feelings that have not been previously integrated into the total personality. I think that there is considerable resonance between free association and the respectful active listening, reflections and polyphony in OD.

In considering the lack of attention to psychoanalytic knowledge in OD training, I wonder whether this reflects a concern that the use of interpretation could lead to an authoritarian skew between professionals and network members, as opposed to seeing it as the offering of an idea to the recipient, as I believe it should be, in the spirit of uncertainty. For tolerance of uncertainty is a principle in psychoanalysis too, and an authoritarian stance is decried in both approaches. And whilst historically psychoanalysis saw interpretation as almost the sole mutative intervention (Strachey, 1934), other factors, such as supportive elements and the quality of the therapeutic relationship (de Jonghe et al., 1994), have long been shown to lead to change in psychoanalysis (Wallerstein, 1989).

I think it would be helpful to explore the similarities and differences between reflective practices and the use of interpretations, and more generally to consider which kinds of psychoanalytic processes and interventions overlap with OD, and which are quite distinct. Of the latter, which ones could complement or impede OD processes?

Dynamic unconscious processes and psychosis

Psychoanalysis would not be psychoanalysis without its focus on the dynamic unconscious. It is clear from accounts in this book that OD facilitates individuals in their networks to find words for concerns, feelings, traumatic events and interpersonal experiences for which there have not previously been conscious words; surely this is transforming the unconscious, or at least the less conscious, to the conscious. Could it then be said that OD network meetings facilitate the transition of individual, social and interpersonal unconscious factors into consciousness? If so, how could OD and psychoanalysis each conceptualise different forms of the unconscious?

Seikkula (Chapter 3, page 53) refers to psychosis presentations as being metaphors for disturbing lived experiences. Integrated into everyday cultural discourse are understandings and language derived from psychoanalysis that describe the multiple ways in which unconscious defences distort disturbing internal and external experiences in a much more nuanced way than the word metaphor alone conveys. Here are just a few: projection, denial, rationalisation, reaction formation, identification with the aggressor, hallucinatory wish fulfilment, idealisation, grandiosity, condensation, and displacement (let alone transference and countertransference). These are established 'facts' of mental functioning that we are all capable of and are of the greatest assistance in unravelling the 'metaphors' of psychosis. In my view, an OD practitioner is handicapped if not adept at recognising these processes, just as a psychoanalytic practitioner is handicapped if they are not able to organise and facilitate network meetings.

The dark side of us humans

Hatred, envious destructiveness and sadomasochism are rarely reported in the OD literature and perhaps some accounts of dialogical processes are somewhat idealised. These 'negative' phenomena are commonly found in psychoanalytic explorations of the human condition and contribute greatly to mental disturbances. How can their relative absence in accounts of OD practice be understood? Does it reflect a tendency to avoid such negative factors, to some extent, with the important focus being on love and respect? Although recoveries in OD are often impressive in terms of freedom from psychosis and the ability to return to work and study, I think that it would be beneficial to conduct more in-depth studies of such individuals, in order to clarify other aspects of functioning, as well as to study those who continue to experience psychosis in spite of the OD approach.

There are few reports in this book of individuals moving on from an OD network approach to a psychoanalytic therapy modified for those vulnerable to psychosis, let alone other therapies. So, an important discussion topic is whether aspects of NAT, as practised in Turku, including its psychoanalytic understandings and psychotherapeutic applications, should be more extensively developed/rehabilitated into OD, to complement the impressive changes in attitude and approach contained in its core principles. This would further emphasise that OD is a platform. Would expertise in addressing 'the negative' lead to further improvement for individuals and families?

Here is a fictitious example, but based on my experience, to make these questions less abstract:

> A man diagnosed with schizophrenia had many hospitalisations and was treated with only medication for years. After brief contact with others he would detach himself – dissociating, hallucinating and feeling confused. In these brief social contacts, he seemed very likeable and innocent. A year of family and individual work led to an increased capacity to engage with others, albeit limited. After three years of individual psychoanalytic therapy, he was gradually able to integrate not so nice aspects of himself and others, and found a violent hateful envy of others, that the dissociation had protected him from (since his younger brother was born). The avoidance of his envy had greatly limited his capacity for relationships.

OD stresses the importance of facilitating and empowering network members to listen to one another and to find resources from within themselves to work their way out of presenting problems; it reduces reliance on professional expertise. However, it should not be overlooked, as the training section of this book emphasises, that considerable expertise is needed for skilful facilitation of the process.

I have raised some possible areas of overlap between psychoanalytic and OD processes, even though psychoanalysis is better known for undertakings with individuals rather than families or networks. I am suggesting that by not paying attention in trainings to, for example, knowledge of unconscious mental processes, OD perhaps avoids a creative tension between the expertise of practitioners and the expertise of network members. My final question is to wonder whether this tension or its avoidance could also apply to other knowledge and skill frameworks, with the risk that those other approaches become rather uncritically deprecated. Part of the intention of this chapter is to address this possibility.

References

Alanen, Y.O. (1997) *Schizophrenia: Its origins and need-adapted treatment.* London: Karnac Books.

De Jonghe F., Rijnierse P. and Janssen R. (1994) Psychoanalytic supportive psychotherapy. *Journal of the American Psychoanalytic Association*, 42(2), p. 421–446. doi. org/10.1177/000306519404200205

Laplanche, J. and Pontalis, J.-B. (1973) *The language of psychoanalysis.* London: Hogarth Press.

Martindale, B. (2017) A psychoanalytic contribution to understanding the lack of professional involvement in psychotherapeutic work with families where there is psychosis. *British Journal of Psychotherapy*, 33(2), p. 224–238. doi.org/10.1111/bjp.12290

Strachey, J. (1934) The nature of the therapeutic action of psychoanalysis. *International Journal of Psychoanalysis*, 15, p. 127–159.

Wallerstein, R.S. (1989) The psychotherapy research project of the Menninger Foundation: An overview. *Journal of Consulting and Clinical Psychology*, 57(2), p. 195–205. doi.org/10.1037/0022-006X.57.2.195

Winnicott, D.W. (1969) The use of an object. *International Journal of Psychoanalysis*, 50, p. 711–716.

34

THE AFFINITIES BETWEEN THERAPEUTIC COMMUNITIES AND OPEN DIALOGUE

Nick Putman
(UK)

In 1946 Tom Main (Main, 1946) coined the term 'therapeutic community' (TC) to describe a radically different way of organising wards in psychiatric hospitals, such that service users could participate fully in the day-to-day running of the ward and offer each other mutual support, with less medical control/intervention. The work of Maxwell Jones (Jones, 1952) at Belmont Hospital in London (later renamed Henderson Hospital) helped to define the model further. Rapoport, an anthropologist who spent time at Belmont Hospital, identified four core principles in the operation of the therapeutic community there: democratisation, permissiveness, reality confrontation and communalism (Rapoport, 1960, cited in Pearce and Haigh, 2017). Although TCs have evolved since these principles were first defined (see Pearce and Haigh, 2017), they have nevertheless played a central role in the development of therapeutic communities, and I think each of them are shared, to some extent, with OD practice.

Democratisation

TCs have flattened hierarchies, which emphasise the capability, agency, responsibility and lived experience of community members (by which I mean the people using the service), where therapists/professionals are not seen as experts. Where decisions need to be made about the community as a whole or an issue relating to one member of the community, everyone's views will be solicited in a meeting. This emphasis on democracy, agency and non-expertise clearly parallels the OD approach, where every voice must be heard, every opportunity for collaborative decision-making is taken, and those identified as being at the 'centre of concern' are seen to be (at least potentially) capable of supporting others in the network.

Although the hierarchy is flattened in TCs, staff have a different role to community members, and whilst as much power is shared as possible, some decisions may need to be taken solely by staff in order to protect community members and the culture/structure of the community. The structure in TCs is necessarily flexible, in order to meet the changing needs of the group (as in the OD approach, where the uniqueness of each crisis is emphasised), and where limits need to be set it is important that the reasons for doing so are made transparent. Transparency is also an important feature of the OD approach.

Permissiveness

Behaviours and attitudes/beliefs that would not be tolerated in other mental health settings are permitted in TCs, provided that people in the community are not harmed (in reality the extent of the permissiveness varied from community to community and over time as new parameters were negotiated). Again, a clear parallel can be seen with the OD approach, where there is an invitation to network members to express themselves authentically and to share more about their experiences/perspectives, however strange these may seem to others and however difficult it may be for others to hear them.

Reality confrontation

Reality confrontation counterbalances permissiveness, enabling TC members and staff to give each other constructive/thoughtful feedback on how they see and affect one another, in the spirit of furthering understanding. We see similar processes in OD network meetings where, through the use of circular questions and other forms of response, practitioners help network members to share more about their perspectives on each other and their relationships, whilst also sharing their own reflections on their experience of being with the network. Practitioners do not attempt to change any particular behaviour, but there is trust that the more network members can share in this way, in a dialogical process, the more likely the experience will be transformative, to the benefit of all in the network. In both OD and TCs, professionals are open to being challenged by the people they work with. Their subjectivity is necessarily a part of the process and they need to take responsibility for their behaviour and communication and be open to others reflecting on it.

Kennard (2008) points out that Rapoport's four principles emerged from a service designed for people diagnosed with personality disorders and may need adapting for services developed for people with psychotic experiences. In particular, he suggests that reality confrontation may be unhelpful for those who are very sensitive to social situations and perhaps experiencing paranoia. This may be the reason why there has been less emphasis on reality confrontation in therapeutic communities set up primarily for people having psychotic experiences, such as the Philadelphia Association households in London and Soteria House in the USA. In these communities the emphasis was on providing genuine asylum; an ordinary dwelling in which a natural healing process can occur when someone is treated with respect in a supportive environment imbued with hope. Mosher et al. (2004), writing about their experiences at Soteria House, argue that "change occurs through the normal interactive processes" (p. 33), and this mirrors the view in OD that change is a natural consequence of dialogue. Mosher in particular stressed the value of a phenomenological approach, which he termed "interpersonal phenomenology" (given the strong emphasis on the relationships that developed at Soteria House) – the desire to meet others without preconceived notions, which again can be found in the OD approach.

Communalism

Communalism was defined by Rapoport (1960) as a "tightknit, interconnected, warm and intimate" (p. 62) network of relationships. It is mirrored in the notion of "belongingness", described by Pearce and Haigh (2017), which develops when those involved in a community can engage authentically with one another and share responsibility for day-to-day matters. TC members are encouraged to take an active interest in each other's progress, and Pearce and Haigh (2017) argue that peer support in TCs is more powerful than staff support. This mirrors the practice in OD, where those facilitating network meetings leave space for network members to address their issues with each other. If this proves possible, it is likely that only a 'light touch' will be needed from the facilitators.

In residential TCs the everyday experience of living together is considered as significant as specific meetings, and so considerable attention is given to the milieu and to the relations that develop when people live, and spend extended periods of time, together. This is different to the practice of OD, especially where someone is living in their own home in the community, such that OD practitioners are generally only with the network during network meetings. Nevertheless, the experiences and stories that are shared in network meetings are often related to aspects of day-to-day life, so these meetings can function as a forum for reflecting on these, as is the case in TC meetings, where issues from day-to-day living are commonly addressed.

Other similarities and differences

In the OD approach, we typically work with the social network of the person at the centre of concern, most commonly close family members, and this is different from the work in TCs, where families/networks are not directly involved. Nevertheless, there is a similar emphasis on the need for community at a time of crisis. In a TC, we are not working with people with a shared history, but community members bring their own lived experience and thus a variety of perspectives, which is valued in TCs in a similar way that polyphony is valued in OD. As in network meetings, there is the opportunity in TCs to explore the historical reasons that may have contributed to the mental health challenges people are experiencing, but the emphasis is most likely to be on how these life experiences continue to affect them and their relationships with others.

Both OD and TCs are essentially relational, as opposed to technique based, approaches. They recognise the healing power of everyday relationships, and the need for these relationships to be consistent. There is an appreciation in both approaches that we are interdependent – that our freedom, to the extent we can experience it, is always situated, and therefore that our capacity to find our way in relation to others is crucial. In OD significant members of the network are typically included in the work, and so issues can be addressed directly, whilst in TCs the hope is that positive developments in relations with others in the TC will translate into the relations that members (seek to) have beyond the community.

In some TCs there may be more conditions attached to participation in the community than there would be in an OD process. Examples are the requirement to attend meetings, a policy of 'no secrets within the community' and the use of contracts and voting in meetings (Pearce and Haigh, 2017). In an OD process, network members are free to attend or otherwise and to share to the extent that they want and feel able. Whilst nobody can or should be forced to participate in dialogue, it might be helpful to consider whether any of the conditions sometimes used in TCs could contribute to an OD process.

Conclusion

It seems that there are more similarities than otherwise between TCs and the OD approach, with the main difference being that family members are not usually involved in the work of TCs and there is less emphasis on the everyday milieu in OD. Some TCs have been set up as an alternative to hospitalisation for people having psychotic experiences (e.g. Soteria House) and I think that, given the similarities in the principles underlying TCs and OD, there is considerable scope for the provision of such residential TCs within an OD service, such that there is an option for people having psychotic experiences to live away from home (when it feels necessary/beneficial to do so), but in a non-hospital setting. This option could potentially still involve the family/social network in network meetings, which could be organised whilst someone was living in the TC.

References

Jones, M. (1952) *Social psychiatry: A study of therapeutic communities.* London: Tavistock Publications.

Kennard, D. (2008) 'A view of the evolution of therapeutic communities for people suffering from psychosis' in J. Gale, A. Realpe and E. Pedriali (eds.) *Therapeutic communities for psychosis: Philosophy, history and clinical practice.* London and New York: Routledge, p. 3–15.

Main, T.F. (1946) The hospital as a therapeutic institution. *Bulletin of the Menninger Clinic,* 10, p. 66–70.

Mosher, L.R., Hendrix, V. and Fort, D.C. (2004) *Soteria: Through madness to deliverance.* Bloomington: Xlibris Corp.

Pearce, S. and Haigh, R. (2017) *The theory and practice of democratic therapeutic community treatment.* London and Philadelphia: Jessica Kingsley Publishers.

Rapoport, R.N. (1960) *Community as doctor.* London and New York: Tavistock Publications.

35

OPEN DIALOGUE AND MUSIC THERAPY

Mario Eugster
(UK)

Introduction

I clearly remember my first encounter with Open Dialogue (OD) and immediately thinking "this strikes a deep chord with music therapy!" This was a vivid first impression and pointed to a convergence of ideas and clinical practice elements between the two approaches. In this chapter, I would like to focus on the concepts of dialogue and polyphony.

Music therapy

Mindful of readers less familiar with music therapy, let me outline some basic principles. In music therapy sessions (individual or group), both therapist(s) and client(s) enter into 'clinical co-improvisation' (which differs from 'purely' musical improvisation). Clients choose from a range of musical instruments and are then invited to express themselves musically. The therapist responds with a range of music therapy techniques, drawn from a wide variety of musical idioms (Nordoff and Robbins, 2007).

Through deep listening to different aspects of the music being created – rhythm, pitch, intensity, pulse, melodic structure and timing – the therapist(s) and client(s) develop a unique, shared musical language. In this co-created musical field, patterns of relating and aspects of internal life (emotions, thoughts, sensations etc.) are worked with collaboratively in order to further therapeutic development (e.g. developing emotional regulation). The therapist uses musical structures and techniques strategically in order to respond to particular therapeutic issues and, depending on the clinical context, the process can be informed by psychodynamic theories and practice, e.g. a mentalisation-based approach (Fonagy and Bateman, 2019).

Early development and dialogue

Music therapy literature and theory refer to communication in early development, and in particular to the work of Daniel Stern (1985) and Colwyn

Trevarthen (1999). Both explored the musical ingredients of pitch, intensity and timing in human communication between parent and infant. The concept 'communicative musicality' (Malloch and Trevarthen, 2008) refers to the musical nature of communication and dialogue and the significance of this for music therapy.

Bakhtin's understanding of dialogue is central to the OD approach and he proposes that dialogue is central to life itself:

> Life by its very nature is dialogic. To live means to participate in dialogue: To ask questions, to heed, to respond, to agree, and so forth. In this dialogue a person participates wholly and throughout his whole life: With his eyes, lips, hands, soul, spirit, with his whole body and deeds.
>
> (Bakhtin, 1984, p. 293)

This view is congruent with the detailed research of Stern (1985) and Trevarthen (1999) into the nature of early communication. Referring to Trevarthen, Seikkula writes that "the original human experience of dialogue emerges in the first few weeks of life, as parent and child engage in an exquisite dance of mutual emotional attunement by means of facial expressions, hand gestures and tones of vocalization" (2008, p. 479). The music therapist Ansdell (2014) develops this idea, by referring to Bakhtin's concept of an utterance:

> A 'musical utterance' is any musical communication addressed to another, and a musical dialogue is any communication that expects an answering response. This can range from infant-carer interactions to sophisticated musical partnerships. In common is the dialogical principle that 'one is not enough'.
>
> (2014, p. 161–162)

Music therapy and psychosis

When considering dialogue in music therapy with people affected by psychosis, music therapists have found that psychotic states tend to lead to particular characteristics in musical expression (DeBacker, 2008; Pavlicevic, 1997). Whilst co-improvised musical language is unique to each therapeutic relationship, we often find a severe collapse in musical dialogue in the context of psychosis, manifest for example in very repetitive musical patterns and a breakdown of 'interactional synchrony', defined as the natural tendency in human communication to find shared pulse and timing (Condon and Ogston, 1966). A person experiencing psychosis might become locked in musical monologue and thus become musically isolated. Therefore, fostering and cultivating musical dialogue is core to the music therapy process.

Equally, for Seikkula, the cultivation of dialogue and polyphony lies at the heart of OD:

> Therapists are no longer interventionists with some pre-planned map for the stories that clients are telling. Instead, their main focus is on how to respond to clients' utterances, as answers are the generators for mobilizing one's own psychological resources.
>
> (Seikkula, 2008, p. 481)

Polyphony in Open Dialogue, music and music therapy

The concept of both inner and outer polyphony is central to the OD approach (Seikkula, 2008). Seikkula maintains that "the mind is voices speaking to each other; it is an ongoing process of dialogues..." (2008, p. 483). As a music therapist, I am intrigued by this view, as the 'ongoing process of dialogues' between musical voices gives rise to meaning and relatedness, as experienced in listening to musical polyphony.

Polyphony is a musical phenomenon found in all musical cultures, whether in Western polyphonic music, such as that composed by J.S. Bach, or the poly-rhythmic music in African traditions or Gamelan music from Southeast Asia.

Polyphony is the weaving together of multiple independent but interrelated voices, resulting in a rich musical tapestry. To illustrate this, let's examine briefly an example from Bach's piano music, Fugue in C-Major from the Well-Tempered Clavier Volume I (see Figure 35.1):

The first voice introduces a musical theme, followed by a second voice, imitating the first voice. These two voices now enter into a dialogue, followed by a third and fourth voice. The resulting web of voices grows into a musical organism in which each voice is equal, but takes different roles and undergoes various transformations. The magic of such a musical composition lies in the living interconnection between each voice, resulting in experiences of beauty and balance. In music therapy, polyphony can be considered as an ideal of musical and human relatedness and interconnectedness.

Music therapy with families developed in the late 20th century, mostly in relation to work with children and their family members (Oldfield, 2015). OD practice can be incorporated into music therapy in the form of family music therapy in adult mental health services. In such a setting family members and therapists can enter into musical co-improvisation, in which aspects of the family's relational patterns and qualities can be musically expressed, resulting in a unique field of 'network music'. The therapists support the co-creation of a musical landscape through deep listening and by musically supporting the family voices to be heard.

The creation of a shared musical language in clinical music therapy impro-visation resonates with core elements of OD:

Fugue I
In C major

BWV 846   Johann Sebastian Bach (1685 - 1750)

Figure 35.1 J.S. Bach, Fugue 1 in C-major (BWV 846) from 'The Well-Tempered Clavier Vol. 1'.

At the beginning, team members are careful to incorporate the familiar language of the network members into their own utterances. As team members respectfully and attentively draw out the words and feelings of each network member, the conversation shifts. As the original network incorporates the team into its membership, new meanings emerge when new shared language starts to emerge between the team and members of the social network.

(Seikkula and Trimble, 2005, p. 462)

Integrating OD network meetings and music therapy allows us to work with both musical and verbal polyphony. Shared musical experiences can provide a focal point for the network, who can often become disoriented when faced with psychosis. As Seikkula and Trimble put it: "In their acute distress, network members often appear stuck in desperate, rigid, constricted ways of understanding and communicating about the problems that absorb them" (Seikkula and Trimble, 2005, p. 462).

In psychosis, musical voices can break away from the network and the sense of shared musical reality can be temporarily lost. This is played out musically in rigid, stuck or fragmented musical patterns, which are out of synch with other voices, resulting in states of musical isolation. Through deep listening and awakening of musical responsiveness between network members, these voices can eventually be reintegrated into the family network, resulting in the experience of dialogue within the family polyphony.

Concluding remarks

The dialogue between music therapy and OD is intriguing, with many potential pathways to develop clinical practice and research. I am continuously fascinated by the exploration of concepts such as polyphony from both perspectives. OD by its nature allows for a creative dialogue between professions and disciplines. This could open exciting new pathways for the future evolution of mental health services.

References

Ansdell, G. (2014) *How music helps in music therapy and everyday life.* Farnham: Ashgate.

Bakhtin, M. (1984) 'Problems of Dostoevsky's poetics' in C. Emerson (ed. and trans.) *Theory and history of literature Vol. 8.* Minneapolis: University of Minnesota Press, p. 283–302.

Bateman, A. and Fonagy, P. (2019) *Handbook of mentalizing in mental health practice.* 2nd ed. Washington, DC: American Psychiatric Publishing.

Condon, W.S. and Ogston, W.D. (1966) Sound film analysis of normal and pathological behaviour patterns. *Journal of Nervous and Mental Disease*, 143(4), p. 338–347. doi.org/10.1097/00005053-196610000-00005

De Backer, J. (2008) A research report detailing the transition from sensorial play to musical form by psychotic patients. *Nordic Journal of Music Therapy*, 17(2), p. 89–104. doi.org/10.1080/08098130809478202

Malloch, S. and Trevarthen, C. (2008) *Communicative musicality.* Oxford: Oxford University Press.

Nordoff, P. and Robbins, C. (2007) *Creative music therapy: A guide to fostering clinical musicianship.* Barcelona: Barcelona Publishers.

Oldfield, A. (2015) 'Family approaches in music therapy practice with young children' in J. Edwards (ed.) *The Oxford handbook of music therapy.* Oxford: Oxford University Press, p. 158–175.

Pavlicevic, M. (1997) *Music therapy in context, music meaning and relationship.* London: Jessica Kingsley.

Seikkula, J. (2008) Inner and outer voices in the present moment of family and network therapy. *Journal of Family Therapy*, 30(4), p. 478–491. doi.org/10.1111/j.1467-6427.2008.00439.x

Seikkula, J. and Trimble, D. (2005) Healing elements of therapeutic conversation: Dialogue as an embodiment of love. *Family Process*, 44(4), p. 461–475. doi.org/10.1111/j.1545-5300.2005.00072.xStern, D. (1985) *The interpersonal world of the infant: A view from psychoanalysis and developmental psychology.* London: Karnac.

Trevarthen, C. (1999) Musicality and the intrinsic motive pulse: Evidence from human psychobiology and infant communication. *Musicae Scientiae*, 3(1), p. 155–215. doi.org/10.1177/10298649000030S109

Section 6

RESEARCH INTO OPEN DIALOGUE

CONTENTS

EDITORS' INTRODUCTION

Any belief that the controlled trial is the only way [of assessing evidence] would mean not that the pendulum had swung too far, but that it had come right off the hook!

We found the above quote of Bradford Hill, the founder of the random controlled trial, in the annual Harveian Oration given in 2008 by Sir Michael Rawlins, who was at that time the chair of NICE in the UK, the National Institute for Health and Clinical Excellence (Rawlins, 2008).

As a further introduction to this section on research in Open Dialogue (OD), we would also like to share the abstract to that Harveian Oration:

> Decisions about the use of therapeutic interventions, whether for individuals or entire healthcare systems, should be based on the totality of the available evidence. The notion that evidence can be reliably or usefully placed in 'hierarchies' is illusory. Rather, decision makers need to exercise judgement about whether (and when) evidence gathered from experimental or observational sources is fit for purpose.
>
> (Rawlins, 2008)

In Chapter 37 Martindale summarises the ongoing research findings from Western Lapland, including a 19-year follow-up study. It is this research which has been receiving worldwide attention, due to the very positive findings, which have inevitably evoked debate as to their wider implications. Prior to this, Martindale (Chapter 36) reviews the evidence base for Need-Adapted Treatment (NAT). Given that outcomes from later cohorts in this research are similar to those from Western Lapland research and that the approaches bear many resemblances, Martindale argues that the positive outcomes from OD research cannot be attributed primarily to factors local to Western Lapland. The extent of the development of OD in several countries, to the satisfaction of service users, their families and staff, clearly demonstrates the possibilities for wider application, and the preliminary data from outcomes in different settings is also encouraging. The chapters by Osborne (40), Lægsgaard (41), Gordon (43) and Martindale and Altwies (44) describe provisional outcomes in services outside Finland.

Freeman et al. (2019) conducted a comprehensive systematic review of the existing qualitative and quantitative research into OD, highlighting the limitations, including the generally low methodological rigor and high risk of bias. They encourage research that better links key ingredients of OD, such as authenticity and trust, with efficacy in outcomes, and also recommend research that focuses on OD as a way of organising services.

Some of the limitations highlighted by Freeman et al. should be addressed by major research projects outlined in the chapters by Razzaque (39) and Pocobello (42) in this section, from the UK and Italy respectively. These will address the question of the transferability of OD to other contexts and how comparable the outcomes are in these contexts to those of Western Lapland. Both the size and range of issues being researched in the British project should meet reservations about the quantity and quality of the existing research evidence. The UK trial also includes peer workers. Their role in network meetings has been discussed in Chapter 25 and aspects of this are being researched in this trial, as well as in a separate research project reported by Osborne (Chapter 40).

Mary Olson, in Chapter 38, describes two fidelity instruments that were developed primarily for research purposes to determine both the quality of work being undertaken in network meetings and adherence to the 12 elements of dialogic practice. She also introduces an Organisational Systems Guide that can help with the development and maintenance of systems that support OD practice.

This book indicates that there is both considerable variation in the length of OD training programmes and in the way OD services are being developed. This will complicate research outcomes and perhaps more standards will need to be developed for both training and service development. It is inevitable though that there will continue to be (significant) differences between services, reflecting both the local culture and variations in the extent of service development. It will be important, then, in evaluating any research conducted in settings developing OD, to clarify the extent of the training and service development, so as to fairly judge the project in hand, but also to be fair to the research from Western Lapland, where the entire service has been fully redeveloped in line with the seven principles of OD and where staff training is to a high level.

Research projects collating feedback from service users, family/network members and/or staff is a particular focus in the chapters by Gordon (43), Twamley (45), Lægsgaard (41) and Pocobello (42), and preliminary findings are largely of positive experiences. Families seem to especially value the opportunity to work collaboratively and the provision of a safe space to talk about issues they have not spoken about before, with people who listen very carefully. Staff members seem in particular to appreciate the values in the OD approach, and the opportunity to work more relationally.

Several of the projects reported investigate the feasibility of developing an OD service in a particular setting. The evidence suggests that, whilst there are always ongoing obstacles/challenges in transforming/developing such a service, it has been possible to make significant progress with service development and the quality of dialogic practice. The chapters by Razzaque (39), Osborne (40), Pocobello (42), Gordon (43) and Twamley (45) in particular focus on this question of feasibility.

Chapter 46 reports on a very interesting kind of research aiming to identify the effective elements within OD. The focus is on the dialogic stance and the research suggests that it is openness and authenticity that are likely to be the key elements. A second strand of research (Chapter 47) uses a current paradigm in the cognitive sciences, which conceives of the self as a self-organising system, brought forth through interactional processes. These two research strands are linked in the theoretical proposal that openness and authenticity in dialogical practice may facilitate the better (re)organisation of the self after a psychotic episode, because they support the basic interactional structures underlying the socially constituted self. This links with long-standing clinical and research interests into the self in psychosis and therapeutic methods addressing the self. Josef Parnas (2012) and Mauricio Peciccia (1998) are particularly well known within the International Society for Psychological and Social Approaches to Psychosis (ISPS) in these respects.

High-quality outcome research does not necessarily lead to the implementation of 'proven' methods, the implication being that there is some outcome research that is welcome and some that is not so welcome, perhaps because it challenges an existing ideology. For instance, quality evidence has existed for decades about the effectiveness of family interventions for people having psychotic experiences and yet these remain rarely applied (Martindale, 2017).

OD is in its early stages as a potentially new paradigm for the provision of mental health services and we hope this research section will excite both further qualitative and quantitative research. Many believe that a good deal of current mental health practice is ideologically too rooted in the biomedical approach, with poor outcomes; they also believe that psychosocial factors receive too little attention and that exploring and researching new paradigms and systems is therefore essential.

References

Freeman, A., Tribe, R., Stott, J. and Pilling, S. (2019) Open Dialogue: A review of the evidence. *Psychiatric Services*, 70(1), p. 46–59. doi.org/10.1176/appi.ps.201800236

Martindale, B. (2017) A psychoanalytic contribution to understanding the lack of professional involvement in psychotherapeutic work with families where there is psychosis. *British Journal of Psychotherapy*, 33(2), p. 224–238. doi.org/10.1111/bjp.12290

Parnas, J. (2012) The core gestalt of schizophrenia. *World Psychiatry*, 11(2), p. 67–69. doi.org/10.1016/j.wpsyc.2012.05.002

Peciccia, M. and Benedetti, G. (1998) The integration of sensorial channels through progressive mirror drawing in the psychotherapy of schizophrenic patients with disturbances in verbal language. *Journal of the American Academy of Psychoanalysis and Dynamic Psychiatry*, 26, p. 109–122. doi.org/ 10.1521/jaap.1.1998.26.1.109

Rawlins, M. (2008) De testimonio: On the evidence for decisions about the use of therapeutic interventions. *The Lancet*, 372(9656), p. 2152–2161. doi.org/ 10.1016/S0140-6736(08)61930-3

36

RESEARCH INTO THE NEED-ADAPTED TREATMENT APPROACH TO PSYCHOSIS

Brian Martindale
(UK)

Introduction

Some might believe that Open Dialogue (OD) is only relevant to a small community in an atypical environment (Western Lapland). I will therefore start by summarising the research results of OD's precursor, the Need-Adapted Treatment approach (NAT) to 'schizophrenia' (Alanen, 1997), summarised in Chapter 2 of this book (page 35), which was instigated in the major Finnish City of Turku, a considerable distance from Western Lapland. It is important to note that the outcomes of later NAT studies were very favourable and commensurate to those of OD (as reported in Chapter 37).

Randomised controlled trials versus cohort studies

Randomised controlled trials (RCTs) treat groups of service users as if they were homogenous in their treatment needs. For this reason, Alanen (1997, p. 124 and p. 141) argued that they are not suited to NAT interventions, and are even unethical. From a NAT perspective, while intervention X might be useful for service user A, it might be counterproductive for service user B, who may need different interventions at different stages, according to their psychosocial problems and development. Therefore, in Turku (in the southwest of Finland), Alanen evaluated outcomes for successive cohorts of service users as NAT developed.

NAT cohort studies

In early NAT cohorts the engagement of service users in long-term individual therapy led to a substantive reduction in hospital bed usage compared to those without therapy (Alanen, 1997, p. 147–148), and in a later cohort (Cohort 3) the improvement seen between years two and five could probably be attributed to the continuation of therapy during this period (Alanen,

Table 36.1 Turku 'schizophrenia' cohort's five-year outcome following family interventions

Year of intake	Sample size	% without psychotic symptoms	% fully able to work	% with no disability pension	Total hospital days in 5 years	Number of suicides
1976–77 (Cohort 3)	56	38	30	49	272	2
1983–84 (Cohort 4)	30	61	57	82	132	1

1997, p. 156 and p. 157). In Cohort 3 family meetings occurred for research purposes and were compared with Cohort 4 where these took place for thera-peutic purposes. Further significant improvements in outcome occurred, for individuals who met strict DSM III-R (Diagnostic and Statistical Manual for Mental Disorders, revised third edition) criteria for schizophrenia (Alanen, 1997, p. 156), as can be seen in Table 36.1:

Particularly noteworthy findings here are the percentage able to work and those without disability pension. As NAT shortened the duration of the psychosis, this probably led to the reduction in those diagnosed with a 'schizophrenic' disorder, as this is defined partly by the duration of psychotic symptoms (Alanen, 1997, p. 157).

Alanen also led the Finnish National 'Schizophrenia' Project to reduce the number of new and longer-term service users with 'schizophrenia' in institutions. The latter decreased by 63% between 1982 and 1992 (Alanen, 1997, p. 159–166). It is notable that, at the beginning of treatment, family-orientated meetings could be organised in 70% of cases (Alanen, 1997, p. 164).

One notable limitation of the NAT cohort studies, and of the OD studies, is that evaluations were not conducted by neutral researchers. To carry greater conviction to the wider mental health research field, this shortcoming needs to be overcome.

Are neuroleptics always necessary?

Later research on Finnish centres using NAT for psychosis compared three centres using a minimal neuroleptic regime with three (the control group) using neuroleptics according to usual practice. In the experimental group 42.9% did not receive neuroleptics at all during the whole two-year period, while the corresponding proportion in the control group was just 5.9%. The clinical outcome of the experimental group was equal to or even somewhat better than that of the control group, with the most important conclusion being that the routine use of neuroleptics in initial treatment is not so essen-tial as is typically thought (Lehtinen et al., 2000).

The need-adapted approach is the context and research background from which OD developed.

References

Alanen, Y. (1997) *Schizophrenia: Its origins and need-adapted treatment.* London: Karnac.

Lehtinen, V., Aaltonen, J., Koffert, T., Räkköläinen, V. and Syvälahti, E. (2000) Two-year outcome in first-episode psychosis treated according to an integrated model. Is immediate neuroleptisation always needed? *European Psychiatry*, 15(5), p. 312–320. doi.org/10.1016/s0924-9338(00)00400-4

37

RESEARCH FROM WESTERN LAPLAND OF OPEN DIALOGUE FOR PSYCHOSIS

Brian Martindale
(UK)

Key aspects of Need-Adapted Treatment were incorporated into Open Dialogue (OD) as it developed in Western Lapland. In this chapter the peer-reviewed published research outcomes of OD will be summarised. Whilst the OD approach forms the basis of *all* psychiatric interventions in Western Lapland, the outcome research in Western Lapland has focused exclusively on people experiencing psychosis.

Hospital stays and the incidence of 'schizophrenia' and 'psychoses'

Between 1985 and 1994, 250 people with non-affective psychosis (Diagnostic and Statistical Manual of Mental Disorders, revised third edition; DSM-III-R) and prodromal 'schizophrenia' (Yung et al., 1996) were identified in Western Lapland (population 72,000) and divided into those treated before and after the introduction of the experimental OD programme in 1990 (Aaltonen et al., 2011, p. 182):

*   The number of new long-stay service users (defined as being an inpatient continually for over a year) fell to zero in 1992 and remained at this level (Finnish national mean 3.5/100,000).
*   The mean hospital stay during the research period was the lowest in Finland (30 days in Western Lapland compared with 49 days elsewhere). 55% of inpatient stays lasted less than 10 days compared with 32% elsewhere.
*   The incidence of new service users with 'schizophrenic disorders' ('schizophrenia' + 'schizophreniform') declined progressively to a highly statistically significant degree throughout the study period, from a mean annual incidence of 30 to 17/100,000.
*   In contrast, the number of *brief* psychotic reactions increased considerably. It is likely that a major consequence of the OD approach is to shift psychosis in a less chronic direction.

Long-term stability of outcomes in acute psychosis in Western Lapland

One study compared a two-year follow-up of service users seen during the period 2003–2005 with two earlier periods, 1992–1993 and 1994–1997 (Seikkula et al., 2011; see Table 37.1), in order to clarify whether similarly good results were obtained after OD had been in place for some years. They were all first episode service users, aged 16–50 across the three periods, with non-affective psychosis classified using DSM-III-R and DSM-IV. The outcomes are as good if not better in the last of the three periods studied, indicating continuing good outcomes after OD has been in place for some years (Aaltonen et al., 2011; Seikkula et al., 2011).

These results indicate that treatment was initiated at a very early stage in the most recent sample (there was a much shorter duration of untreated psychosis) and that this correlated with a reduction in 'schizophrenia' diagnoses but an increase in the incidence of brief psychotic episodes. Effective

Table 37.1 Two-year follow-up results for three periods following the introduction of OD in Western Lapland (adapted from Seikkula et al., 2011)

Measure	1992–1993 N=34	1994–1997 N=46	2003–2005 N=18
Mean duration of untreated psychosis in months	4.3	3.3	0.5
Mean number of hospitalisation days	25.7	9.3	13.6
Mean number of family treatment meetings	26.1	20.7	23.3
Those started on neuroleptic medication	26%	26%	50%*
Those with ongoing use of neuroleptics at 2-year follow-up	15%	11%	28%
Those having individual psychotherapy	33%	44%	67%
Those with no psychotic relapses (in each group more than 80% had no residual psychotic symptoms)	74%	83%	72%
Percentage on disability allowances	26%	9%	16%
Studying, employed or seeking employment	62%	78%	72%
Mean age (years) at intake	26.6	26.8	20.2
'Schizophrenia' diagnosis	38%	41%	22%
Brief psychotic episode diagnosis	15%	24%	39%

*Seikkula et al. (2011, p. 199) indicate that this percentage is probably because some people experiencing psychosis responded to just a few network meetings without neuroleptics and did not partake in follow-up research interviews.

early interventions probably mean that psychotic breakdowns are less likely to deteriorate further into 'schizophrenia'.

The authors point out that the early initiation of interventions, the involvement of service users' social networks, and the quality of staff relationships with all concerned has led, over the years, to meaningful contact with a significant percentage of the local population. This has contributed to an increase in the trust of the overall population in psychiatric treatment and a reduction in stigma. Aaltonen et al. (2011) sees this to be an aspect of what he calls an increase in 'social capital'.

Long-term outcomes in Western Lapland

a) Five-year follow-up

A five-year follow-up study of the first two inclusion periods, 1992–1993 and 1994–1997, has also been published (Seikkula et al., 2006). In the latter period, which started after the full development of OD, the five-year outcomes were as good as the two-year outcomes, with 82% having no residual psychotic symptoms, 76% having returned to studies or full-time employment, and only 14% receiving disability allowance. During the first two years 17% experienced at least one relapse and in the following three years 19% did so. Only 29% had used neuroleptic medication in some phase of the treatment.

b) 19-year follow-up

All service users experiencing psychosis for the first time who were included in the three Western Lapland samples between 1992 and 2005 (N=108) were followed up for an average of 19 years (Bergström et al., 2018; see Table 37.2). Finnish national health register information was used to compare outcomes in Western Lapland with the entire Finnish national cohort of service users experiencing first episode psychosis during the same time period (treatment as usual = TAU).

These results indicate considerable long-term benefits from the OD approach, even for those who needed hospitalisation. It is noteworthy that there is a correlation even within this group, between *less* use of neuroleptics for individuals and better outcomes.

In a separate study of long-term patterns of service use in Western Lapland, Bergström et al. (2017) reported that people who presented with physical aggression had more admissions, spent longer in treatment and used neuroleptics more, raising questions for further research into the applicability of OD to people with more aggressive presentations. The latter concern has also been raised by Gordon et al., in Chapter 22.

The research results from Western Lapland challenge many of the usual conceptions on which interventions are typically based for those with

Table 37.2 Psychiatric treatment and disability pensions in 2015, on average 19 years after the start of treatment (from Bergström et al., 2018)

	OD total (N=108)	OD hospital (N=75)	TAU (N=1,763)	Statistics*	
	(%)	(%)	(%)	x^2	p
30 or more hospital days from onset to follow-up	18.5	54.5	94.4	32.4	.000
Neuroleptics started at onset	20.4	25	70.1	305.1	.000
On neuroleptics at end of follow-up	36.1	47.1	81.1	47.8	.000
In active treatment at follow-up	27.8	35.3	49.2	5.1	.02
Disability pension allowance at follow up	33	44.1	61	28	.000

*These comparisons are between the OD *hospital group* and the TAU group as national data on TAU were only available for those who had been hospitalised.

psychosis: the need for hospitalisation, the necessity of neuroleptics in all cases, the tendency to treat service users individually without involving family and friends, and the attitude of inevitable long-term handicap (it should be noted that these practices are also challenged elsewhere, especially where early intervention services are being developed, such as in the UK). To carry greater conviction, further outcome studies need to be carried out by independent researchers in other settings that support OD practice and where practitioners have been well-trained in OD.

References

Aaltonen, J., Seikkula, J. and Lehtinen, K. (2011) The comprehensive Open Dialogue approach in Western Lapland: I. The incidence of non-affective psychosis and prodromal states. *Psychosis*, 3(3), p. 179–191. doi.org/10.1080/17522439.2011.601750

Bergstrom, T., Alakare, B., Aaltonen, J., Mäki, P., Köngäs-Saviaro, P., Taskila, J. and Seikkula, J. (2017) The long-term use of psychiatric services within the Open Dialogue treatment system after first-episode psychosis. *Psychosis*, 9(4), p. 310–321. doi.org/10.1080/17522439.2017.1344295

Bergström, T., Seikkula, J., Alakare, B., Mäki, P., Köngäs-Saviaro, P., Taskila, J.J., Tolvanen, A. and Aaltonen, J. (2018) The family-oriented Open Dialogue approach in the treatment of first-episode psychosis: Nineteen-year outcomes. *Psychiatry Research*, 270, p. 168–175. doi.org/10.1016/j.psychres.2018.09.039

Seikkula, J., Aaltonen, J., Alakare, B., Haarakangas, K., Keränen, J. and Lehtinen, K. (2006) Five-year experience of first-episode nonaffective psychosis in open-dialogue approach: Treatment principles, follow-up outcomes, and two case studies. *Psychotherapy Research*, 16(2), p. 214–228. doi.org/10.1080/10503300500268490

Seikkula, J., Alakare, B. and Aaltonen, J. (2011) The Comprehensive Open-Dialogue Approach in Western Lapland: II. Long-term stability of acute psychosis outcomes in advanced community care. *Psychosis*, 3(3), p. 192–204. doi.org/10.1080/17522439.2011.595819

Yung, A.R., McGorry, P.D., McFarlane, C.A., Jackson, H.J., Patton, G.C. and Rakkar, A. (1996) Monitoring and care of young people at incipient risk of psychosis. *Schizophrenia Bulletin*, 22(2), p. 283–303. doi.org/10.1093/schbul/22.2.283

38

OPEN DIALOGUE ADHERENCE AND FIDELITY TOOLS

Mary Olson
(USA)

Introduction

Following the US National Institutes of Mental Health guidelines for therapy and organisational-change research development, I, together with colleagues from the University of Massachusetts Medical School, have developed psychotherapy and systems fidelity assessment guides, along with two companion measures, a fidelity adherence scale and a rating manual. As presented here, these carefully derived research products have already proven quite promising in furthering new and creative pathways for Open Dialogue (OD) research and training worldwide.

Psychotherapy guide

As a guide for assessing psychotherapy fidelity in network meetings, *The Key Elements of Dialogic Practice in Open Dialogue: Fidelity Criteria* (Olson et al., 2014) is a summary of the necessary elements. It identifies both the structural components (1–2) and conversational actions of the therapists (3–12) requisite to foster dialogical-network interaction. For a full description, please see our text cited above, which includes many examples as well as in-depth definition of the key elements. This paper has been translated into 15 languages. The key elements are as follows (Table 38.1).

Fidelity adherence scale and rating manual

Based on *The Key Elements of Dialogic Practice* (Olson et al., 2014), we have also developed two companion pieces, a Likert-style fidelity rating scale, called the *Dialogic Practice Fidelity Scale* (Ziedonis et al., 2018), and the *Dialogic Practice Fidelity Rating Manual* (Ziedonis et al., 2018). Both research materials were developed following the need to create concrete scales to assess the adherence items and to provide more clarity for the reviewers on how to rate recorded network meetings.

Table 38.1 The 12 key elements of fidelity to dialogic practice in OD

1. Two (or more) therapists in the team meeting
2. Participation of family and network
3. Using open-ended questions
4. Responding to clients' utterances
5. Emphasising the present moment
6. Eliciting multiple viewpoints
7. Use of a relational focus in the dialogue
8. Responding to problem discourse or behaviour in a matter-of-fact style and attentive to meanings
9. Emphasising the clients' own words and stories, not symptoms
10. Conversation amongst professionals (reflections) in the treatment meetings
11. Being transparent
12. Tolerating uncertainty

Table 38.2 Some criteria for assessing the infrastructure to support dialogic practice

1. Prioritising a network approach
2. Leadership that models respect, authenticity and collaboration
3. Reimbursement to work in dialogical teams
4. Staff well-trained in dialogic practice
5. A welcoming warm, caring environment for people seeking services
6. Capacity to provide and connect clinical and community services
7. Organisational support for the tolerance of uncertainty and the role of dialogue in crisis teams
8. Capacity to provide immediate help and access to need-adapted services
9. Collaborative, shared decision-making in network meetings, e.g. about medication, hospitalisation and treatment planning
10. Genuine value placed on OD as a mindful way of being

Organisational systems guide

We have also drafted an organisation system guide (Ziedonis and Olson, 2015), identifying 10 criteria for a larger organisational culture and treatment infrastructure that can support dialogic practice. It is the OD 'North Star' for organisations: written for everyone involved in OD initiatives, it provides clear direction for those with the most influence on shaping initiatives – administrators, team leaders and clinical and training directors – and allows researchers to assess the setting and how well it facilitates OD and dialogic practice. The criteria are included in Table 38.2.

Clinical trial at Grady Hospital, Atlanta, Georgia, USA and ODDESSI, UK

These psychotherapy and systems fidelity assessment materials have made it possible to undertake new and more rigorous OD research. The University of Massachusetts research team that developed these research materials has been putting them into practice as part of a study to further test and refine the fidelity tools and obtain pilot data in advance of an ongoing clinical trial of OD at Emory University Medical School and Grady Hospital in Atlanta, USA. The initial phase has been funded by the US Foundation for Excellence in Mental Health Care. A core team at Grady has strongly and enthusiastically embraced the approach, while adapting it to their own context. The experience at Grady, and the sense of empowerment this way of working has afforded both service users and staff, has suggested that OD can translate, with fidelity, into an urban-based system that serves primarily a low-income, African American community (Olson, 2017). These fidelity and adherence rating scales have also been the prerequisites for the ODDESSI study in the National Health Service in the UK, described in Chapter 39.

With the ascendancy of a reductionist, biomedical psychiatry, there has over recent decades been a downplaying of relational practices everywhere, a trend that has most dramatically affected disenfranchised populations served by public clinics, agencies and hospitals (Coffey et al., 2001). In contrast, OD can humanise and democratise public psychiatry, and thus represents a much-needed alternative approach. Yet there has been a persistent question as to whether OD can really work outside of Western Lapland. With the arrival of psychotherapy and systems fidelity assessment guides, together with ODDESSI, in particular, it will be possible to answer this question with scientific rigour.

References

Coffey, E.P., Olson, M.E. and Sessions, P. (2001) The heart of the matter: An essay about the effects of managed care on family therapy with children. *Family Process*, 40, p. 385–399. doi.org/10.1111/j.1545-5300.2001.4040100385.x

Olson, M. (2017) Aliveness and social justice: Teaching the principles and practices of Open Dialogue. *Mad-in-America.* [online] Available at: www.madinamerica.com/2017/03/aliveness-social-justice-principles-practice-open-dialogue/ [Accessed 23 May 2020].

Olson, M., Seikkula, J. and Ziedonis, D. (2014) The key elements of dialogic practice in Open Dialogue: Fidelity criteria. *The University of Massachusetts Medical School*, Worcester, MA. [online] Available at: http://umassmed.edu/psychiatry/globalinitiatives/opendialogue/ [Accessed 23 May 2020].

Ziedonis, D. and Olson, M. (2015) 10 organizational criteria of Open Dialogue. Worcester, MA: *The University of Massachusetts Medical School.*

Ziedonis, D., Small, E. and Larkin, C. (2018) *Dialogic practice fidelity rating manual.* San Diego, CA: University of California.

39

THE UK ODDESSI TRIAL

Russell Razzaque
(UK)

Background

ODDESSI stands for 'Open Dialogue – Development and Evaluation of a Social Network Intervention for Severe Mental Illness'. It is a national multi-site cluster randomised controlled trial – together with a parallel qualitative analysis – funded by the UK National Institute of Health Research (NIHR) with a £2.4 million grant. It is the largest OD study in the world, with trial teams being rolled out across six different UK National Health Service (NHS) Trusts. The services will be working with anyone referred in a crisis, thus people of all diagnostic categories – not only those with psychosis.

The reason for such a large-scale study lies in the number of people in the UK wanting to see OD happen. Hundreds of current and ex-service users had been meeting in groups across the country for years advocating OD to NHS managers and commissioners – indeed I have run five gatherings myself with over 300 attendees in each. A growing body of clinicians have also been increasingly inspired by its philosophy; attending workshops, reading literature, talking to colleagues and urging their organisations to look at this way of working. In 2016, for example, the Royal College of Psychiatrists General Adult Faculty set up an OD online subgroup. The response from management has been consistent rejection, stating the insufficient evidence base. The general criticism was that the improved outcomes reported in Western Lapland could be unrelated to the change in clinical practice to OD – and that, without any randomised evidence, a wholesale shift in this direction could not be justified.

Some proponents of need-adapted treatment and OD suggest that randomised controlled trials (RCTs) can only be designed to draw "one size fits all" conclusions (Alanen, 1997), the very opposite of the need-adapted and OD approaches, which are personalised ones. At an International Psychosis meeting of OD practitioners and trainers in 2014, held in Denmark, I informally discussed the need for an OD RCT to have any hope of propagating it, resulting in varying degrees of interest and scepticism, much of which I shared. I wanted to see OD happen for people in my country, and if this was the key to bring it about, I argued we had a responsibility to organise one. There was broad agreement that such a study would need a strong qualitative aspect too,

248

so that a narrative could be written alongside the raw data, describing the human experience of OD beyond the numbers. A long journey has been travelled since then, involving considerable intensive ongoing collaboration with Jaakko Seikkula, Mary Olson and Doug Zeidonis, and other key trainers and leaders in the field.

Recruiting senior academics took less time than expected, especially with the strong backing of Steve Pilling at University College London, and support from the Clinical Trials Unit at King's College London. A panel of distinguished professors from these universities, and from Middlesex University and Birmingham University, joined together to help design the trial and apply for a major NIHR programme grant. The final agreement only came about after the latter was satisfied that our power calculation (the number of people needed in the study in order to achieve a significant finding) was sufficient. This turned out to be 644 people.

Design of the study

ODDESSI is a five-year programme, consisting of five work streams:

Work stream 1

This concerns developing local OD services and involves working with clinicians in six trusts: appointing people, writing operational policies, setting up team business and meeting cycles and operationalising a fully fledged NHS OD service. A key objective is ensuring continuity of care organised around dialogical network meetings, with consistent staff in attendance.

Work stream 2

This is a pilot evaluation of two teams to model fidelity. The teams are based in northeast London and Kent.[1] The evaluation was due to run for six months from July 2018 and has been successfully completed. The key objectives set were that a) an OD service can operate in the NHS, b) we can demonstrate adherence and fidelity to OD in these local services, and c) service users can be recruited into a trial to measure their outcomes. These objectives were all met fully and, as a result, the trial was given the go ahead to complete the full programme over the following three years.

Work stream 3

This is the RCT itself, bringing all the remaining teams online. All six teams will be operational and recruiting soon. The core outcome measures are relapse rates and hospital admissions. We want to demonstrate that people are less likely to remain in services long term once they have OD, as their probability of relapsing fully would be lower. There are many further measures of mental and physical health including those of the wider social network. Staff recruitment and retention will be one important aspect of the economic analysis.

The problems of engaging those with psychosis will be addressed as the trial will accept all referrals in each chosen area as part of a cluster randomised design. This means that particular geographical catchment areas are assigned randomly to either OD or control and all those in the OD area will receive OD when referred for urgent crisis care. As that is the front-line service provided in that area, all referred will start and continue their care in this way, including psychosis presentations. Some Trusts have an exclusion for first episode psychosis, due to local commissioning arrangements, but this is not universal across the trial, and so there will be a significant proportion of service users who will be seen with such issues. Consent for research evaluations will take place for each service user after the crisis is over, as agreed in our ethics approval.

Work stream 4

This is a qualitative analysis, involving multiple interviews and focus groups with all involved, generating a detailed picture of the experiences of both those receiving and providing an OD service.

Work stream 5

This explores and evaluates the peer worker role (see Chapter 25 for more information about the peer worker role in Open Dialogue).

Training

Details of the training programme developed for this project are in Chapter 18. All participating Trusts have sent staff to the course, and as of 2019 we have trained over 300 staff from all disciplines and a significant cohort of peer workers. In 90% of teams, the team manager is one of those being trained. Training a higher level of manager such as the clinical or medical director has had a particularly powerful effect on boosting support for the research and clinical practice.

Challenges

The experience of the training so far, and with several of the initial families that we have started to work with, has been very promising, with powerful feedback from both clinicians and families. All are aware of how different this form of care is to traditional ways of working. Almost universally, those who have worked traditionally express profound gratitude for the new experiences. Challenges lie ahead in the trial, including how the continuity of care that

OD demands can be maintained operationally, and how the culture can be sustained over the years as staff change, as training takes considerable investment and time.

A key driver to overcoming these obstacles has been the passion that OD has unlocked among the people who encounter it. As a result, there is a great deal of energy involved in finding ways to ensure this endeavour succeeds and can be sustained. If we manage to replicate anything like the findings of our predecessors and mentors in Western Lapland, then this will very likely become the future of mental healthcare in the UK and beyond. It is this dream that keeps so many of us committed to this endeavour.

Note

1 Kent is a county in the southeast of the UK.

Reference

Alanen, Y. (1997) *Schizophrenia: Its origins and need-adapted treatment.* London: Karnac.

40

RESEARCH INTO A PEER-SUPPORTED OPEN DIALOGUE SERVICE IN THE UK

James Osborne
(UK)

Introduction

The first UK NHS Peer-supported Open Dialogue (POD) service was launched in the UK county of Kent in February 2017. POD is a UK adaption of the Finnish OD model in which people with lived experience, employed as peer support workers, are trained in OD along with qualified staff and then form an integral part of the network meetings (see Chapter 25 for more information on peer workers in OD). This approach is closely aligned to the New York Parachute Project outlined in Chapter 44. Although the service has become part of the ODDESSI trial, described in Chapter 39 of this section, the research reported here commenced before the ODDESSI trial.

The service receives referrals from general practitioners or accident and emergency departments of people requiring mental health services due to any form of mental health crisis, including people experiencing psychotic symptoms. The team makes contact and arranges the first network meeting within 24 hours, and the same POD clinicians take responsibility for seeing the service user and their network throughout their care.

With the launch of the service we embarked upon a National Institute of Health Research (NIHR) study, funded by The Health Foundation. The aim was to investigate the feasibility of POD as a treatment offered by secondary mental health services in Kent and Medway NHS Partnership Trust (KMPT), as well as to examine the feasibility of the measures used to evaluate POD.

Among the specific objectives are:

1 To examine the number of hospital admissions and the length of hospital stays for service users receiving POD.
2 To examine service user clinical functioning, wellbeing, experience and impact on daily routine during the course of POD.
3 To examine the perceived support received by the family, carers and social network.

4   To better understand the peer support worker role and their experiences of being involved in POD.
5   To broadly examine the costs of the POD approach.
6   To detail the views of Trust personnel on the implementation of POD in the Trust.

Study design and methods

The study involves a mixed methods design of quantitative and qualitative research. The primary quantitative research collected data from electronic medical records and questionnaires covering clinical presentation, wellbeing, functioning and satisfaction. Participants aged 18–65 entering the POD service (N=50) were recruited over 18 months, with the addition of family and social network members. Several quantitative outcome measures were collected through repeated, validated scales completed by participants and POD clinicians at baseline, three months and six months to understand if the POD intervention was feasible and clinically effective in an NHS setting. As a feasibility study there was no comparison group at this stage.

The embedded qualitative research examined experiences of NHS staff. Focus groups were carried out with POD clinicians specifically to understand their experience of working in this model, their experience of working with the family or social network and the role of peer support workers. Managers of KMPT took part in focus groups to understand the challenges of implementing POD in the NHS, its value and sustainability. Transcripts of these group sessions were then subject to a qualitative thematic analysis.

Results

At the time of this publication, recruitment is complete but findings have not yet been analysed. Shortfalls will be discussed below, but early data look promising. Service user and family or network satisfaction consistently appear high, along with the family feeling more supported than previously. There are also clear indications that hospital admissions reduce and mental wellbeing and social functioning improve. Initial findings suggest that there is strong staff satisfaction and that POD-trained clinicians adhere closely to the model.

Discussion and reflection

We recognise that the study does not have the rigour of a randomised controlled trial; however, it does begin to highlight some interesting benefits from POD in the UK, not just for the service user, but also their family/network and clinical staff.

It has also provided valuable learning about undertaking research into this particular model, especially when starting research at the onset of a mental health crisis. The study was initially discussed with participants early on in the intervention and consent to participate was sought. Despite careful thought with POD clinicians about the research and its introduction into network meetings, the process shone a light on the complexities of researching an OD model at the point of crisis. POD clinicians spoke of feeling uncomfortable about the consent process and described it as a 'monological' insertion, not well placed at the point of crisis. Follow-up measures also represent a challenge due to people deciding they wanted to move on from the service. Future OD studies will benefit from paying close attention to the method of recruitment, obtaining consent and follow-up data collection.

With no benchmarking around training, set-up and operationalisation of a POD team in the UK, this study represents an early attempt to look beyond some of the direct benefits for people using a POD service in order to learn more about the factors facing NHS mental health Trusts when considering implementing OD. These include both the redesign of services and the complex interfaces with traditional models of psychiatry that inevitably occur when POD is part of the system instead of being the system.

41

OPEN DIALOGUE FOR PSYCHOSIS IN FIVE DANISH MUNICIPALITIES – RESULTS AND EXPERIENCES

Mett Marri Lægsgaard
(Denmark)

Introduction

Between 2014 and 2016, we conducted a study for the Danish National Board of Social Services on the implementation and outcome of OD for psychosis in five Danish municipalities. The five municipalities evaluated OD as a service, and based on the results from our study, the Board recommended that OD be implemented in additional Danish municipalities, using our implementation guide to support this. The full study has been published in Danish (Lægsgaard et al., 2017) as both a report and an implementation guide. We now present a summary in English.

Study design and participants

The study had two main aims:

- to evaluate the impact of OD on people experiencing psychosis; and
- to investigate factors influencing the implementation process.

The study was designed as a theory-based evaluation according to the principles of Contribution Analysis, which aims at inferring causality in real-life evaluations where an experimental design has not been possible (Mayne, 2012).

A total of 103 people were included in the study. All participants were aged over 18 years and had a diagnosis in the F20–29 range in the International Classification of Diseases ICD-10 (schizophrenia, schizotypal and delusional disorders). They had all been in contact with the psychiatric system within the past two years and were currently in contact/receiving support from social services in the municipality.

Training of staff

Danish OD experts converted the seven original principles into a practical manual, focusing specifically on the planning and running of network meetings, i.e. the roles and actions of staff (The National Board of Social Services, 2014). Network meetings had one facilitator and included one or two additional staff members acting as a reflecting team. A total of 28 experienced social workers were trained in the seven principles of OD and in performing OD in accordance with the manual. The training consisted of five days of theory, instruction and role-playing. The training also included 100 hours of subsequent group supervision, and a certification process involving experts evaluating a video recording of a network meeting facilitated by a trainee. All 28 social workers passed the certification.

Results

We expected OD to influence the recovery and general well-being of the participants. We used two instruments to measure this outcome: the Mental Health Recovery Measure (MHRM) is a 30-item scale that assesses self-perceived recovery in persons with a severe mental illness. The score ranges from 0 to 120 points (Young and Bullock, 2005). The WHO-5 Well-Being Index (WHO-5) is a 5-item scale that assesses current mental well-being. The score ranges from 0 to 100 points (Bech, 2012). The two questionnaires were administered to the participants before and after their engagement in the OD process (maximum three months after their last network meeting). The OD processes included 2–9 network meetings in a time span from one to 19 months. 58% of participants had only two meetings.

Results showed a positive development on both instruments. The MHRM mean score increased from 67.3 to 74.0 (a 6.7-point increase, SD 13.4), which corresponds to an effect size of 0.41 (Cohens D). 37% of the participants had at least a 10-point difference in before–after scores (clinically significant). The WHO-5 mean score increased from 44.6 to 51.8 (a 7.2-point increase, SD 22.1), which corresponds to an effect size of 0.32 (Cohens D). 47% of the participants had at least a 10-point difference in before–after scores (clinically significant). Positive development measured by the two scales correlated, meaning that the same participants had changes in both recovery and general well-being. Participants with the lowest baseline ratings on the two scales were more likely to show a positive development.

We also used the Client Satisfaction Questionnaire to measure participants' overall self-assessment of outcome (Larsen et al., 1979). Almost all participants expressed great satisfaction with OD. We conducted a survey asking participants, network members and staff how they experienced each network meeting, as well as qualitative interviews with participants, members of personal and professional networks and staff to investigate their experience of specific elements of OD. A great majority of participants thought that staff had a flexible attitude and focused on their needs. Participants and network members also thought that the social network perspective was consistently present and that the meeting structure facilitated new ways of being in dialogue, generating new possibilities for acting and interacting in the network. In conclusion, the results from the questionnaires and the qualitative interviews indicated that:

a the implementation of OD corresponded to the basic principles; and
b most of the participants in the study were satisfied with OD and found that central elements of the network meetings made a positive difference for them.

Implementing Open Dialogue

We monitored the implementation process by means of questionnaires and interviews. We identified a range of experiences relevant to the future implementation of OD but can only mention a few here. For a broader perspective on implementing OD in the Scandinavian countries, see Buus et al. (2017).

The implementation of OD required an adaptation of the principles to the specific local setting, e.g. the principle of immediate help. Although the participants in the present study suffered from severe mental health problems (within the F20–F29 ICD range), they were not currently hospitalised, and most were not in acute crisis. In fact, it took a great deal of motivational work to recruit persons to the study – as the usual OD principle of immediate help was not appropriate, it was replaced by motivational work towards participation in network meetings. This required consideration of how to organise OD such that there is a higher level of flexibility in planning and conducting network meetings than is usual in social services – to meet the actual needs of the service user.

In this project, each participant's social network was defined as including both a personal and a professional network, and the manual instructs staff to encourage participants to consider including all such network members. However, most network meetings included only the participant, the professional team, a parent and a contact person from the municipality. The intent was to include a broader network, but the organisational structure and culture made this difficult.

The study leads to one central conclusion: OD is a principle-based approach and therefore implementation of OD is very dependent on the local organisation, the support of local leaders and cooperation across sectors. Nevertheless, our results show that even this manualised version of OD, implemented in different settings with varying levels of organisational support, had a positive impact on the well-being of a large minority of participants in the study.

Also, most participants, network members and staff considered OD to be a valuable approach that facilitated new ways of talking and interacting in the network.

References

Bech, P. (2012) WHO-5. [online] Psykiatri-regionh.dk. Available at: www.psykiatri-regionh.dk/who-5/Pages/default.aspx (Accessed 23 May 2020).

Buus, N., Bikic, A., Jacobsen, E., Müller-Nielsen, K., Aagaard, J. and Rossen, C. (2017) Adapting and implementing Open Dialogue in the Scandinavian countries: A scoping review. *Issues in Mental Health Nursing*, 38(5), p. 391–401. doi.org/10.1080/01612840.2016.1269377

Lægsgaard, M., Balleby, M., Nørbæk, A. and Pilegaard, K. (2017) *Evaluering af Åben Dialog i fem danske kommuner [Evaluation of Open Dialogue in five Danish municipalities]*. [online] Available at: https://socialstyrelsen.dk/udgivelser/kvalitet-i-den-kommunale-indsats-over-for-borgere-med-svaere-psykiske-lidelser-aben-dialog [Accessed 4 August 2020].

Larsen, D.L., Attkisson, C.C., Hargreaves, W.A. and Nguyen, T.D. (1979) Assessment of client/patient satisfaction: Development of a general scale. *Evaluation and Program Planning*, 2(3) p. 197–207. doi: 10.1016/0149-7189(79)90094-6

Mayne, J. (2012) Contribution analysis: Coming of age? *Evaluation*, 18(3), p. 270–280. doi.org/10.1177/1356389012451663

The National Board of Social Services (2014) *Metodemanual for Åben Dialog [Open Dialogue Manual]*. [online] Available at: https://socialstyrelsen.dk/udgivelser/metodemanual-for-aben-dialog [Accessed 23 May 2020].

Young, S. and Bullock, W. (2005) 'Mental health recovery measure (MHRM)' in T. Campbell-Orde, J. Chamberlin, J. Carpenter and H. Leff (eds.) *Measuring the promise: A compendium of recovery measures*, 2nd ed. Cambridge, MA: Evaluation Center at Human Services Research Institute, p. 36–40.

42

RESEARCHING WHETHER FINNISH OPEN DIALOGUE TRANSFERS TO THE ITALIAN MENTAL HEALTH SYSTEM[1]

Raffaella Pocobello
(Italy)[2]

Introduction

This chapter presents the research design and the preliminary results of a project evaluating the transferability of the Finnish Open Dialogue (OD) approach into the Italian mental health system. The Italian OD programme (Pocobello et al., 2016) started in February 2015, with a two-year project funded by the Ministry of Health involving eight mental health departments (MHDs) across Italy, selected according to their mental health director's interest in developing an OD approach. The project was coordinated by the Department of Prevention of the local health service of Turin and evaluated by the National Research Council, and the introduction of OD to Italy is described more fully in Chapter 20.

Research design

A participatory and mixed methods research design was implemented as part of the OD programme, as recommended by Greenhalgh et al. (2004). The research programme follows the OD implementation process in Italy and is articulated in three main phases:

Phase 1: professionals' view and system antecedents

In this phase the research questions were:

• Do professionals accept OD practice?
• What do they think are the critical issues in the transferability of OD to their MHD?

First, we conducted interviews with the MHD directors to explore their views on the OD approach, focusing on perceived opportunities for and obstacles to transferring OD into their departments. The perspective of the professionals involved in the training was explored using a questionnaire. The hindering factors were then discussed by MHDs in a workshop with a group of international OD experts.

Phase 2: training evaluation

In this phase the research questions were:

- Was the training effective?
- Did the skills learned during the training transfer to actual OD practice in the workplace?
- At the end of the training, did trainees' clinical practice adhere to the OD fidelity standards?

The OD foundation training by expert trainers took 10 months and started in December 2015 (see Chapter 20 for more detail on this training). It involved 80 professionals (divided into two groups). The training evaluation had different phases and used a multi-methods approach:

(a) participatory observation during the training;
(b) the evaluation of the impact of the training on professionals, analysing essays on their experience of the training;
(c) the transfer of OD clinical and organisational principles from the training to the workplace, evaluated by means of a questionnaire; and
(d) the adherence of clinical interventions to OD, using OD fidelity scales (see Chapter 38). Preliminary results of the OD fidelity assessment were shared and discussed in all the MHDs.

Phase 3: pilot study

In this phase the primary research question was:

- Is OD transferable clinically and organisationally into the context of Italian MHDs?

And more specifically:

- Do trained professionals succeed in treating at least 66% of all new cases of a predefined area using the OD approach?
- Does clinical practice reflect OD fidelity criteria?

- What processes and factors were related to a successful OD implementation? We looked at the number of meetings, whether the families could choose where the meetings took place (including in their homes), the numbers of professionals from each discipline involved and the professionals' attendance at training. We also looked at rates of hospitalisation and the use of pharmacological interventions as well as psychological and social treatments.
- What are the short-term outcomes (symptoms, psychological and social functioning, and social network size) related to the practice of OD in the Italian context?
- Are service users and families involved in OD satisfied?
- Is it feasible to collect the necessary data and gain permission for the recording of network meetings?
- Finally, we assessed the reliability of data ratings between independent raters.

All the persons referred to mental health services for the first time (age range 16–64) within a defined area of each department were enrolled during the first month of the study and followed up for 12 months. Independent of diagnostic criteria, symptom functioning and social network dimension were assessed at the beginning of the OD treatment process and again at months six and 12. After each network meeting, information about where the meeting took place, who participated, and the use of other services and therapies was collected by professionals. Service user satisfaction was investigated by means of two visual scales. Fidelity to key OD elements was assessed by two independent raters analysing videotapes of OD sessions. The results of the pilot study are forthcoming.

Preliminary results

Professionals' views and system antecedents

Changes don't occur when health professionals don't accept the innovation being implemented (Fleuren et al., 2004). We found that professionals perceived OD to be highly compatible with their values, the norms they would like to follow, and their perceived needs at both an individual and organisational level. Professionals stated that operationalising the key principles of OD may help them improve their practice and see that OD is in line with Basaglia's legacy[3] (Foot, 2014). One MHD director pointed out:

> [F]or me it [OD] is an interesting theoretical framework… it is aligned with the reforms to Italian psychiatry with the law 180… thus, we are already prepared, in some ways, to adopt it.

This compatibility is a valuable predictor of the successful assimilation of a new practice (Greenhalgh et al., 2004). However, OD was also described by professionals as a complex and challenging innovation, which might mean there are obstacles to its implementation (Greenhalgh et al., 2004). Furthermore, professionals' lack of knowledge about dialogical practice, as well as certain organisational aspects, such as shift work and the absence of teams dedicated full time to OD, were identified as obstacles. To address these critical issues, professionals outlined the importance of training, clinical adherence, OD-dedicated teams and a positive mental attitude of sharing, respect and trust in their clinical co-workers.

Training evaluation

Our findings suggest that the OD training was effective in eliciting a positive attitude in trainees and in enabling them to learn the approach. Italian professionals experienced the training as a deep professional and emotional journey, and the assessment of OD fidelity was mainly satisfactory. However, we found some differences in the level of adherence between departments and some professionals had difficulty in formulating open questions, eliciting polyphony and having a relational focus in the dialogue.

Pilot study

The pilot study involved 72 persons in need of help for mental health issues. The OD teams successfully enrolled and treated 69.2% of all new service users in the areas being researched, meeting the required standard of transferability (minimum 66%). The reasons for non-enrolment were either service users not wanting to be involved in a research project or not wanting to involve their families. However, service users who did engage in an OD process, and their family members, expressed a high level of satisfaction when the network meetings were evaluated. These preliminary results suggest that OD is transferable clinically and organisationally into the Italian MHDs.

Reflections

OD appears feasible for the Italian context (Pocobello and el Sehity, 2017). However, we need to wait for the results of the pilot study to determine (1) how faithful clinical practice was to OD as assessed by OD fidelity criteria, (2) the processes involved in successful and unsuccessful OD implementation, and (3) the short-term outcomes, the feasibility of collecting OD outcomes and the reliability of ratings between independent raters.

In the meantime, an OD national network needs to be established to promote quality assurance and to attract resources for training, supervision and research.

Notes

1 This contribution was realised with the support of the Italian Ministry of Health, CCM-Programme 2014.
2 I am grateful to Giuseppe Salamina and Chiara Rossi for the coordination of the Italian OD project and to Tarek el Sehity for his significant contributions to the research.
3 Franco Basaglia was an Italian psychiatrist who promoted the closure of psychiatric hospitals and mental health reform in Italy. Thanks to his contribution, Italy was the first country to close psychiatric hospitals, with a law (n. 180/1978), also called 'Basaglia Law'. Psychiatric hospitals were replaced with radically different networks of community services.

References

Fleuren, M., Wiefferink, K. and Paulussen, T. (2004) Determinants of innovation within health care organizations. Literature review and Delphi study. *International Journal for Quality in Health Care*, 16(2), p. 107–123. doi.org/10.1093/intqhc/mzh030

Foot, J. (2014) Franco Basaglia and the radical psychiatry movement in Italy, 1961–78. *Critical and Radical Social Work*, 2(2), p. 235–249. doi.org/10.1332/204986014X14002292074708

Greenhalgh, T., Robert, G., Macfarlane, F., Bate, P. and Kyriakidou, O. (2004) Diffusion of innovations in service organizations: Systematic review and recommendations. *Milbank Quarterly*, 82(4), p. 581–629. doi.org/10.1111/j.0887-378X.2004.00325.x

Pocobello, R. and el Sehity, T. (2017) *Evaluation of Open Dialogue in the context of the Italian mental health services. Technical report for the Ministry of Health.* National Research Council, Rome.

Pocobello, R., Salamina, G., Rossi, C. and Alonzi, C. (2016) Open Dialogue in Italy: From project to programme. *The UK Peer-Supported Open Dialogue Bulletin (fourth POD Bulletin).* [online] Available at: http://eepurl.com/bWeBNz [Accessed 23 May 2020].

43

A FEASIBILITY STUDY OF ADAPTING OPEN DIALOGUE TO THE US HEALTH CONTEXT

The Collaborative Pathway at Advocates, Massachusetts, USA

Christopher Gordon
(USA)

Context

The Collaborative Pathway (CP) serves persons aged 14–35 years who are experiencing current or recent psychosis, regardless of diagnosis (see Chapter 22 for more information on this programme). The programme, based on Open Dialogue (OD) principles, opened in 2012. The pathway in Framingham, Massachusetts, USA, is in a not-for-profit mental health agency: *Advocates*. The leadership and clinical staff trained for two years, achieving certification, at the Institute for Dialogic Practice in Massachusetts, directed by Mary Olson and Jaakko Seikkula. The programme blends revenue streams of private insurance and grant support, receiving support from the Foundation for Excellence in Mental Health Care, the Cummings Foundation, and the Massachusetts Department of Mental Health.

The service

The CP provides one year of service with pairs of clinicians engaging in network meetings, primarily in the home. When the psychiatrist is involved, network and individual meetings occur in a clinic office. The team also arranges for individual psychotherapy and other services as needed. The programme is supported by a 24/7/365 mobile crisis team, whose leaders are also trained in OD. All participants in the programme first engaged in a standard psychiatric evaluation and risk assessment and provided informed consent. We understand that these requirements interfered with optimal OD practice as conducted in Western Lapland in which a spirit of dialogue is present from the very first encounter. In the US, either due to research requirements or due to a more litigious atmosphere of care, these modifications may be necessary.

Feasibility study

This account is a summary of the published feasibility study of work with our first 14 families (Gordon et al., 2016). The participants' average age was 23 years, and duration of illness was 41.1 (+/− 40.7) weeks. We were primarily interested in whether, and how, OD could be practised in an urban, multi-ethnic, publicly funded centre within a North American city. We evaluated feasibility and effectiveness by surveys at baseline and at three, six and 12 months, using a variety of quantitative and quality evaluations – for details see Gordon et al. (2016). Through record reviews, we assessed psychiatric medications prescribed, school and work participation and psychiatric hospitalisation in the six months prior to, and during, the 12-month engagement in the CP service. We tracked adverse events, including any suicidal acts, other acts of violence, and involuntary hospitalisations. Independent researchers conducted six in-depth qualitative interviews with participants and their families (Gidugu et al., 2020). Though the staff were trained by Mary Olson, the research was conducted before the availability of the OD adherence and fidelity tools described in Chapter 38.

Outcomes of the feasibility study

Participants at intake were diagnosed by the treating psychiatrist as within the schizophrenia spectrum disorders (12/14) and bipolar disorders (2/14). At the end of one year, the diagnostic impression of the treating psychiatrist had evolved on the basis of additional information to schizophrenia spectrum disorders (7/14); bipolar disorders (5/14); autism spectrum disorders (1/14); and obsessive-compulsive disorder (1/14).

On average, 12.5 network meetings occurred in the year, and 36% of these involved a psychiatrist. Service user satisfaction and perceptions of shared decision making were high throughout the year. Clinical outcomes were generally positive, with clinically significant improvement in symptoms, functioning and need for care. We had no substantial adverse outcomes, apart from six short-term psychiatric hospitalisations, two of which were involuntary. In terms of self-determination and collaborative processes, participants used network meetings to make a variety of decisions about medications: some reduced or eliminated antipsychotic medications, others adjusted their dosages or choice of medications and some began antipsychotic medications. Staff satisfaction was high.

Lessons learned

We have now served 41 families. Lessons learned include the following:

1 Training was expensive and time-intensive, but highly valued.
2 Preliminary psychiatric evaluation and risk assessment were well tolerated and did not, in our view, compromise the integrity of the programme.
3 Insurance covered only a fraction of the total cost.
4 This model supports empowered shared decision making around medication use and results in various choices about medication by the service users.
5 Families and individuals highly value network meetings as powerful forums for mutual support, understanding and connection. In particular, the following were appreciated:
   • support to avoid hospitalisations;
   • a safe space to say the otherwise unsayable;
   • making meaning of the experience of psychosis in familiar, human terms;
   • the appreciation of the perspectives of all network members; and
   • the development of authentic relationships with the clinical team.

Many participants also mentioned the value of the clinicians' reflections, as both an embodiment of transparency and a demonstration of warmth and care.
6 Staff commented that the model *slows down* the pace of clinical practice, deferring conclusions about the nature of the problem, and making space for solutions and ideas to emerge, especially from the network itself.
7 Some people experience terrible clinical turbulence and psychic pain, which this model sometimes does not alleviate – even then, many families, and people at the centre of concern, express greater satisfaction with their engagement and partnership in this model, compared with standard care.
8 Principal barriers to bringing the model to scale include the costs of OD not covered by insurance and the related problem of clinicians having sufficient time and flexibility to provide care.

References

Gidugu, V., Rogers, E.S., Gordon, C., Elwy, A.R. and Drainoni, M.-L. (2020) Client, family, and clinician experiences of Open Dialogue-based services. *Psychological Services.* Advance online publication. doi.org/10.1037/ser0000404

Gordon, C.D., Gidugu, V., Rogers, E.S., DeRonck, J. and Ziedonis, D. (2016) Adapting Open Dialogue for early-episode psychosis to the US healthcare environment. *Psychiatric Services*, 67(11), p. 1166–1168.

44

THE PARACHUTE PROJECT NYC –
THE PROJECT AND OUTCOMES
OF THE BROOKLYN MOBILE TEAM

Brian Martindale and Edward Altwies
(*UK and USA*)

The project

Brian Martindale

Between 2012 and 2015 there was an ambitious project to transform New York City mental health services in what was called the Parachute Project NYC. The intention was to forestall the excessive concentration on hospitalisation for mental health crises through the provision of crisis respite centres, call-in centres and ongoing family/network dialogic practices, developed along the lines of those implemented in Scandinavia and Germany, where peers and clinicians worked together in teams.

After being awarded a 17.6 million US dollar grant, the project was launched and followed by ethnographic researchers who have provided summaries (Hopper et al., 2019) and more detailed accounts (Parachute NYC, 2015) of their findings in the hope that many valuable lessons will be learned for future implementations. The ethnographers identified three factors which affected the implementation adversely: a) challenges involved in training and supervision, b) systemic indifference to the project's vision, and c) network members' insecure livelihoods. The importance of addressing the first two issues has been repeatedly stated at various points in this book. The third issue was the finding that many network members in the project did not have access to basic material needs such as housing, benefits, job training and paid time off work to attend network meetings, which would have been more readily provided in Scandinavia and Germany. This severely hampered/delayed the development of dialogic network meetings.

Outcomes of the Brooklyn mobile team

Edward Altwies

This section focuses on outcomes for a subgroup of service users (see selection criteria below) who experienced psychosis and who were in contact with a subgroup of mental health workers from the Parachute NYC Brooklyn mobile team.[1] The primary interventions were:

1   **Network meetings** attended by the participant and at least one member of their social network at the network's place of choice – most often the service user's home. Usually these meetings were co-facilitated by a peer specialist and licensed clinician in a similar manner to network meetings in Western Lapland. Most of the network meetings lasted at least 75–90 minutes.
2   Additional community-based **one-to-one meetings** with the peer specialist or the clinician.
3   Individual home-based **psychiatric care**, offered to all participants, with a psychiatrist who was only involved in the project on a part-time basis.

Selection criteria

The writer selected only service users with whom he was directly involved, and in 25 of 30 instances was the primary clinician, usually working with a peer specialist. Additionally, only the service users who took part in at least five network meetings or individual meetings were included in the review.

Findings at intake to project

Age and education: The mean age of the 30 service users was 20.5 years. The age range was 16–30 years old. Of the 18 service users who were 18 years or older, 15 had obtained a high school diploma or general equivalency degree. Six participants had attended college and one was a college graduate.

Migration and ethnicity: Twenty-five of the 30 service users were immigrants or were born in the US to parents who had immigrated. The other five identified as African-American.

Previous hospitalisation and medication: Four service users had never been hospitalised before. The remaining 26 service users were all referred directly from acute psychiatric inpatient units, having been diagnosed with psychotic disorders and prescribed medication at the time of discharge.

Research period and data collection

The research period was from the time of enrolment in Parachute NYC until either discharge or project termination, whichever came first. The average research period was 10.7 months (range 6–17 months). Descriptive, treatment and outcome data were gathered from a careful review of clinical records as well as post-discharge/termination phone interviews with service users and family members.

Results/outcomes

Number of meetings: Over the course of treatment, the group averaged 9.2 network meetings and 5.1 individual meetings (the range was 2–32 and 0–25 respectively).

Hospitalisations: During the 12-month period following enrolment in Parachute NYC, eight of 30 service users were hospitalised compared to 26 of the 30 participants in the 12-month period prior to enrolment. These eight people had 11 hospitalisations, with a total of 174 hospital days, compared to 34 hospitalisations and a total of 516 hospital days during the 12-month period prior to enrolment. Thus, the average number of hospital days during the 12-month period prior and the 12-month period subsequent to enrolment decreased from 17.2 to 5.8 respectively.

Medication: The average medication dose for the 26 service users taking medication at the time of enrolment was 4.2 risperidone equivalents. During treatment, 15 service users decided to stop taking medication on their own, with limited input from the team, and three participated in tapering off, in collaboration with the team psychiatrist. The average dose for the eight service users taking medication at the time of Parachute NYC discharge was 2.4 risperidone equivalents. The average dose for all 26 service users decreased to 0.7 risperidone equivalents.

Discussion

The writer conducted a careful chart review to collect the demographic data listed above, diagnosis on discharge from inpatient services, medication and hospitalisation data. An important finding was the reduction in overall hospital days in the 12 months subsequent to enrolment in the project as stated above. A potentially significant finding is that only four service users accounted for 133 of the 174 total hospital days (76%) following enrolment and that these service users had a very low engagement in network meetings – at the time of rehospitalisation they had participated in two or less meetings. Those that did engage in network meetings had much lower hospitalisation rates.

Regarding medication, only eight of the original 26 service users taking medication at time of enrolment were taking any medication at Parachute discharge. The prevailing wisdom in the usual treatment paradigm is that such a high rate of 'non-compliance' would result in high rates of rehospitalisation in the group as a whole. This rationale is often used as a justification for coercive tactics by providers to increase medication compliance. A possible mediating factor was that the high level of home-based engagement through individual and network meetings led to a robust psychosocial intervention that prevented a higher rehospitalisation rate. Of course, there could be other explanations for these findings, including these being the natural course of the conditions. However, these outcomes are comparable to the other published

US-based OD outcome study (Gordon et al., 2016), summarised in the previous chapter (Chapter 43).

This study had important limitations including lack of fidelity criteria, small sample size and lack of a control group. More rigorous studies are needed to address such limitations. However, these outcomes do point to the possibility that collaborative and psychosocial interventions inspired by OD (which de-emphasise medical model psychoeducation and coercive tactics for medication compliance) can lead to reduced and/or low rehospitalisation rates in community samples.

Note

1 These team members were: Keyanna Delisser, Janet Espinal and Jessica Cirilo.

References

Gordon, C., Gidugu, V., Rogers, S., DeRonck, J. and Ziedonis, D. (2016) Adapting Open Dialogue for early-onset psychosis into the U.S. health care environment: A feasibility study. *Psychiatric Services*, 67, p. 1166–1168. doi.org/10.1176/appi.ps.201600271

Hopper, K., Van Tiem, J., Cubellis, L. and Pope, L. (2019) Merging intentional peer support and dialogic practice: Implementation lessons from Parachute NYC. *Psychiatric Services*. [online] Available at: https://ps.psychiatryonline.org/doi/10.1176/appi.ps.201900174 [Accessed 10 December 2019] doi.org/10.1176/appi.ps.201900174

Parachute NYC (2015) *Tracing the origins, development, and implementation of an innovative alternative to psychiatric crisis (White Paper)*. [online] Available at: bit.ly/2Xr0apP [Accessed 23 May 2020].

45

OPEN DIALOGUE RESEARCH IN IRELAND

Iseult Twamley
(Ireland)

Introduction

Open Dialogue (OD) implementation in Ireland commenced with a week's training in 2012 from the Finns Mia Kurtti and Birgitta Alakare. Six years on, we have two in-house OD trainers (trained with Open Dialogue UK) and an established programme of training and supervision. OD has developed (within one area of our service) as a distinct care pathway from assessment to discharge. We have worked with over 300 service users and their networks to date. Our team is based in West Cork, a rural community mental health team working with a relatively small population. Our project was initiated through collaboration between service users, mental health staff and management. Our focus was recovery-oriented service improvement within our adult service. We felt that OD, with its emphasis on network inclusion, collaborative decision making and transparency, was in line with our organisational values (and what stakeholders were asking of us). We were looking to change the experience of all our service users (including those with experience of psychosis).

Phase 1 of the implementation was a pilot project of dialogic practice with a small number of service users and networks, to explore the feasibility and acceptability of the approach.

In response to research which identified the need for an integrated pathway, the project expanded in 2016 to create Phase 2: an OD care pathway for routine referrals to mental health services within one specific sector (population approximately 20,000). This created a marked shift in practice, from a few ad hoc referrals to dedicated staff working on a dedicated day in this OD pathway (with some possibilities to meet on other days as needed). Regular reflective supervision was critical to support staff with this change.

Research

We have taken a naturalistic approach to our research – a principal motivator is to inform the project's ongoing development. The research is led by the author as clinical lead and Dr Maria Dempsey from University College Cork (UCC).

Research into service users and families

Phase 1: A master's research project by Nicola Keane at UCC, together with the principal researchers, used interpretative phenomenological analysis (IPA) to explore the experiences of Phase 1 service users and families (Keane, 2017).

Findings: This research found that service users had positive experiences of the approach. In particular, and deemed pivotal to their recovery, were enhanced communication, a sense of relationship with staff, and the development of a shared understanding of mental health within their network.

Phase 2: The second study by Niamh Doyle as her DClinPsy thesis (2019) explored how service users, currently engaged in our OD-informed clinic, made sense of their mental health and their experience of our OD service. Six individual semi-structured interviews were conducted and analysed using IPA.

Findings: Participants provided evocative accounts of meaning making in network meetings, drawing from experiences of non-dialogical services to make valuable comparisons. Their narratives support OD as a humanising approach to mental health services, facilitating, rather than imposing, meaning, which can engender relational and individualised narratives that reduce self-blame.

Research into staff attitudes and experience

To evaluate staff experience, focus groups on staff attitudes and experiences of OD implementation occurred before training and at intervals across three years (Twamley, 2018). We were interested in the responses of staff to an approach so prima facie different from standard clinical training for most mental health professions.

Findings: Recurrent thematic cross-sectional analysis identified changes in attitudes, language and reported practices over time, leading to a sense of 'culture shift'. Staff discussed changes in discourse and practice, in how they understood and met service users' distress, and in how they worked with each other. They spoke of the importance of 'not knowing' and reflective practice, of a way of working that changed them personally as well as professionally, and also of the challenges experienced working within the existing system, outside of the OD pathway.

Staff experiences of working within the Phase 2 OD pathway were the subject of another master's research project by Colm Hayes at UCC (Hayes, 2017). Thematic analysis of staff interviews showed OD was experienced as an approach that places value on contextualising service user experience. A collegial working environment was portrayed, one that simultaneously encouraged service user autonomy and practitioner growth. Challenges were

273

also identified, and in particular the task of shifting practice to adhere to the principles of OD (e.g. tolerating uncertainty).

Further projects

In further research, as part of his DClinPsy (2019) thesis, Dr Dan Hartnett interviewed 14 OD practitioners across seven countries with respect to their views and their clinical practice with both OD and Trauma Informed Care (TIC).

Findings: Results revealed that several elements of OD are perceived as particularly supportive of and sensitive to working with trauma, in particular the pace, responsivity and reflections within dialogic practice. Some participants emphasised that within the OD approach service users are free to construe their experiences as being trauma related or not. This increased control over meaning making may serve as an avenue for greater service user empowerment, which may be less present in TIC models, which may position a trauma narrative more centrally. Systemic issues were also highlighted, though, particularly the interface between network meetings and wider health and social services systems.

All of these research projects are under preparation for publication. We are now conducting a clinical audit of the OD care pathway within our service, comparing with treatment as usual, using quantitative and qualitative outcomes. Our project has attracted attention in Ireland and the story of a young service user and her network's experience of working with us was featured in a national television documentary on Schizophrenia (RTE, 2017). The first Irish one-year foundation training started in 2020.

Questioning research!

Our experiences have raised questions for us in relation to OD research. As the saying goes: "Not everything that counts can be counted, and not everything that can be counted counts". A small-scale service improvement project, working across clinical presentations, cannot hope to reach a standard of 'evidence' that will sway the many who question the approach. Also, the reality is that OD is a 'front-loaded' intervention, with teams working closely and intensively with families/networks at the point of crisis (following the Western Lapland model where crisis is defined as a referral to mental health services). Short-term evaluations will not demonstrate the value of the approach as convincingly as the longer-term Finnish outcome studies. Qualitative data of the type we have collected has been affirming and educational as we continue to develop our practice, but in some contexts has little persuasive value.

Further implementation of OD requires financial investment in training, a restructuring of clinical roles and a shift in service delivery, all of which can be a hard sell, particularly in the context of changing management policies and priorities. We have learnt (and our research has borne out) that the cultural paradigm shift implicit in the implementation of dialogic practice requires a commensurate paradigm shift within organisational/hierarchical structures, and a willingness to value stories over symptoms, not just in the clinical room but also within service planning. Our future audit aims to address both service deliverables (e.g. hospital days, referrals, etc.) and markers of recovery-oriented practice (e.g. sharing our clinical notes with service users). We would like to further develop the co-production of research with our service users and network members. We are also interested in fostering international collaborations.

References

Doyle, N. (2019) 'Treated as a person, not a case': Exploring meaning-making in an Open Dialogue informed mental health service. (Unpublished DClinPsy thesis) UCC, Cork.

Hartnett, D. (2019) Practitioner perspectives on trauma informed care and the Open Dialogue approach to mental health care. (Unpublished DClinPsy thesis) UCC, Cork.

Hayes, C. (2017) 'Between two worlds': Exploring practitioner experiences of delivering the Open Dialogue approach in an Irish mental health setting. (Unpublished master's thesis) UCC, Cork.

Keane, N. (2017) An Open Dialogue-informed approach to mental health service delivery: A pilot study of the experiences of service users and support networks. (Unpublished master's thesis) UCC, Cork.

Radio Telifis Eireann: RTE 1 (2017) Schizophrenia: The voices in my head. Broadcast 19 September 2017.

Twamley, I. (2018) Community Mental Health Staff Experiences of Dialogic Practice Implementation: unpublished study.

46

ANTHROPOLOGICAL RESEARCH INTO OPEN DIALOGUE IN BERLIN

Lauren Cubellis
(Germany)

I have conducted 22 months of ethnographic research on the daily practice of Berlin-based clinicians – on how Open Dialogue (OD) principles and techniques are incorporated into the work of crisis intervention teams and how the more theoretical aspects of 'dialogism' can be interpreted as therapeutic principles. This research constitutes the material for my doctoral dissertation in anthropology and will be developed for publication over the next three years.

Participant observation allowed me to take part in the daily practice of these teams, including network meetings (where I participate as a member of the reflecting team), supervision, staff meetings and everyday socialising, as well as more than 350 hours of OD training in Berlin and the surrounding area.

I conducted regular semi-structured interviews with members of the crisis intervention teams, and with medical doctors, health insurance providers and OD training programme participants. Spurred by the commitment of these teams to working dialogically, I collected professional history narratives of training participants and practitioners to better understand the trajectories and investments of those involved with OD work.

The multiple dimensions of this ethnographic endeavour – combining presence, training and reflexive practice – afford a reading of the cultural environment under which OD is being implemented in Berlin. This contextualising work enables me to examine how the social role of such community-based health organisations is situated in relation to larger institutions, such as hospitals and health insurance companies. By looking at daily practice and the larger socioeconomic context, this research explores the real-world contingencies under which OD-informed practitioners struggle to preserve the principles of dialogic practice, while adapting to the changing pressures and circumstances of the surrounding healthcare context.

What has become increasingly clear during my research is that OD in Germany is sensitive to structural and institutional constraints and additionally responds to the cultural history of psychiatric practice in ways unique to the local context. The history of psychiatry under national socialism in Germany positions OD as a uniquely human rights-based approach, and its rejection of coercion, restraint and forced medication take on additional significance for its German practitioners in the light of this history. Whereas many OD projects have been small, top-down implementation endeavours, the German OD landscape is more akin to a grassroots saturation: country-wide training has been going on regularly for a decade, there is an extensive trainer network and integration at various levels of the healthcare system. This allows for differently positioned practitioners to speak across geographical distance and professional divides with a shared understanding of the practice.

While institutional structures remain slow to change, and reimbursement structures offered by insurance companies shape what degree of implementation is possible, the expansion of OD in Germany suggests a unique and broadly sustainable integration of the model in the German psychiatric landscape. Over time, the German case may offer invaluable insights for the practice of OD on a larger scale.

47

OPENNESS AND AUTHENTICITY IN THE OPEN DIALOGUE APPROACH

Laura Galbusera and Miriam Kyselo
(Germany)

In our first theoretical research project on Open Dialogue (OD) we aimed at a better understanding and clarification of the principles underlying its efficacy (Galbusera and Kyselo, 2018). Among OD's core principles, we focused on *dialogue*, as the dialogical process stands out as likely to be a main healing factor in the approach. We shed light on one element that yields and sustains dialogue: the dialogical therapeutic stance. We carried out a conceptual analysis, systematising and disentangling all heterogeneous descriptions of the dialogical therapeutic stance found in the OD literature. Our analysis found two necessary and sufficient principles that underpin and define a dialogical therapeutic stance: *openness* and *authenticity*. We believe that this conceptualisation might usefully inform OD practice and theory, and eventually help to advance research on psychosis therapies.

Our second theoretical research project adopted an interdisciplinary approach aimed at seeking possible explanations for why dialogue is effective in the treatment of psychosis (Galbusera and Kyselo, 2019). We drew on a current paradigm in cognitive science, i.e. the enactive approach, which conceptualises the self as a self-organising system, brought forth through interactional processes. These interactional processes have been specified as *distinction* and *participation* (Kyselo, 2014), where a core aspect of psychotic experience is understood as an intersubjective existential struggle between being a distinct subject and participating with others (Kyselo, 2016). We drew on our OD work described above, where we defined the dialogical therapeutic attitude as being constituted by two necessary and sufficient factors: *openness* and *authenticity*. We then brought the OD approach and the enactive approach together by suggesting that dialogue might be a specific kind of relation that (in principle) supports individuals in the processes of social participation and individual differentiation. At the core of this link, we suggest that the very constitutive aspects of a dialogical stance, i.e. openness and authenticity, per se entail an aspect of distinction (authenticity) and of participation (openness). A dialogical therapeutic stance (because of its very

278

structure) might thus foster and support a sense of a balanced self. We believe that this interdisciplinary theoretical work might constitute a useful basis for empirically investigating the effect of dialogical interactions on a person's sense of self.

References

Galbusera, L. and Kyselo, M. (2018) The difference that makes the difference: A conceptual analysis of the Open Dialogue approach. *Psychosis*, 10(1), p. 47–54. doi. org/10.1080/17522439.2017.1397734

Galbusera, L. and Kyselo, M. (2019) The importance of dialogue for schizophrenia treatment: Conceptual bridges between the Open Dialogue approach and enactive cognitive science. *HUMANA.MENTE Journal of Philosophical Studies*, 12(36), p. 261–291.

Kyselo, M. (2014) The body-social: An enactive approach to the self. *Frontiers in Psychology*, 5, p. 986. doi.org/10.3389/fpsyg.2014.00986

Kyselo, M. (2016) The enactive approach and disorders of the self – the case of schizophrenia. *Phenomenology and the Cognitive Sciences*, 15, p. 591–616. doi.org/ 10.1007/s11097-015-9441-z

EPILOGUE

Brian Martindale
(UK)

So, we are now at the end of our journey through the history and current practice of OD, and it is time to reflect; reflection following dialogue is central to OD. Of course, our reflections may well vary considerably, based on the extent of our prior familiarity with (practising) OD and perhaps other factors too.

I find myself reflecting on my motivation for initiating this book. It stemmed from my experience that fully engaging family members (and key others) *from the very beginning of contact with services* often leads to much improved outcomes. It also leads to totally different processes that, in my experience, are usually far more satisfying to the individual and his or her family than those in mental health services with a more individualistic focus. The book has a number of testaments to this.

When working as a psychiatrist in an Early Intervention in Psychosis (EIP) service, I was very familiar with the need-adapted approach of Yrjö Alanen (Alanen, 1997), which involved families in situations where someone was experiencing psychosis, but I was not nearly so fully acquainted as I am now with the developments of the very special training and principles of OD (which remain need-adapted).

In bringing the idea of the book to fruition, it was therefore a great relief for me to be put in touch with Nick Putman who became my co-editor of this volume. His intimate experience of OD as clinician and trainer will be clear to readers of this book and I also wish to acknowledge his writing skills and his attention to detail, both factors that are so necessary in editorial work. Just as important have been his links with OD practitioners throughout the world to help create this truly multi-author book.

In my re-reading of Nick's prologue, written at an earlier stage, it is not surprising to find that my epilogue, written as the book nears completion, echoes many of the themes he introduced. We both hope that the book will play a significant part in transforming the image of OD as being largely connected to, and thus a peculiarity of, a small part of Finland, to one of OD being of great import to the wider international mental health field. The feasibility of introducing some, if not all, of the principles of OD around the globe has been clearly demonstrated in this book, and in very varied settings.

Though this book has focused on those experiencing psychosis, we have aspirations that it will play a substantive part in the evolution of new *systems* of provision for *all* mental health care.

In his foreword to this book the United Nations Special Rapporteur refers to the

> ever increasing research evidence pointing to the limited effectiveness and possible harm of mainstream mental healthcare based on a bio-medical approach to individual mental health disorders that often ignores and undermines broader societal issues and human rights concerns.

As a psychiatrist, who also spent years in training and practice as a psycho-therapist and psychoanalyst, I have long felt discomfort and disquiet with the predominant paradigm that the Special Rapporteur refers to. When I started working in EIP services, I found that my fellow EIP professionals, though not fortunate to have had my training, had previously shared similar dis-quiet, intuitively feeling that there were essential elements missing in the ser-vices they had been providing, until the development of EIP services with principles such as early and flexible engagement, a higher level and wider range of support, including psychological therapy for the individual and his or her family, and an increased focus on relapse prevention and recovery of functioning. OD considerably extends and adds to these principles.

We hope that further qualitative and quantitative research outcomes of the practice of those who are well trained in OD will bear out the emerging findings and thereby support OD's wider inclusion as a platform for organising ser-vices. The word *platform* is essential, as it highlights the need to retain the key principle of OD as a need-adapted approach which can support many kinds of responses. I am confident that the integration of a variety of approaches within an OD service will become increasingly refined over time. In addition to this, lessons need to be learned from previous attempts at wider implemen-tation, such as the Parachute Project in New York City (Hopper et al., 2019).

I emphasise that these are my hopes, hopes that are well tempered by the knowledge that professionals tend to only select evidence they like and find reasons for ignoring evidence they do not like (Dare, 1996). An important example is that it has been conclusively shown, over several decades, and before OD was even developed, that quality family interventions considerably reduce relapse rates in psychosis (Mari and Streiner, 1994). Such interventions have long been a part of national guidelines and yet decades further on family interventions are still rarely available for people experiencing psychosis (Kuipers, 2011).

To my mind one of the biggest challenges in the further development of OD will be to shift the predominant focus on the individual in mental health training to one that is more naturally inclusive of the individual's network. If OD were to facilitate this to become the norm rather than the exception, it will have helped perform a Kuhnian revolution in the mental health field, shifting practitioners from being often unwitting reinforcers of alienation to that of facilitators of social inclusion.

References

Alanen, Y. (1997) *Schizophrenia: Its Origins and Need-Adapted Treatment.* London: Karnac.

Dare, C. (1996) Evidence: Fact or fiction. *Psychoanalytic Psychotherapy*, 10, Supplement, p. 32–45.

Hopper, K., Van Tiem, J., Cubellis, L. and Pope, L. (2019) Merging intentional peer support and dialogic practice: Implementation lessons from Parachute NYC. *Psychiatric Services*, 71(2), p. 199–201. doi.org/10.1176/appi.ps.201900174

Kuipers, E. (2011) Cognitive behavioural therapy and family intervention for psychosis – evidence based but unavailable? The next steps. *Psychoanalytic Psychotherapy*, 25(1), p. 69–74. doi.org/10.1080/02668734.2011.542966

Mari, J. and Streiner, D. (1994) An overview of family interventions and relapse on schizophrenia: Meta-analysis of research findings. *Psychological Medicine*, 24(3), p. 565–578. doi.org/10.1017/s0033291700027720

United Nations (2017) *Report of the Special Rapporteur on the right of everyone to the enjoyment of the highest attainable standard of physical and mental health (A/HRC/ 35/21).* [online] Available at: https://reliefweb.int/report/world/report-special-rapporteur-right-everyone-enjoyment-highest-attainable-standard-0 (Accessed 1 June 2020).

INDEX

Länsi-Pohja *see* Western Lapland
Lapland *see* Western Lapland
late interventions 70
law (legal dimensions; legislation):
Finland 37, 46; Germany 147, 152;
Italy, Basaglia Law 155, 263; USA 171
Lee, Kirsty (and family), experiential
account 70, 78–80
legal issues *see* law
Leonardo da Vinci project 126
life experiences (extreme/traumatic) 39,
41, 52–65
listening: deep 24, 226, 228, 229;
responsive 25–6
London: Early Intervention in Psychosis
service 161–2; Henderson (formerly
Belmont) Hospital 221; ODDESSI
trial 249; Philadelphia Association
107, 222–3; training in 107, 113, 118,
122–4, 125, 128, 162
long-term: hospital stays in
Western Lapland 240; psychotic
experiences 62–4

Main, Thomas 221
manualisation 110
Massachusetts (USA): Advocates 144,
165–70, 179, 264–7; University of
Massachusetts 245, 247
medical model *see* biomedical model
medication 19; antipsychotic *see*
neuroleptic (antipsychotic)
medication; Parachute Project
269, 270
mental health care in the community *see*
community care
Mental Health Departments (MHDs),
Italian 154, 155, 156, 259–60, 261,
262
Mental Health Recovery Measure
(MHRM) 256
Michels, Rolf, and colleagues 70, 81–4
migrants and immigrants 176–8; families
176–8; Parachute Project NYC 269;
Sweden 176–8
mobility 18
motivation: service user 257; trainees
133
multifamily (interfamily) group therapy
196, 210, 212–15
music: Dan's interest in 99, 100, 101;
therapeutic use 196, 226–30

Nash, John 71
National Health Service *see* NHS
National Institute for Clinical Excellence
(NICE): antipsychotic drugs 199;
CBT 207; early intervention in
psychosis 162
National Institute of Health Research
(UK - MIHR) 249, 252
National Institute of Mental Health
(USA - NIMH) 97, 199, 245
national network (Italy) 136, 263
National Research Council (of Rome)
154, 259
National Schizophrenia Project in
Finland (1981 –1987) 38, 216
national socialism (Germany) 276–7
Need-Adapted Treatment/intervention
(NAT) 10, 123, 180, 196, 237–9;
experiential account 89; Finland 10,
38–40, 42–3, 199, 209–11, 218, 237,
280; randomised controlled trials
(RCTs) 237, 248, 249; research 237–9,
248, 249
negative capability 23
negative phenomena (humans)
218–19
negative symptoms 198, 200
Nelson, Leslie (peer worker) 180–1,
183, 194
network (family/social) incl. network
meetings 14–17, 18–31; Advocates
(Mass. USA) 144, 165–70; Berlin
hospital 148–50; in different contexts
and countries 148, 150, 167–8, 172,
173, 179–84, 191–2; families and
individual valuing meetings 266; need-
adapted therapy and 209; Parachute
Project NYC 270; peer workers and
181; research and 234; systemic
therapy vs OD and 204; team role 55;
therapeutic communities and 222–4;
training and 109, 110, 111, 112–13,
114, 115–16, 117, 126; Western
Lapland 9, 13, 14, 15, 21
'Network Mental Health' (Netzwerk
psychische Gesundheit – NWpG)
150
neurobiological model *see* biomedical/
biological/neurobiological model
neuroleptic (antipsychotic) medication
2, 19–20, 198–200, 238, 242; cases 87,
101; Finland/Western Lapland 9–51,

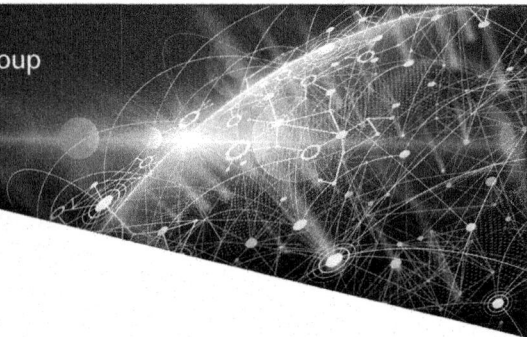